# THE NEW
# QUILTING &
# PATCHWORK
# DICTIONARY

**Other Books by Rhoda Ochser Goldberg**
*The New Knitting Dictionary*
*The New Crochet Dictionary*
*Needlepoint Patterns for Signs and Sayings (with Marion Pakula)*

# THE NEW
# QUILTING &
# PATCHWORK
# DICTIONARY

## RHODA OCHSER GOLDBERG

QUILTING TECHNIQUES • TOOLS AND ACCESSORIES •
FRAMES • FABRICS • TEMPLATES • BORDERS •
FILLERS • PATCHWORK AND APPLIQUÉ PATTERNS •
ENLARGING AND REDUCING • FINISHING • *And More*

CROWN PUBLISHERS, INC. · NEW YORK

*This book is dedicated to Jason Patrick O'Connell, my first grandson and the newest patch in my Album Quilt of Life.*

Published by Crown Publishers, Inc., 225 Park Avenue South, New York, New York 10003

CROWN is a trademark of Crown Publishers, Inc.

Manufactured in the United States of America

Library of Congress Cataloging-in-Publication Data
Goldberg, Rhoda Ochser.
   The new quilting and patchwork dictionary: quilting techniques, tools and accessories, frames, fabrics, templates, borders, fillers, patchwork and applique patterns, enlarging and reducing, finishing, and more / by Rhoda Ochser Goldberg.
      p.   cm.
   Includes index.
   1. Quilting—Handbooks, manuals, etc.   2. Patchwork—Handbooks, manuals, etc.   I.Title.
TT835.G63 1988
746.9'7—dc19                                                                                          88-3836

ISBN: 0-517-56965-5

10 9 8 7 6 5 4 3 2 1

First Edition

# CONTENTS

# ACKNOWLEDGMENTS

I gratefully acknowledge the assistance I received from my many friends and relatives, the professional and not so professional "friendly" quilters, the quilting products and accessory manufacturers and distributors who gave so freely of their time, knowledge, equipment, and the many products needed to produce a book of this scope and size.

I must thank the members and officers of the Suffolk County Chapter of the Embroiderers Guild of America, the Long Island Chapter of the Embroiderers Guild of America, the Eastern Long Island Quilters Guild, and the Long Island Quilters Society for making the majority of the samples photographed for this book. The wonderful quilters who belong to these groups gave their time and talents purely for the love of their craft and the desire to promote and teach quilting.

A special word of gratitude must go to the people of the sewing and quilting industry, who, without reservation, compensation, or limitation, provided me with the finest tools, equipment, materials, and sewing accessories necessary to create the samples. Generously, the dedicated representatives of these companies even referred me to their competitors so that I could show quilters everything available to further the knowledge and enjoyment of this art. In every instance, a phone call was enough to generate cooperation and assistance.

I must thank Helen Anderson, for giving me permission to use and photograph her original pattern "Ohio School House," and a very special woman, Laura Lipski, for providing me with samples of her new and antique quilt blocks when my deadline was near and panic was close behind. A thank-you must be given to Bobbie Brannin, who not only provided samples but acted as a matchmaker between me and many of the fine quilters who contributed to this book.

I will always hold dear the friendship of Marion Pakula, my first writing partner and teacher.

This list would be incomplete without a major acknowledgment of my editor, Brandt Aymar. Without his assistance, hand holding, and "pun-tastic encouragement, I would never have been able to complete this book.

**Samples were made by the following quilters:**

Helen Anderson, East Quogue, New York
Bobbie Brannin, East Williston, New York
Barbara Charles, West Islip, New York
Nancy Coster, Lindenhurst, New York
Pat Crispi, Lindenhurst, New York
Mary Di Giantonio, Lindenhurst, New York
Eylene Egan, West Babylon, New York
Martha Fee, Northport, New York
Nellie Fizzvoglio, West Babylon, New York
Terri Gauvain, St. Louis, Missouri
Virginia Genna, Hackettstown, New Jersey
Gloria Gralla, Flushing, New York
Laura Lipski, Lindenhurst, New York
Betty Lombardi, Huntington, New York
Bernice Malatzky, Bronx, New York
Mary Mase, Shelter Island, New York

Anita Miller, Cliffside Park, New Jersey
Jacqui G. O'Connell, Patuxent River, Maryland
Agnes Palazzo, Central Islip, New York
Gail Rogers, Sayville, New York
Marjorie Rogers, Sayville, New York
Aurelie Stack, Mattituck, New York
Linda Tapfar, Shelter Island, New York
Lorin Tuttle, Eastport, New York
Sarah Vickary, Smithtown, New York
Veronica Wightman, Brightwaters, New York
Bonnie Lynn Young, Ephrata, Pennsylvania
Jane Zorn, Smithtown, New York

Alan Goldberg (Photo Assistant)
Ross Kass (Photo Assistant)
Jacqueline O'Connell (Model)

*Materials and supplies for making the samples were generously provided by the following companies:*

**Ben Franklin,** 42 Indian Head Road, Kings Park, New York 11754 (*This store is a wonderful local example of a retail source for fabric and quilting supplies.*)

**Coats & Clark,** New York, New York (*all quilting threads used to make the samples*)

**Fabrics By Lineweaver,** 3300 Battleground Ave., Greensboro, North Carolina 27410 (*all solid-color classic cotton fabrics, muslin, and paisley prints used to make the samples. This firm was chosen as an outstanding mail-order source for fabrics.*)

**gingher® Inc.,** Greensboro, North Carolina (*all scissors used in demonstration photographs and to prepare samples. This firm manufactures a complete line of precision cutting instruments for sewing, embroidery, and quilting.*)

**Pellon Corporation®,** New York, New York (*all Quilters Secret, Wonder-Under, Stitch-n-tear used for the samples and instructional material*)

**Marie Products®,** Tucson, Arizona (*all stretcher strips used to prepare the samples, Rocky Giraffe,*

*Quilt Square with stand, Early American Quilting Floor Frame*)

**The Stearns Technical Textiles Co.,** Cincinnati, Ohio (*all the Mountain Mist batting products used in the samples and instructional and informational chapters, Ensure washing products*)

**Susan Bates® Inc.,** Chester, Connecticut (*all quilting needles, needle threaders, and Anchor embroidery floss used to make the samples*)

**Viking-White Sewing Machine Company,** Minneapolis, Minnesota (*the Viking [Prisma 900] sewing machine was used in the preparation of many pieced and machine-appliqué samples shown in this book. This is their premier machine, a complete line of fine sewing machines.*)

**VIP Fabrics,** New York, New York (*all calico prints and Christmas prints used to prepare the samples. This firm was chosen as an outstanding source for quilting fabrics sold in retail and craft stores.*)

**W. H. Collins, Inc.,** Whippany, New Jersey (*all notions and sewing and quilting accessories used to prepare the samples*)

# INTRODUCTION

The art of quilting has roots deeply embedded in tradition. It provides a design vehicle for the serious artist and a challenging series of techniques for the craftsperson or needleworker. You can combine hand and machine stitching, embroidery, garment construction, and sewing. Quilting can be worked within a group (the famous quilting bee), combining the craft with a social gathering, alone, or even carried to an airport or other waiting room.

There are so many techniques to be tried and mastered and so many patterns to work that I can only describe quilting as the most exciting and versatile craft you can learn.

The "typical" quilter is a creative person who wants a simple craft that can be challenging. This person is a parent at home, a worker outside the home, a teenager, a grandmother. The quilter is willing to spend large sums of money on coordinated decorator fabrics, or hoards leftover scrap materials and worn-out clothing. This typical person loves to work on a complex five-year project, or to make an accessory for the home or wardrobe in twenty-four hours; she wants a warm, usable product or a decoration.

The typical quilter is any one of the above or a combination of each at different times.

This art form dates back to the Middle Ages, when the Crusaders used an early form of quilting to line their armor for warmth. It is speculated that they saw the craft in some form in the Middle East.

In Europe we find examples of quilting from the fourteenth century, used for warm bedcovers and clothing. The articles were often embellished with fancy embroidery on a solid-color background fabric.

In the fifteenth century we see the introduction of appliqué—pieces of fabric cut into pictorial shapes and stitched to a fabric surface as a decoration.

By the seventeenth and eighteenth centuries, elaborate embroidery and appliqué work was combined with silks, satins, and velvets to produce quilted clothing and bedding for royal families. The French were known for this particular fancy execution of the quilting art.

The American pioneer is generally credited with the origination and development of patchwork—the most popular form of quilting in the United States today. Necessity was truly the mother and the father here. Faced with long, cold winters and limited resources, these frugal women used scraps of worn clothing to create bedding covers. They stitched together odd-shaped bits and pieces of fabric to form a larger piece of fabric or quilt top. These are known to us as the crazy quilt patterns. Soon, inventive women embellished the surface of the fabric with embroidery stitches for additional strength and decoration.

Later, fabric was cut into regular geometric shapes and pieced (sewn together) to form patterns or blocks, many of them named and passed down from generation to generation. The blocks were joined to create beautiful block and allover patterns.

The social event called the quilting bee started when women gathered in groups to work the construction or actual quilting, socialize, and gossip. This was the primary social contact for many pioneer women.

As the pioneers pushed westward they carried these precious patterns and shared them with others along the route. The average female child began her quilt collection at the age of six or seven, often completing a dozen quilts by the time she reached the marriage age of fifteen or sixteen. Her last quilt as a single girl was usually a "marriage quilt."

Some of these early examples of American patchwork have survived, to be found today in prized collections and museums. Many are signed and dated.

The "plain people" or Amish settlers were masters of the quilting art. The patterns are a reflection of their simple way of life and religious convictions. The earliest Amish quilts, dating to the eighteenth century, were made of wool and cotton fabrics in geometric patterns; the colors came from natural dyes. Today, Amish women are still famous for quilting and practice the art with the same standards of excellence attributed to their ancestors.

In this book, there are about 1,000 patchwork patterns charted and broken down into the individual shapes to enable you to actually work each block into a quilted square. If you make 30 of the patterns into 12" blocks with 1" borders, you have a quilt for a twin bed; if you get carried away, 245 pattern blocks will cover a bed 35 feet wide.

Various quilting forms and techniques are explored in separate chapters. I have also included basic instructions for the beginning quilter and templates for all the patchwork patterns shown. There are also chapters on terminology, tools, construction, and assembly. This is your quilting dictionary, from A to Z.

# The Basics

## GENERAL PLAN

Before a quilt can be made, it is essential to establish a general working plan. This is idea time and involves choosing the pattern, techniques to be learned, basic color scheme, and fabric. After you have this thought out, write it down.

## QUILT LOG

The first time I saw a quilt log, I thought it was the cleverest thing I had ever seen and I vowed to begin keeping one. I spent hours with the quilter reminiscing about the facts it revealed about times in my youth and times before I was born. Her stories and remembrances practically jumped from the pages as she told me about each quilt. It was a documented history of the life and times of an entire family. I almost felt that I was reading a diary.

A quilt log also enables the quilter to refer back to specifics when maintenance or repair is necessary or a pecuniary value has to be placed on the quilt.

I use a plain loose-leaf binder for my quilt log. Each quilt is listed on its own page (or pages), which contains the following information:

1. **Dates.** When the quilt was started, when it was finished.
2. **Size.** Size of the bed and size of the quilt.
3. **Name.** For whom the quilt is made (if known).
4. **Pattern design.** This can be a rough drawing: the name of a traditional pattern; the name of the book, magazine, or other source in which it appeared; or a photocopy of the actual working pattern.
5. **Templates.** A set of paper templates taped in an envelope, or just a thin piece of tracing paper traced over the templates but not cut apart, will do nicely. This takes extra time, but it will pay off if you ever want to repeat part or all of the pattern.
6. **Fabric.** I try to include a small piece of each fabric, with the manufacturer's name (if known), the place it was purchased, where (if a scrap or remnant) it was first used, the price per yard, and the estimated yardage for the quilt.
   These facts are essential if you ever need to replace or duplicate part of a quilt, price it for sale or insurance, or just want to know how much it cost to make. Years later, you'll be amazed to see the difference in costs, owing to both choice (upgrading quality as technical proficiency increases) and inflation.
7. **Time chart.** If you are working for resale, a time sheet is essential. If you want to place a value on your time for insurance purposes, this is a form of documentation. If you just want to know how much time it took to complete a particular quilt, this is useful and sometimes a revelation. Just so you'll know, keep a time sheet for at least one quilt.
8. **Quilting pattern.** Detail the type of quilting used (outline, diagonal, etc.). If a pattern such as Feather, Wreath, or Rope was used, include a drawing or tracing.
9. **Batting.** Document the type of batting used: brand name, manufacturer, and fiber content.
10. **Border.** The border should be described in detail. If it is pieced or appliquéd, draw the pattern. Plain borders with detailed quilting patterns are best remembered with a tracing.
11. **Binding.** Include a piece of the binding in your fabric collection. It is part of the quilt.
12. **Photograph.** Since quilts and individual blocks are given as gifts, I always recommend taking a photograph of the finished piece or quilt; a simple "clothesline snapshot" is good enough. **Do not omit it!** It may be your only real record of many months of hard work.

## DRAFTING THE QUILT PATTERN

All the quilt patterns in this book are drafted on graph paper. You can enlarge or reduce them to any desired size by following the instructions in "Enlarging and Reducing Patterns" (page 18). Most individual quilt blocks measure 6" to 18" on each side, but smaller and larger sizes are acceptable.

When you have drafted the chosen pattern to the desired finished size, draw a scale diagram of the entire quilt-top design, using graph paper. Decide whether you want to place the blocks side by side, alternate them with plain blocks, or separate them with lattice strips.

If desired, place a border on the diagram. Many quilters use borders to frame a quilt or bring it up to size.

## TEMPLATES

The template is a reusable pattern for both the segments that make up a block and the overall designs for quilting. Templates are made of plastic, metal, cardboard, or heavy paper. They can be purchased from quilting and craft or fabric stores.

Satisfactory templates can be made from common shirt cardboard, poster board, plastic coffee-can lids, plastic sheets made for this purpose, and, my favorite, old X-ray film plates. The shirt cardboard and poster board wear out quickly, so you'll need several of each shape, and plastic lids are limited in size, so I use the X-ray film or plastic sheets.

To make your own template, first draw the shape *accurately* to size on a sheet of graph paper. If you are using cardboard, the shape can be transferred with carbon paper and cut out with scissors. **Do not use your fabric scissors to cut paper**; they will become dull very quickly.

If you are using a plastic sheet or X-ray film, lay it over the drawing and trace with a waterproof marking pen. This too can be cut out with household scissors.

## MARKING THE FABRIC
### Patchwork Block

Place the fabric wrong side up on a flat surface. Put the template on the fabric, aligning it with the grain of the fabric, *not* the bias.

Trace around the template with a pencil or transfer pen. Do not forget that this is always the seam line and a ¼" margin must be marked around it, with the help of a ruler or quilter's quarter (see "Tools and Accessories," page 4), before you cut the fabric.

### Appliqué

To transfer the pattern from a template for a piece to be appliquéd, place the fabric *right side up* on a flat surface. Then proceed as for patchwork transfer.

## CUTTING AND PIECING

Always cut the fabric with extreme care. Use the best scissors you can get, and keep them sharp. Remember to add a ¼" seam allowance around each piece before cutting it out.

Join the pieces by hand or machine according to your drafted pattern.

Press each seam as you work. The seams are usually pressed to one side (in one direction). Seam and press each block.

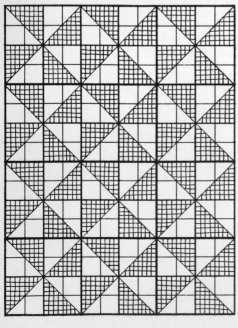

## ASSEMBLING THE BLOCK QUILT TOP

After the pattern has been pieced or appliquéd to form a block, the blocks must be attached to form the quilt top. This is often called "setting the quilt."

The simplest method is to set one block next to another. This often forms an allover pattern that may appear quite different from the single block.

The second method is to alternate the pattern block with a plain block, much like a checkerboard.

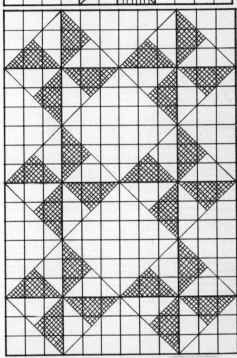

The third method is to set the blocks on the diagonal. This requires half blocks to square the sides.

Another popular way to set the blocks is with lattice strips. This gives the illusion of framing each block, and adds to the finished size of the quilt with little extra time or effort expended.

## BORDERS

The border is the frame of the quilt. It must be wide enough to show off the main design, but never so wide that it overwhelms the pattern. A border can be light or dark, narrow or wide, patterned or plain.

Usually, pieced borders are put on pieced quilts, appliquéd borders on appliquéd quilts, but it is not unusual to find a combination of these techniques in a quilt.

The plain border can be placed on both pieced and appliquéd quilts and can be embellished with ornate quilting patterns. The Amish do this most effectively. (See "Borders," page 264, and "Border Quilting Patterns," page 76.)

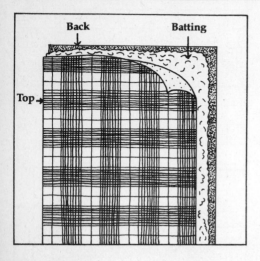

Back    Batting

Top →

## ASSEMBLING THE QUILT

The quilt is made of three parts: the top, the batting or filling, and the backing. This is usually called the quilt or "quilting sandwich."

### Filler

A filler or interlining is the center of the quilt sandwich. It provides the warmth for the quilt and enhances the quilting stitches by producing puffiness around each stitch.

The filler can be as thin as a flannel sheet or any of the many thicknesses available in cotton, wool, or Dacron batting. Most quilters today use Dacron, because it will not shift or become lumpy when the finished quilt has to be washed. (See "Tools and Accessories," below.)

### Backing

The backing can be made of one large piece of fabric or several lengths of fabric pieced together. **Note:** A 100% cotton bedsheet makes a wonderful backing and can be purchased on sale year round.

Remember that the quilting pattern will show on the backing. A patterned fabric will obscure these stitches; a solid fabric will enhance them.

# TOOLS AND ACCESSORIES

The quilter does not need very many tools to work the craft, just the basic sewing implements. However, I must admit that I love to collect and use many of the tools and accessories that make each aspect of quilting easier and quicker to master.

## BATTING

I have chosen the **Mountain Mist®** line of quilt batting for its superior product quality, extensive variety, national name recognition, and availability. The following were chosen for exclusive use in the preparation of all samples used in this book.

**Polyester Batting** has become the standard for quilters with all levels of experience. It is a soft 100% polyester and highly recommended for all-around use in most quilting projects. This is made in crib, twin, full, and queen sizes.

**Quilt-Light™** is a lightweight quilt batting with a reduced loft for the appearance of the old-time quilts so popular today. It is all polyester and is made in crib, full, and queen sizes.

4

Cotton quilt batting is made of all bleached natural fibers. It has been used for generations by traditionalists who prefer an all-natural look and feel. It is made in the two larger quilt sizes.

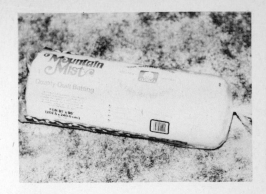

Fatt-Batt is an extra-loft, very soft 100% polyester batting. It is twice as thick as regular batting, which makes it the perfect comforter and outerwear filler. The Fatt-Batt is made in crib, twin, full, and queen sizes.

## BEESWAX

This is rubbed across the thread to make it stronger and keep it from tangling. It comes in cake and molded forms, with or without a case. (The case is recommended, to keep the beeswax clean.)

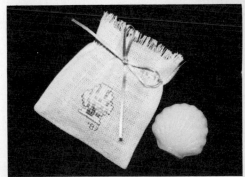

## CARBON PAPER

This is the standard medium for transferring a design from one surface to another. When working with fabric, use dressmaker's carbon only.

## CARDBOARD

A good supply of cardboard is necessary for making the templates used in quilting. It is the best material for a single block pattern where only limited use is necessary. For multiple use I recommend using plastic sheets or tin for templates.

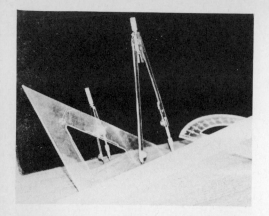

## DRAFTING TOOLS

It is definitely helpful but not essential to have a few drafting tools in your bag. Angles are easier to measure with a protractor, circles are easily drawn with compasses and measurements are quickly figured with an architect's scale rule.

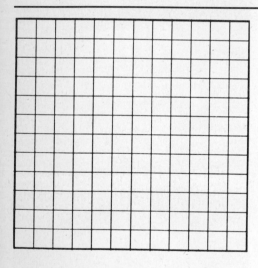

## EMBROIDERY FLOSS

Six-strand embroidery floss is used for all types of embroidery, from cross-stitch to crazy quilting. It is manufactured in a magnificent range of colors.

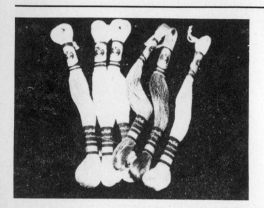

## GRAPH PAPER

All the patterns in this book are drawn on graph paper. To enlarge or reduce any pattern, just copy it onto graph paper with a larger or smaller grid. (See "Graph Paper," page 270.)

## HOOPS

The quilting hoop works on the same principle as the embroidery hoop: it is just larger and heavier. It consists of two wooden circles or ovals about 20" to 30" in diameter. It can be mounted on a floor stand, clamped to a table, or used in the lap. It works best for smaller items, but can be used for quilting larger pieces worked in sections.

## MASKING TAPE

Sewing accurate parallel lines is one of the most difficult tasks for the quilter to learn. Masking tape, available in ¼" to 3" widths, is temporarily placed directly on the fabric as a guide. **Note:** Do not leave tape on the fabric for any length of time. It may leave marks or become difficult to remove.

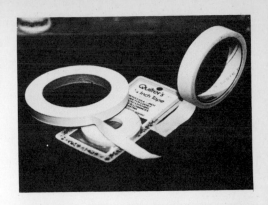

## NEEDLES

The quilting needle is a short, sharp needle available in sizes 7, 8, 9, 10, and 12. Embroidery sharps can be used but are generally considered too long, and often have large eyes that can leave holes in the fabric. Sizes 7 and 8 quilting needles are the most commonly used. The new platinum-dipped quilting needles glide smoothly through the fabric and are fun to try, but for general use I feel that the expense is too high.

## NEEDLE THREADERS

They help get the thread into the eye of the needle. These are a necessity after the age of twenty-one, perhaps before.

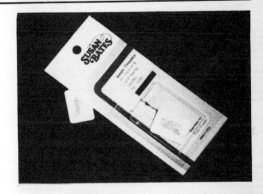

## NONWOVEN AND FUSIBLE FABRICS

There are a number of products that I have used and recommend highly for beginning quilters and those learning a new technique. All the products mentioned here are made by Pellon® and are readily available in fabric and craft stores.

**Quilters Secret®** is a preprinted nonwoven fusible backing for the quilter who is looking for a way to cut 2" or 4" geometric shapes without templates, needs large quantities of one shape, or needs assistance in sewing straight seam lines. The seam allowance and cutting lines on the nonwoven fabric help make perfect matching lines and angles. This is a wonderful aid for the "nervous novice"—just iron it onto the fabric, cut, and sew.

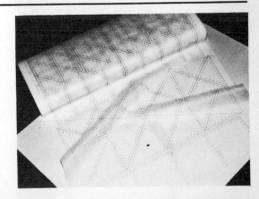

**Wonder-Under™** is a paper-backed transfer web that fuses fabric to fabric. The Wonder-Under™ is pressed to the wrong side of the fabric. Shapes can then be drawn on the paper backing. Cut out the shape, peel off the paper, and press (fuse) the resulting appliqué in place. It certainly makes appliqué easy to work. It is also good for securing hems.

**Stitch-n-tear®** is a tear-away backing used to add stability to a design area when working embroidery and appliqué by machine.

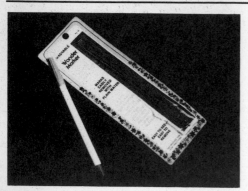

## PENS AND PENCILS

Until a few years ago the entire description of this essential tool would have been one sentence long. You still need a common No. 2 pencil for general use. However, a whole family of related marking devices is now readily available.

There are a number of pens and pencils for marking on plastic. Some are permanent and will not wash off; others are water-soluble, and the markings are easily removed with a damp tissue.

The many available fabric markers could fill a wall display in a fabric shop. My favorites include the **Vanishing Fabric Marker**, which makes a purple mark that fades away without water, and the **Wonder Marker**, which makes a blue mark easily removed with plain tap water applied with a spray bottle. The **Nonce Marking Pencil** is a white-marking water-soluble pencil good for dark fabrics. The dressmaker's marking pencil is filled with chalk and is used like an ordinary pencil.

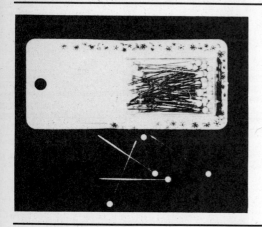

## PINS

Steel dressmaker pins are most commonly used for any sewing-related craft. For quilting, I recommend quilting pins. They are made with a long, fine, sharp shaft and have a rounded plastic head, making them easier to see and use.

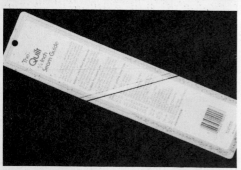

## QUARTER MEASURE

After the template is placed on the fabric and traced, a ¼" seam allowance must be added. This can be accomplished with a ruler and marking pen or pencil, but this technique is time-consuming and often inaccurate. A ¼"-wide bar of plastic or wood, called a ¼" seam guide or quilter's quarter, is a very useful tool for adding this seam allowance quickly and accurately.

The accessory shown in the photo is aptly named the **Wonder Wheel**. To use this tool, simply place the point of the pencil through the hole in the center of the metal disk and slowly move it around the edge of the template. This works well on curves and long straight lines.

## QUILTING FRAME

If you have the room, a quilting frame is the quilter's ultimate luxury tool. Nothing is as convenient for quilting a large item or working on a quilt in a group. See page 13.

## ROTARY CUTTER

The rotary cutter is a wonderful cutting tool that makes a sharp cut through many layers of fabric at the same time. It is recommended for straight-line cuts (strip quilting and most geometric shapes). A self-sealing cutting board or thick piece of mat board must be used to protect your table or other cutting surface.

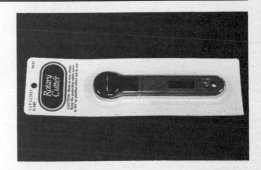

## RULERS

Everything is measured in quilting. You should have a variety of rulers available at all times. I suggest 6" and 12" rulers for drawing patterns and the "quick check" as you work; a yardstick, made of metal for accuracy; and a T-square ruler for squaring up your patterns and fabric.

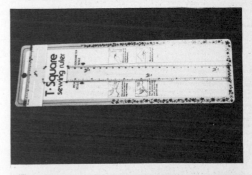

A plastic ruler printed with a graph (grid) is a wonderful all-purpose tool to add to your workbasket. This ruler enables you to make large graph grids, square up patterns, make right angles, and even draw a circle. It is essential for use with a rotary cutter.

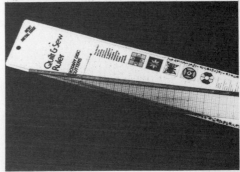

## SCISSORS

I am frequently asked, "What kind of scissors should I buy?" My answer is always "The best you can afford."

The gingher® line of scissors is considered by many in the textile industry, home sewers, and, of course, quilters the premier line of scissors manufactured today.

These are some of the most important tools the quilter will use. Each type of scissors has a special function. *Never cut paper or plastic with scissors used to cut fabric.*

The following are examples of different types of scissors and their uses.

**8″ bent trimmers** are chrome-plated general-use scissors, for cutting all weights of fabric of natural and synthetic fibers. I found eight layers of cotton fabric no contest for the scissors in this photograph.

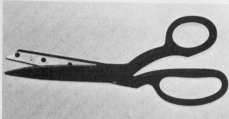

**8″ featherweight bent trimmers** have a black nylon frame with stainless-steel blades. They are used for general cutting of all weight fabrics.

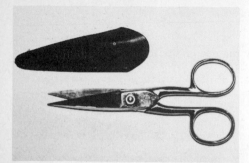

**5″ tailor's points** are chrome-plated scissors used for trimming, quilting, and general craftwork.

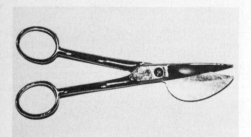

**6″ appliqué scissors** are a wonderful chrome-plated tool used for close trimming. The duckbill edge provides greater protection for the fabric when you cut around an appliqué.

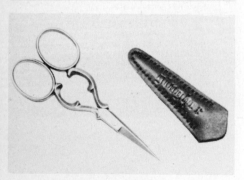

**3½″ embroidery scissors** are my favorite among the dozen pairs of embroidery scissors in my collection. It is part of a set of four pairs in the "Collector's Series." They are made in different finishes (black oxide carbon steel, nickel-plated carbon steel with gold-plated handles, pewter-finish stainless steel with antique gold-plated handles, and pewter-finish stainless steel). If you do fine needlework, invest in one of these show-stoppers.

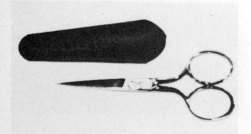

**4″ embroidery scissors** are chrome-plated all-around embroidery scissors used for cutting thread and fine needlework.

**4″ thread clip** has a black nylon frame with stainless-steel blades and is used for clipping thread (not for cutting fabric.) This is excellent for use with the sewing machine.

## SEAM AND STITCH RIPPER

Removes your mistakes quickly and safely. This is a **must** in my sewing basket.

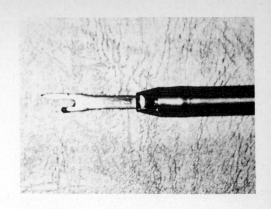

## SEWING MACHINE

The sewing machine was invented in the mid-nineteenth century, and has been used for piecing quilts almost from the beginning. The arguments for and against the use of a machine have also raged since its invention.

The philosophy of working by hand is not negated by the use of any tool. I consider the sewing machine just another tool. The handwork purist maintains that hand sewing is the only legitimate form of the art. To them, the introduction of a mechanical device removes the end product from the hand-sewn category. Both sides can advance valid arguments. Each quilter must choose for him- or herself.

Great improvements have been made since the sewing machine was invented. The first machines were powered by a foot treadle. Then came the electrical motorized machine. Plain stitching was enhanced by the cams of the fifties.

Now, as you can see in the photograph, the newest models have a computerized panel for preprogrammed stitches, stitch length and width, and types of fabric. The machine I use, the Viking (Prisma 990), even has a cassette called the "sewing advisor" for the times when you are uncertain which stitch is best. This machine will automatically set the correct stitch length and width for the fabric you are using. A second cassette contains decorative stitches and complete alphabets and numbers for detailed and intricate embroidery. You can add a message and sign and date your quilt with this feature. The machine is lightweight and entirely self-contained.

Once you learn to use today's sewing machines you can put your talents into the design preparation and handwork aspects of becoming a fine quilter, artist, and creator.

## STANDS

Quilting requires the use of both hands, so a good floor stand to hold your hoop or stretcher strip bars is absolutely essential. The stand in the photo, called a **Rocky Giraffe,** is the best all-around utility stand I have ever used. It is made of rock maple, is fully adjustable, and collapses to accompany me to courses and seminars.

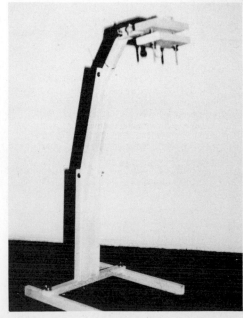

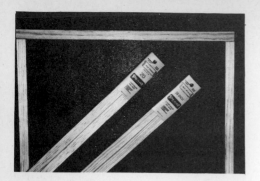

## STRETCHER STRIPS

I recommend the use of stretcher strips for quilting blocks, rectangles, and smaller items. They are made in sizes from 4" up.

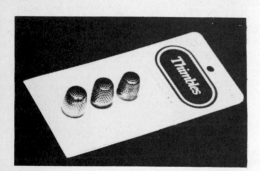

## TACKS

Common thumbtacks can be used to pin a piece of quilting to a wooden frame or stretcher strips. They rust, leave large holes in the fabric, and are difficult to remove. I recommend using quilter's tacks, fine, sharp ½" pins with plastic-ball heads that make them easy to insert and remove.

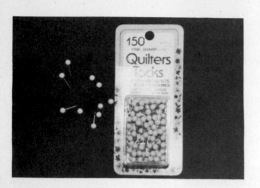

## THIMBLE

For some quilters, the use of a thimble is an absolute necessity. Some even use two thimbles, one on the third finger and one on the thumb. Others consider them a clumsy nuisance, preferring to build calluses on the forefinger.

Thimbles are usually made of metal. In my collection, I have thimbles made of nickel, pewter, and silver, and one made of gold, which I wear on a bracelet.

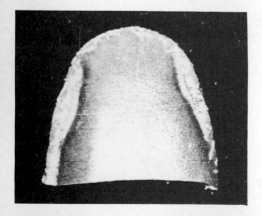

Many experienced quilters and most beginners find the leather finger thimble more comfortable.

One of the newer thimbles, shown, is made of moldable plastic. It is placed in boiling water for a few seconds, until it becomes soft. Then it is placed on the finger and pressed until it molds to the exact shape of your finger.

## THREAD

If it is available, always use mercerized cotton or cotton-covered polyester quilting thread. For quilting, try to use the same color as the background fabric.

For joining patchwork or appliqué, I prefer to use heavy-duty or **Dual-Duty-Plus®** thread. The usual length of thread to use is 24" to 30" for quilting. If the thread is longer, it will knot or tangle.

## TRACING PAPER

Tracing paper and drawing paper should always be kept available for copying and transferring the patterns. I have often used tracing paper in place of carbon paper by rubbing graphite pencil over the reverse side of the paper and tracing over the pattern drawn on the front side.

## WASHING PRODUCTS

This is another of the few times I have felt the need to mention a brand name. All quilts and quilted accessories get soiled. Sometimes it is necessary to remove work markings. I have found **Ensure® Quilt Wash** to have no equal for the care and cleaning of quilts and comforters. **Note:** I use Ensure to wash embroidery, hand-washable sweaters, and lingerie. I hope that someday the manufacturer will put this product on supermarket shelves.

# HOMEMADE QUILTING FRAME

For quilting large items, the ultimate accessory is the quilting frame. The size of the frame can also be the ultimate liability. If you have the space, buy or make one. Many types are manufactured today. The frame chosen for the photograph is attractive and also adjustable from crib-to queen-size quilts.

## TO MAKE A QUILTING FRAME

The sawhorse quilting frame is the easiest to construct. This frame can be quickly taken apart for storage under a bed or in a closet, and is functional and sturdy. I must admit that it isn't very attractive, but it is a good first frame and can be made for a few dollars. Follow the diagram for the setup.

### Materials

2 pairs sawhorse brackets (available at lumber and hardware stores)
8 legs: 2" x 4" x 28" common pine
2 notched crossbars: 2" x 4" x 36"
2 long bars: 2" x 2" x width of quilt + 12" (no longer than 10')

**Step 1** Build the sawhorse legs according to the bracket instructions or follow the diagram.
**Step 2** Cut the notches from the 2″ x 4″ x 36″ pieces to fit the long bars as shown.
**Step 3** Cover the long bars with a double layer of muslin and stitch in place as shown.
**Step 4** Assemble as shown.

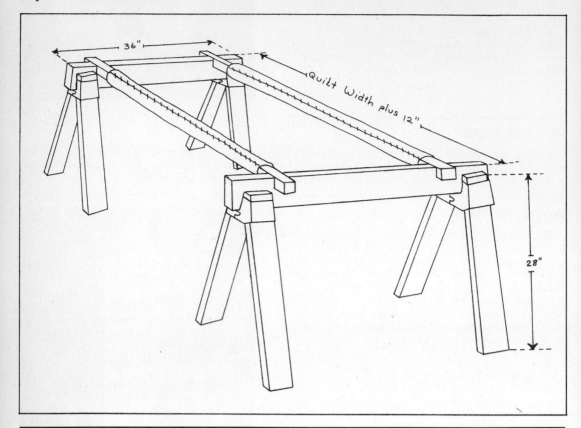

# FABRIC

Traditional quilts are made of 100% cotton (broadcloth or percale). Solid colors are used exclusively in Amish and Hawaiian quilting, calicos mixed with solids for most patchwork and appliqué.

Synthetic fabrics and blends are very popular and available in a magnificent range of colors and prints, but they lack the feel of 100% cotton and are more difficult to stitch.

If you have or find a remnant in a store and can't determine the fabric content by feel, try the burn test on a scrap of the fabric. Cotton will burn slowly and leave a fine ash, while a blend will burn slowly and leave a smoky, hard edge.

You can use chintz, satin, velvet, corduroy, and wool for specialty quilts. Stay away from loosely woven or heavyweight fabrics like burlap, poly knits, linen, sailcloth, and canvas. Some will shred or stretch when stitched; the others are too heavy and unmanageable.

The following are samples of fabric chosen for fine quality, color range, and pattern. (See "Acknowledgments," page vii.)

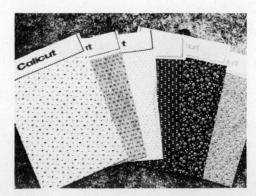

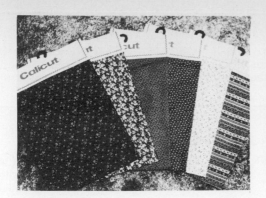

## ESTIMATING YARDAGE

It is necessary to estimate the amount of fabric you need for a quilting project before you go to the store to make your purchase. It is a pity to waste money by buying more fabric than you need, but it is a disaster to start the last block and discover that you need a few more inches of fabric to finish the quilt.

To figure fabric requirements mathematically requires a basic knowledge of geometry. First, find the area of each template (including seam allowances). Since I haven't any batteries for my calculator and really cannot function well in the world of geometric formulation, I suggest the old favorite "paper template, pencil, and count" method for finding the area of each piece. Then multiply by the number of pieces required, and finally divide by the fabric width.

**Step 1** Using the enlarged pattern block as your guide, make a set of full-size templates (with a ¼" seam allowance). Mark each piece with the number of times it appears in *each* fabric in the pattern.

**Step 2** Mark a 1" grid on each pattern template. Count the number of squares. Any part of a square is counted as a whole square. See how the 4" x 6" triangle in the diagram equals 14 square inches (area of triangle).

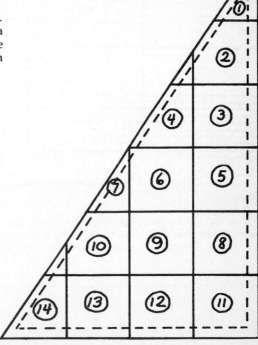

**Step 3** Multiply the number of times the piece appears in one fabric in the pattern (found in step 1) by the number of square inches determined in step 2. For example, if the triangle appears four times, 14 x 4 = 56 square inches.

**Step 4** Count the number of blocks needed for the quilt. For the example, say that there are 12 blocks in the quilt top. Multiply the number of blocks (12) by the area (56). This will give you the total square inches of fabric needed for this pattern piece: 56 x 12 = 672 square inches.

**Step 5** Finally, divide this number (672) by the fabric width in inches. If the fabric measures 45" wide, 672 ÷ 45 = 14.9". Round off this number to the nearest higher inch: 15.

**Step 6** For safety, add about 10% to this final calculation before making any fabric purchase. In this example, 10% equals about 1½". This pattern piece would require a piece of fabric 45" wide by 16½" long for the entire quilt top.

**Step 7** Repeat for each template in the pattern block.

# BASIC PATTERN CATEGORIES

Most patterns can be divided into units or grids. These form the basic pattern categories: four-patch, five-patch, seven-patch, and nine-patch, or the number of units or grids by which a pattern can be equally divided.

## FOUR-PATCH

The four-patch pattern is divided into 4 squares on a grid. This can then be subdivided into multiples of four (divided in half, the result is 16 squares; in fourths, 64 squares).

The majority of patchwork patterns fall into this category.

## FIVE-PATCH

The five-patch pattern is divided into 25 squares on a grid (5 across and 5 down). This may then be subdivided into 100 or more squares. Although it would be more logical to call this a twenty-five-patch, for simplicity it is always called a five-patch.

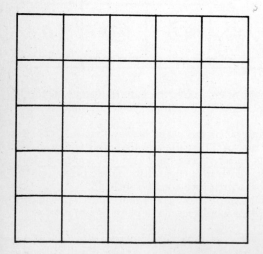 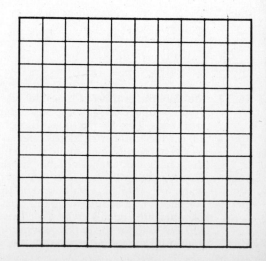

## SEVEN-PATCH

Seven-patch patterns are divided into 49 squares on a grid (7 units across and 7 units down). Again for simplicity, it is always called a seven-patch pattern rather than the logical forty-nine-patch.

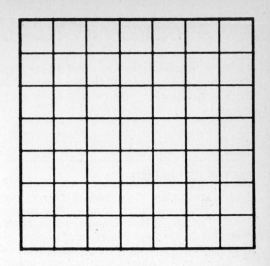

## NINE-PATCH

The nine-patch pattern is divided into 9 squares on a grid. It may be subdivided in half to make 36 squares, in thirds to make 81 squares, or in quarters to make 144 squares. This is the second most popular patchwork category.

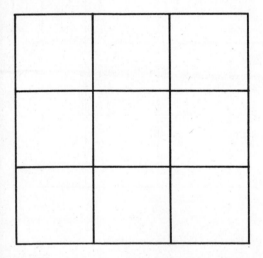

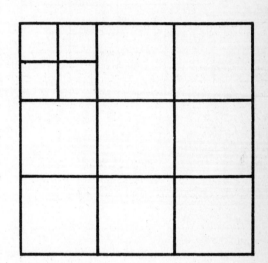

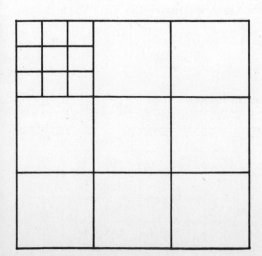

17

# ENLARGING AND REDUCING PATTERNS

All patterns in this book are drafted on graph paper. This has been done to make enlarging and reducing the patterns and making working templates easy to do using the grid method. This technique requires no artistic talent or knowledge of drawing.

## METHOD I (GRID)

**Step 1**  Select a pattern from this book. These are already drawn on a grid (graph paper). If you choose a pattern from another source (not graphed), you must either trace it on graph paper or trace it on tracing paper and mark a grid over your tracing.

**Step 2**  I do not stock graph paper in every grid size, although it is readily available in ½", ¾", and 1" grids for sewing and related work. I use ¼"-square grid graph paper generically and, using the ¼" markings, draw a heavy line in the size I want over the ¼" lines. For example, to make ½"-grid graph paper, draw over every two lines horizontally and vertically; for ¾" grid, draw over every three lines, etc.

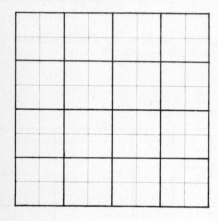 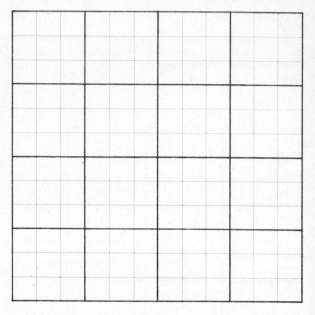

Prepare your finished-size-grid graph paper. Mark a grid having the same number of squares as the pattern.

Plan before you draw. If the chosen pattern has 12 squares, a 1" grid will produce a 12" block, a ¾" grid a 9" block.

You can use the following chart to compute the size of a block. Count the number of squares in the pattern (across or down) and check the size of your finished grid squares on the chart. Where the two numbers intersect is the finished size of the block.

### Number of Squares in Pattern

|        | 10    | 12    | 14     | 15     | 16   | 17     | 18     |
|--------|-------|-------|--------|--------|------|--------|--------|
| ½"     | 5"    | 6"    | 7"     | 7½"    | 8"   | 8½"    | 9"     |
| ¾"     | 7½"   | 9"    | 10½"   | 11¼"   | 12"  | 12¾"   | 13½"   |
| 1"     | 10"   | 12"   | 14"    | 15"    | 16"  | 17"    | 18"    |
| 1½"    | 15"   | 18"   | 21"    | 22½"   | 24"  | 25½"   | 27"    |

**Step 3** Number and letter the squares on both grids.
**Step 4** Copy each line from the smaller grid to the corresponding square on the larger grid.

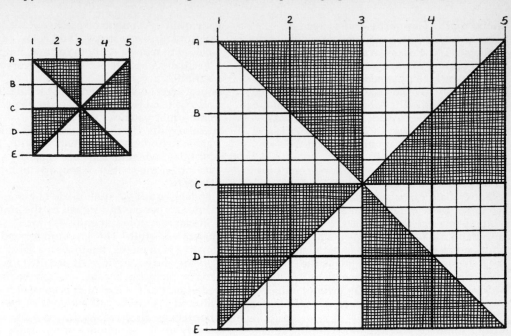

**Step 5** To make a template, repeat these steps for each piece or just cut apart the larger grid on the lines you have drawn. *Do not forget to add a ¼" seam allowance to each piece.*

---

## METHOD II (OPAQUE PROJECTOR)

The opaque projector works like an ordinary slide projector except that it does not limit you to a slide or transparency. It is a wonderful tool for enlarging or reducing any printed material, drawing, or photograph to be traced on paper. I usually project the image on graph paper to save a few steps in preparing the pattern.

---

## METHOD III (PANTOGRAPH)

The pantograph is an adjustable drawing tool made of four strips of wood or plastic that are assembled in a scissorslike manner. A drawing that is traced at point A will be enlarged by a pencil at point B. A simple reversal of the point and pencil will result in a reduction.

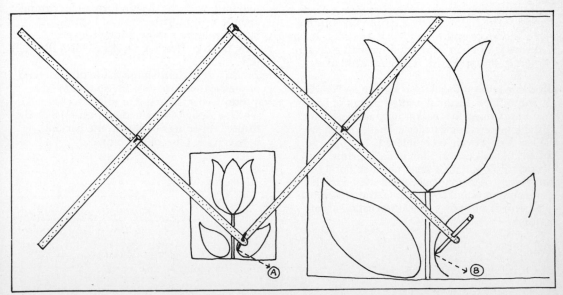

# VOCABULARY

**album quilt**  This quilt is constructed of individual blocks, usually made by different people. The blocks can follow a central theme or be unrelated samples of an individual's work. Each block would be signed in ink or embroidery by the maker.

**Amish quilting**  The Amish people are famous for a distinctive style of pieced patchwork. The design is always a simple geometric and the fabrics are always unpatterned wool or cotton.

**appliqué**  This method of working comes from the French, meaning "applied." A piece of fabric is laid on or sewn to the surface of another piece of fabric. An appliqué is the shape or piece to be applied.

**autograph quilt**  This quilt is made of individual blocks and can be appliqué or patchwork. The common link is the autograph inscribed on each block.

**backing**  The back or bottom layer of a quilt. It can be made of a single piece of wide fabric or joined strips of fabric.

**baste**  To pin or sew with long running stitches to temporarily attach one or more pieces or layers together.

**batting**  This is the filler or stuffing layer, placed between the top and backing to create an interlining. It can be made of wool, cotton, or synthetic fibers and is available in many thicknesses. Although it is also sold by the bag, the sheet form is always used for making a quilt. (See "Tools and Accessories," page 4.)

**bias**  Fabric is woven with vertical and horizontal threads. The diagonal line across these threads is called the bias. A fabric cut on the bias is easily stretched. Since it is difficult to sew a straight line on the bias, it is usually used for curved lines that must be stretched or eased into place.

**binding**  This is used to finish the raw edges of a quilted work. Usually, a piece of bias-cut material is sewn around the raw edges of the quilt sandwich.

**block**  A quilt block is one complete design unit of many that make up the quilt top. It can be pieced or appliquéd. Blocks are sewn together, side by side, or bordered with strips of fabric. The entire quilt top may be a block.

**border**  The frame of fabric strips surrounding the blocks or entire quilt top is a border. It can be made of plain fabric, quilted with a design, pieced, or appliquéd. It is often used as a binding.

**broderie perse**  This is also known as Persian embroidery. Pictorial printed pieces of fabric are appliquéd to a background fabric, giving the illusion of embroidery. These pieces are also decoratively embroidered.

**calico**  An all-cotton cloth usually printed in bright colors with a small motif or floral print.

**comforter**  A heavy quilt, filled with a thick stuffing or animal down or feathers. Because it is thick and puffy, it is often called a puff quilt.

**crazy quilt**  Appliqué or patchwork, it is made of random sizes, shapes, and colors of fabric placed to make a random pattern. Embroidery is usually added to secure and decorate the surface.

**embroidery**  A decorative topstitching. May also be used to cover and secure the edges of crazy quilt patches.

**freedom quilt**  In colonial times this quilt was given to honor a young man's twenty-first birthday, when he achieved majority and was no longer the chattel or property of his parents.

**friendship quilt**  A quilt made of blocks by different people and signed by the quilter. Similar to autograph quilt.

**masterpiece quilt**  This is a quilt formed of many small pieces, made with a great amount of care and proficiency. It usually took years to complete and became a family heirloom.

**medallion quilt**  This quilt is constructed around a central motif with one or more borders on all sides.

**memory quilt**  A memory or mourning quilt was made from pieces of clothing from a person who had died. This was a popular Victorian item when grief was an art. The modern-day memory quilt is usually made from outgrown children's clothing as a memory of childhood. This is a happy quilt.

**miter**  A miter is the right angle formed by making a diagonal seam when turning a corner on a border or binding.

**one-patch**  A design made from pieces of one size and shape.

**patchwork**  The general common term used for joining small pieces of fabric together to form a larger piece of fabric. Also called piece or pieced work.

**quilt**  The generic term for a bedcover consisting of the three layers called the quilt sandwich.

**quilt sandwich**  This is made by combining a top or decorative layer of fabric with a middle filling layer and a backing layer of fabric.

**reverse appliqué**  A decorative technique often used to embellish clothing. Layers of different-colored fabric are sandwiched together, with the design formed by cutting away one or more layers and turning the fabric under to expose another layer.

**setting the top**  Joining blocks to form the quilt top.

**template**  A pattern shape made of cardboard or plastic, used to trace the shape on fabric.

**trapunto**  This is a relief or raised technique in which a design is formed by putting a cord through openings or slits in the backing, between the lines of stitching.

# MEASUREMENTS

The measurement debate between the American linear system (inches, feet, and yards) and the British/European metric system continues to confuse quilters and craftspersons around the world. The Briton has difficulty reading the pattern measurements or purchasing fabric for a quilt pattern published in the United States. The American cannot follow the Italian trapunto pattern or calculate fabric requirements on patterns published in the United Kingdom or Europe.

The United States has been trying to convert to the metric system for more than ten years. The tremendous resistance here has forced most manufacturers to print dual measurements and store owners to post equivalency charts to help make the eventual conversion possible and familiarize the post–school-age customer with the metric system.

In this book, I have used the conversion formula: inches x 2.54 = centimeters; or, in reverse, to find the number of inches: centimeters x 0.4 = inches.

The following equivalency charts show the conversion measurements commonly used in quilting instructions. They can be used as a simple aid for those quilters who are in the confused majority (along with the author) and do not carry a calculator to the store or library.

## Length Equivalency

| Inches | Centimeters |
|--------|-------------|
| 1/8 | 0.3 |
| 1/4 | 0.6 |
| 1/2 | 1.3 |
| 5/8 | 1.6 |
| 3/4 | 1.9 |
| 1 | 2.5 |
| 1½ | 3.8 |
| 2 | 5.1 |
| 3 | 7.6 |
| 4 | 10.2 |
| 5 | 12.7 |
| 6 | 15.2 |
| 7 | 17.8 |
| 8 | 20.3 |
| 9 | 22.9 |
| 10 | 25.4 |
| 12 | 30.5 |
| 18 | 45.7 |
| 24 | 61.0 |
| 30 | 76.2 |
| 36 | 91.4 |
| 48 | 121.9 |
| 60 | 152.4 |
| 72 | 182.9 |
| 84 | 213.4 |

## Linear and Metric Measurements of Bed Sizes

| Type of Bed | Size in Inches | Size in CM |
|-------------|----------------|------------|
| Crib | 27 × 52 | 68.5 × 132.0 |
| Cot | 27 × 75 | 68.5 × 190.5 |
| Highriser | 30 or 33 × 75 | 76.2 or 83.8 × 190.5 |
| Daybed | 36 × 75 | 91.4 × 190.5 |
| Twin | 39 × 75 | 99.0 × 190.5 |
| Double | 54 × 75 | 137.1 × 190.5 |
| Queen | 60 × 75 or 80 | 152.4 × 190.5 or 203.2 |
| Dual-King | 78 × 75 | 198.1 × 190.5 |
| King | 80 × 80 | 203.2 × 203.2 |

## Linear and Metric Measurements of Quilt Sizes

| Type of Bed | Quilt Size in Inches | Quilt Size in CM |
|-------------|----------------------|------------------|
| Crib | 40 × 60 | 101.6 × 152.4 |
| Cot | 40 × 80 | 101.6 × 203.2 |
| Highriser | 60 × 84 | 152.4 × 213.3 |
| Daybed | 64 × 84 | 162.5 × 213.3 |
| Twin | 72 × 84 or 90 | 182.8 × 213.3 or 228.6 |
| Double | 84 × 84 or 90 | 213.3 × 213.3 or 228.6 |
| Queen | 94 × 90 | 238.7 × 228.6 |
| Dual-King | 112 × 90 | 284.4 × 228.6 |
| King | 112 × 90 | 284.4 × 228.6 |

# The Quilting Dictionary
# "A to Z"

## AMISH QUILTING

The world of the Amish community centers around the belief that faith and daily life are inseparable. They are committed to the Lord and believe their way of life is the embodiment of their faith. They follow a strict code of rules, shunning modern technology and dress and most interaction with the outside world.

The traditional quilting of the Amish women is very distinctive in pattern, color, and execution. Colors must be permitted by the church, and reflect the nature of plants and flowers. The quilt tops may be pieced or appliquéd. The elaborate quilting or surface stitching is considered a nondecorative, functional method of combining the three layers that create a quilt. Amish stitching is accepted as among the finest in the world.

The following pages show examples of some typical Amish patterns.

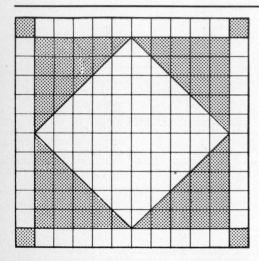

### DIAMOND IN A SQUARE

This simple pattern, consisting of one large square tipped to form the center diamond, with large triangles placed at the corners in a contrasting color to make a square, and framed with one or more borders, is one of the oldest known Amish quilt patterns. The center diamond is usually quilted in an intricate circular pattern, with a less lavish adaptation of the design placed in the borders.

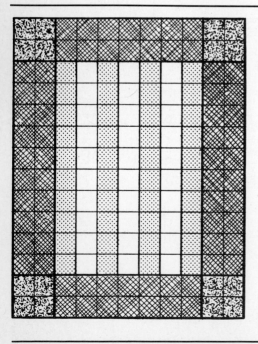

### BARS

The Amish bar patterns can be a simple combination of even vertical strips of fabric. They are usually surrounded by the classic Amish borders or varied by the insertions of narrow bands or even patterned strips such as the classic Wild Goose or Nine-Patch.

The next group of patterns are often called the multiple-patch designs. The small pieces used make this group an excellent source for scrap quilting and a very good beginner or teaching group of patterns.

## FOUR-PATCH

As the name suggests, four-patch patterns are a series of blocks formed by combining four pieces of fabric.

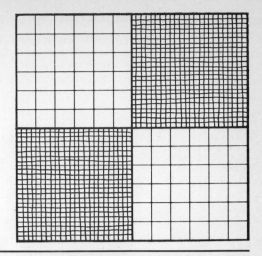

## DOUBLE FOUR-PATCH

The double four-patch combines two blocks of four-patch with two solid blocks of the same size. This forms a four-block square.

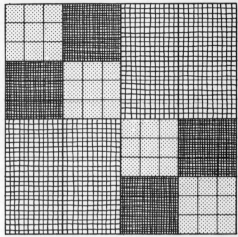

## NINE-PATCH

The nine-patch block combines nine patches of fabric pieced in the same manner as the four-patch blocks, with rows of three horizontal by three vertical patches forming the square.

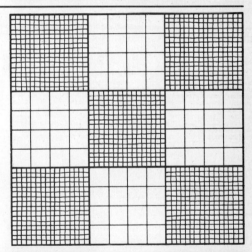

## DOUBLE NINE-PATCH

A double nine-patch pattern combines five nine-patch blocks with four solid squares to form the larger square.

23

## SUNSHINE AND SHADOW

This pattern is created by placing bold, vibrant light and dark solid colors cut from small squares of fabric in a series of ever-expanding rows of diamonds. It is usually a scrap quilt pattern.

Traditionally, one or more borders surround the central diamond pattern. The borders usually contain the very detailed quilted motifs, and the squares are simply seam-quilted or crosshatched.

This pattern is also worked in printed fabrics outside the Amish community and is called Trip Around the World.

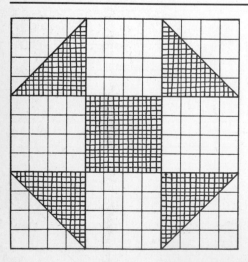

## SHOO-FLY

The Shoo-fly pattern block is a basic nine-patch with cutoff corners. A Shoo-fly quilt would alternate solid quilted blocks with the pattern blocks and have the traditional quilted borders.

## DOUBLE T

The Double T patterns are found in the midwestern Amish communities, where a more liberal approach to quilting is practiced. As the name suggests, these patterns are simply a letter "T" that is mirror-imaged in two directions.

 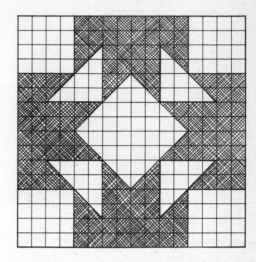

## BASKET

Basket patterns are also found more often among the midwestern Amish. They are varied in design, but traditional in the use of color. Most basket quilt tops alternate the pattern block with a solid intricately quilted block of the same size. The traditional border is also heavily adorned with quilting.

## ROMAN STRIPE

This traditional pattern is most adaptable to strip quilting. Note: In a quilt made in this pattern, look for the *sparkle* stripe—one stripe of a different or more intense color.

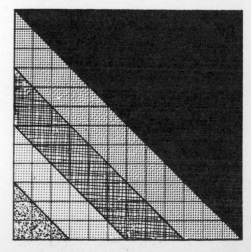

The following photographs show samples of Amish and Amish-style quilting.

Double four-patch in a nine-patch

Double four-patch in a nine-patch quilt

Amish Diamonds and Squares

Bear's Paw

Bow Ties

Indian Plums

Amish Basket

Amish Diamond Basket

Album Star (Odd Fellow Chain)

Roman Stripe

# APPLIQUÉ

*Appliqué* is from the French word meaning "applied." It is simply the art of putting one piece or shape of fabric on another by stitching.

Appliqué has a long history, dating back to the Chinese, Egyptians, Indians, and Europeans. Some of the earliest forms of appliqué in America can be traced to the early 1700s, when it probably evolved from the need to repair a torn or worn fabric. Fabric was scarce and so expensive that decorative techniques were developed to keep these household articles and clothing in usable condition for as long as possible.

Since the days of the colonists, appliqué has come a long way from the original patch-to-repair concept. Reverse appliqué, stuffed appliqué, machine appliqué, traditional appliqué, Hawaiian appliqué, three-dimensional appliqué, and broderie perse are but a few of the techniques that fall into the larger generic category of appliqué techniques.

They all have two basic concepts in common. First, one shape of fabric is placed on another. Second, the design is pictorial rather than geometric or graphic. It can be realistic or impressionistic.

## HAND APPLIQUÉ

Always choose closely woven fabrics for appliqué. Cotton broadcloth, muslin, and calico are good choices, since they will not fray easily and are sturdy enough to withstand the handling necessary in working appliqué. Try not to use polyester or other synthetic blends, knits, or loosely woven or heavyweight fabrics.

The appliqué design can be a small motif or a large pictorial scene. The design or pattern can be chosen from a book, magazine, or pattern company or adapted from a coloring book or photograph. Read "Enlarging and Reducing Patterns" (page 18) and "Templates" (page 259). When the design is drawn to the correct size and the templates are cut, you are ready to begin.

**Step 1** Prepare a ground fabric. This can be a piece of muslin or cotton broadcloth.

**Step 2** Choose the fabric for the appliqué. Use some tricks in this step. For example, a tiny leaf print provides a good illusion for a tree shape, a miniature floral print for a meadow, or a pale tie-dyed blue for a sky.

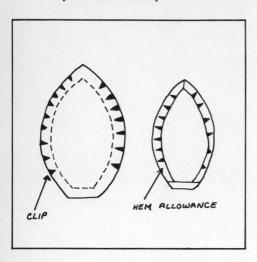

**Step 3** Place the template on the right side of the fabric. This will leave the seam line visible when you turn it under for hemming. Trace around the template, leaving about ¾" between patterns. Draw a ¼" hem allowance, to be turned under when hemming. If you have a good eye, you can cut out the shape while estimating the ¼" hem allowance.

**Step 4** Plan the setup. Lay the pieces in place according to the design. Where pieces overlap, remember to place the foreground piece on top of the background piece—the roof is on top of the house, the leaf on the tree, etc. Even on a small item, think out your order of placement. For example, to appliqué a toy truck remember that the wheels are on the truck, the hubcaps on the wheels, and the fenders over the wheels.

**Step 5** Clip the curves and turn the hem allowance under to the back. Some people prefer to turn, clip, and press the piece before stitching, while others turn the hem under as they sew. Both methods are correct; try both and choose the more comfortable method. **Note:** Some edges do not have to be hemmed. For example, if the raw edge of a piece will be tucked under the hemmed edge of the next piece, it can be tacked or basted in place.

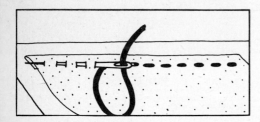

**Step 6** Baste all the pieces in place.

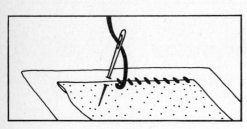

**Step 7** Secure the appliqué pieces, using a hem stitch or a blind hem stitch. The thread should match the appliqué piece.

**Hem Stitch**

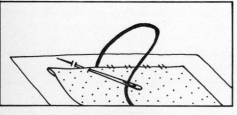

**Blind Hem Stitch**

## MACHINE APPLIQUÉ

Machine appliqué is a method of applying one fabric to another. It is a technique, not a substitute for hand appliqué. This is an art form that must be learned and practiced. Always remember, you are topstitching and the stitches will show. There are several ways to work machine appliqué.

## Method I

**Step 1** Prepare the fabric as in hand appliqué, leaving a ¼" hem allowance all around the piece.

**Step 2** Turn under the hem allowance and clip the curves where necessary.

**Step 3** Pin or baste the appliqué in place on the foundation block.

**Step 4** Topstitch ⅛" in from the turned edge.

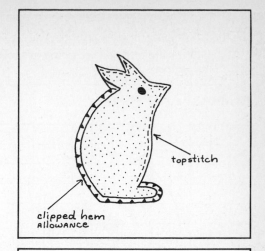

topstitch

clipped hem
allowance

## Method II

**Step 1** Follow method I, steps 1 to 3.

**Step 2** Using the zigzag stitch on your sewing machine, sew on the turned hem line.

ZIG-ZAG

## Method III

**Step 1** Prepare the fabric as for hand appliqué, leaving a ½" to ¾" hem allowance. *Do not turn the hem allowance under.*

**Step 2** Pin or baste in place.

**Step 3** Using the zigzag, satin, or other decorative machine embroidery stitch, sew on the hem allowance line.

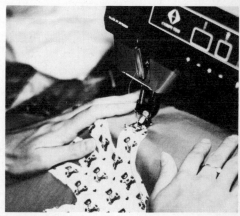

**Step 4** Cut away the excess fabric close to the line of machine stitching. **Note:** The appliqué scissors used in the photograph allow you to snip close to the stitching while protecting the fabric from an accidental cut.

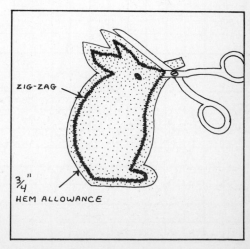

ZIG-ZAG

¾" HEM ALLOWANCE

The following appliqué patterns can be worked by hand or machine and can be used as blocks, wall hangings, and borders. Each pattern is drafted on graph paper for easy enlargement to your desired size. (See "Enlarging and Reducing Patterns," page 18.)

The patterns are grouped according to subject and can be combined in many ways to create larger and more complex patterns.

## ANIMALS AND FISH

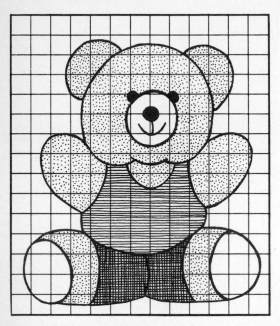

Bear 1

Bear 2

**Bear 3**

**Bear 4**

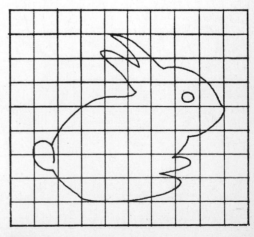

**Bunny 1**

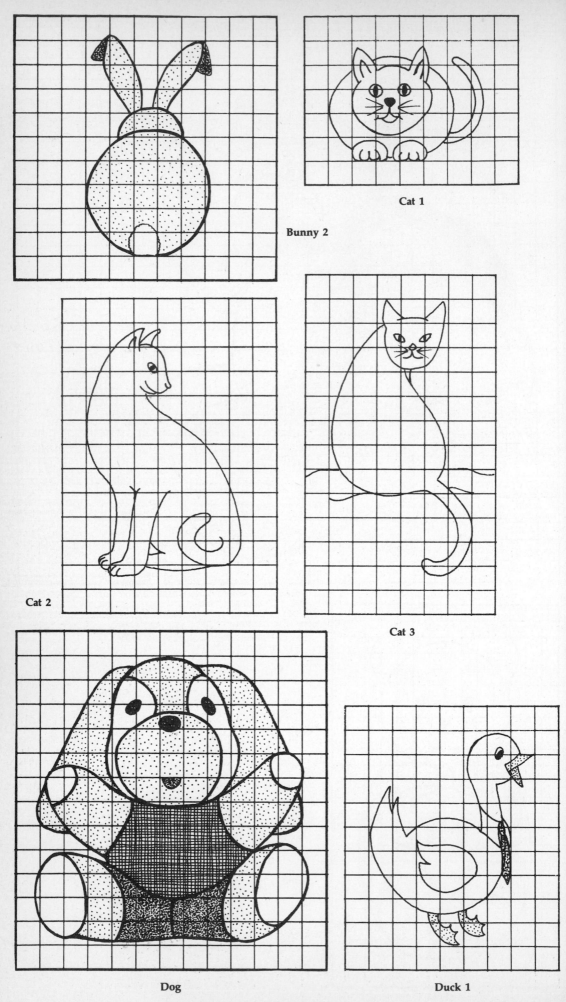

Bunny 2

Cat 1

Cat 2

Cat 3

Dog

Duck 1

Duck 2

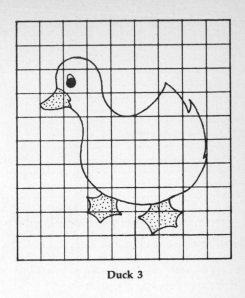

Duck 3

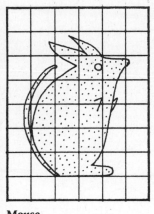

Mouse

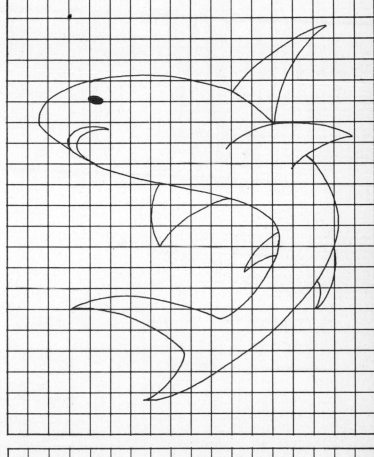

Fish (Shark)

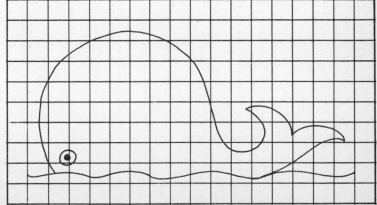

Fish (Whale)

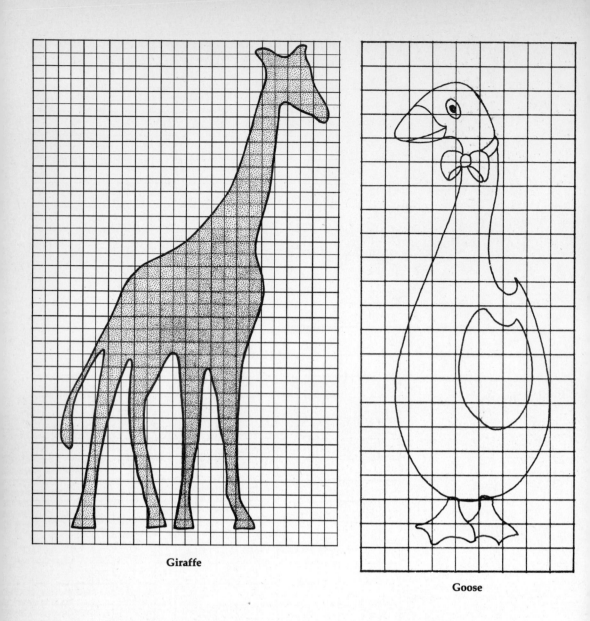

Giraffe

Goose

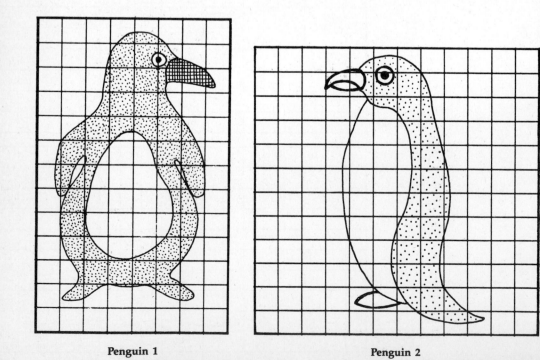

Penguin 1

Penguin 2

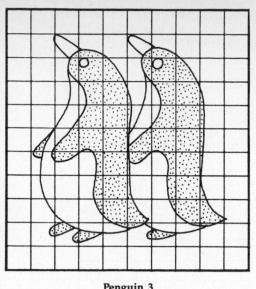

Penguin 3

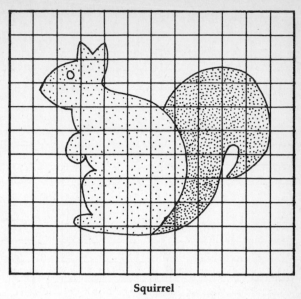

Squirrel

## DESSERTS

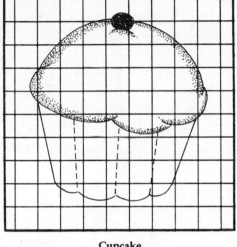

Cupcake

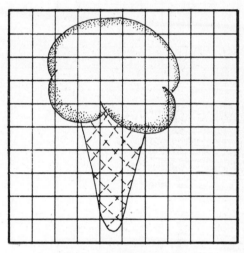

Ice Cream

## FLOWERS AND LEAVES

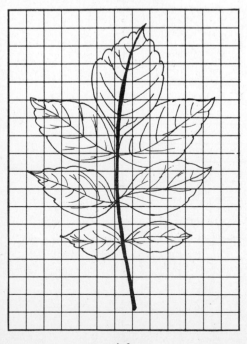

Ash

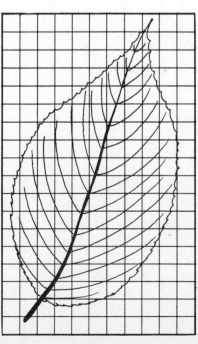

Elm

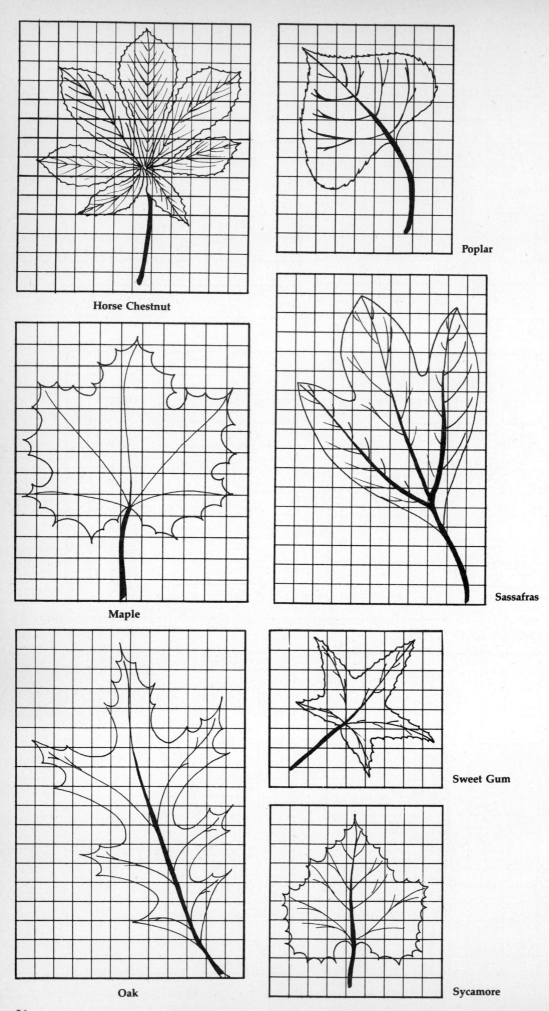

Horse Chestnut

Poplar

Maple

Sassafras

Oak

Sweet Gum

Sycamore

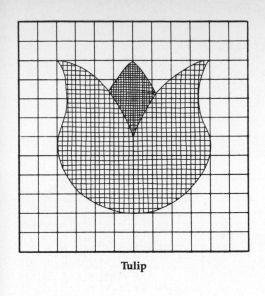

Tulip

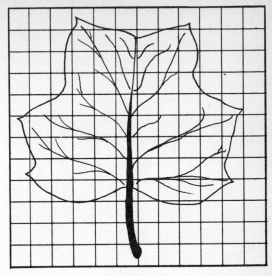

Tulip Tree

## THE HUTCH

Every quilt exhibit seems to have at least one trompe l'oeil kitchen wall hanging. This pattern was drawn from bits and pieces I have seen over the years. To make it your own, just rearrange it: add or subtract dishes and utensils to reflect your desires or lifestyle. This is a project that is fun to plan and work.

# MY GARDEN IN OCTOBER

This pattern is an adaptation of a wall hanging made by a quilter in the autumn of her life, reflecting on her "garden of life." The fabrics were from scraps of her children's clothing, saved over the years. I have chosen to show about a quarter of the pattern, but you can make it as wide as you want and add many more shelves.

# FALL LANDSCAPE

This wall hanging was adapted from a photograph and worked in appliqué using the colors indicated below and fabrics printed with leaves on the tree, trees on the mountain, and small flowers in the foreground.

The pattern can be enlarged to create a twin-size quilt using 1 square = 2" and adding a 16" border on four sides.

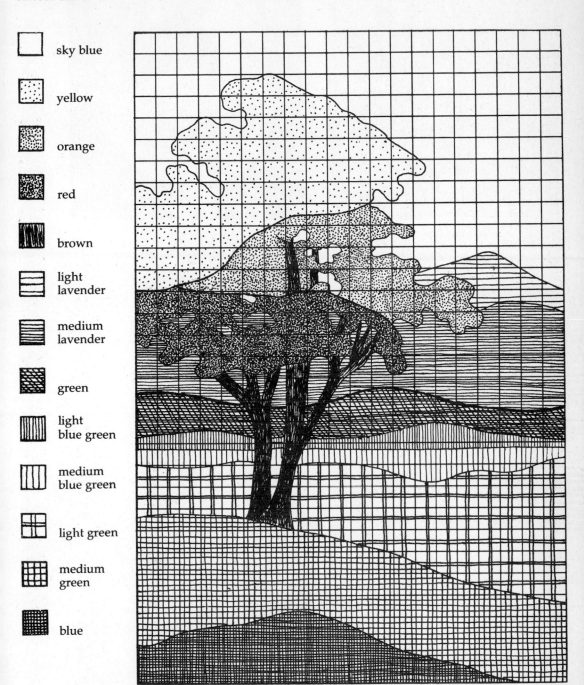

sky blue

yellow

orange

red

brown

light
lavender

medium
lavender

green

light
blue green

medium
blue green

light green

medium
green

blue

The following photographs show examples of appliqué blocks.

**Fall Leaves appliqué**

**Duck 2**

**Antique Sunbonnet 1**

**Antique Sunbonnet 2**

**Ohio Rose pattern**

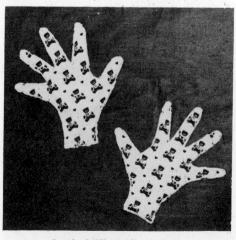
**Justin Miller's Handprints**

# CATHEDRAL WINDOW QUILTING

Cathedral window quilting is the traditional name for a fascinating three-dimensional technique using squares of unbleached muslin folded and refolded to form multilayered squares. These squares are joined with small squares of print or calico fabric to form a unique interlocking diamond-and-circle pattern. No filler or batting is used, and no quilt stitching or lining or edging is required.

## TO MAKE A SQUARE
## Method I

**Step 1**    Cut a square of preshrunk unbleached muslin 7" square. **Note:** The square of muslin is about 4 times as large as the finished square, so by changing the size of the muslin square you can change the finished cathedral block.

**Step 2**    Cut a cardboard template 6" square. Place the template in the center of the muslin and fold a ½" seam allowance over the cardboard. Press in place. Remove the cardboard and mark the center with a pin or pencil dot.

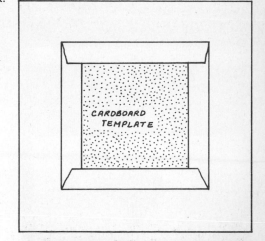

**Step 3**    Fold the four corners to the center and pin in place. Press lightly.

**Step 4**    Repeat step 3. Tack all four center corners together securely through all thicknesses to the back. The square now measures approximately 3" x 3".

**Step 5**    Make a number of squares, repeating steps 1 to 4.

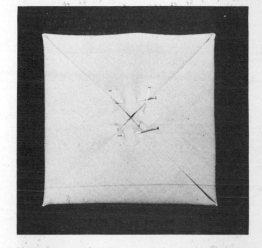

**Step 6**    To join, place two squares together (folded sides facing) and sew with an overcast stitch along the sides.

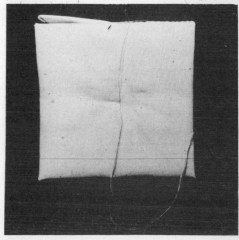

**Step 7**    Open the two squares and place on a flat surface, fold side up.

**Step 8**    To make the windows, cut a 2" square template from cardboard or plastic. Using this template, cut a 2" square piece of colored print fabric. A well-stocked scrap basket will come in handy for this project.

**Step 9** Place the 2" piece of print fabric diagonally over the seam on the diamond shape formed by the two adjoining squares. **Note:** The square of fabric may have to be trimmed to fit.

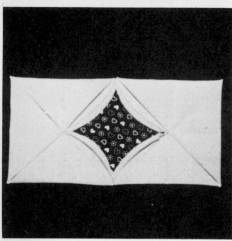

**Step 10** Roll the folded edge of the muslin over the print fabric window and slip-stitch in place. Repeat with each side, tacking the corners about ¼" from the tip as you work. **Note:** Some quilters prefer to secure the window with a running stitch.

**Step 11** Make strips of windows in this manner. Join the strips to make a larger piece of fabric, adding the colored windows on the seam line between the rows as you work.

## Method II

**Steps 1 and 2** Work as for method I.
**Step 3** Fold the muslin in half with the seam allowances on the outside. Using a close overcast stitch, sew the edges together on each side, working from the open top edge down 1¼" toward the folded edge.

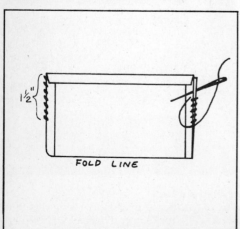

1½"

FOLD LINE

**Step 4**  Turn right side out and refold to leave the seams at the center. Slip-stitch the two open folded edges together from the center out 1¼".

**Step 5**  You now have a square that measures approximately 4¼". Press lightly to square the corners.

**Step 6**  Fold the four corners to the center and pin. Tack the four center corners together through all thicknesses of the square. This square now measures approximately 3".

**Step 7**  Make a number of squares, then proceed from step 6 of method I.

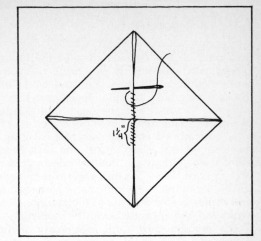

## Method III

This is often called the "speed method," because it can be worked by hand or with a sewing machine.

**Step 1**  Cut a 7" square of muslin.

**Step 2**  Fold the muslin in half and stitch a seam (½" seam allowance) along both short side edges.

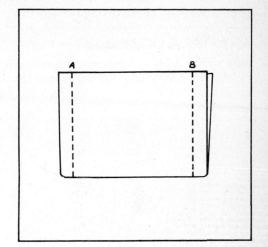

**Step 3**  Trim the corners at the fold and press the seams open.

**Step 4**  Right sides facing, bring the two seams (A and B) together and pin. Stitch across (½" seam allowance), leaving an opening for turning to the right side.

**Step 5**  Trim the top corners and press this seam open.

**Step 6**  Turn right side out and close the opening with slip stitches. Press lightly. The square now measures approximately 4¼".

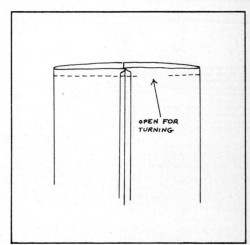

**Step 7**  Mark the center of each side with a pin. Draw a line as shown in the diagram from A to B, B to C, C to D, and D to A. This is the seam line for joining the squares.

**Step 8**  Repeat these steps to make a number of squares. Place two squares together, smooth sides facing. Match the seam lines on both squares and stitch.

**Step 9**  Join a row of squares, then join the rows in the same way.

**Step 10**  Bring the four corners to the center of each square and pin in place. Tack the four corners together through all thicknesses to the back.

**Step 11**  Cut a 2" piece of print fabric and place over the seam line formed by the two adjoining squares, then proceed to step 10 of method I to make the windows.

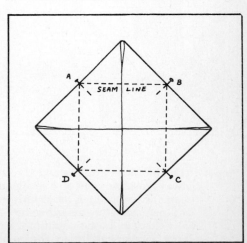

# CRAZY QUILT

The crazy quilt is considered to be the first form of pieced patchworking. It was made from scraps of worn clothing and leftover bits and pieces of fabric. These were arbitrarily joined together to form a quilt.

In the Victorian age the crazy quilt again found popularity. This time, it was not a product of necessity, but rather a fancy ornamental covering. Fancy fabrics—velvets, silks, satins, and lush brocades—were used. Ornate embroidery adorned each scrap and piece of fabric. The quilts were often made of 12" to 16" blocks that were joined and bordered. Flowers and butterflies were some of the favorite motifs embroidered and appliquéd over the quilt surface.

The modern crazy quilt uses many of the same techniques. The scrap-bag approach is often tempered with planned design relationships.

## TO MAKE A CRAZY QUILT

**Step 1**  Cut a piece of muslin to the size of the finished block (usually 12" to 16") plus a seam allowance for joining the blocks together. This is called the foundation block.

**Step 2**  If this is to be a planned arrangement, select the scraps of material and arrange them according to your design, allowing a ½" overlap. If you are not satisfied, move and trim the pieces.

If this is a random arrangement, begin by placing the first scrap of fabric in one corner of the foundation block, right side up. Baste it in place with small running stitches. I prefer to start at the lower left corner, building up and to the right as I work, but starting at any corner will produce the same result.

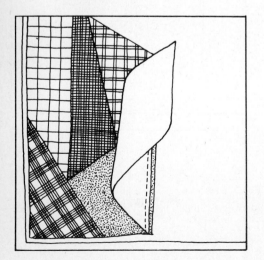

**Step 3**  Put the next scrap of fabric over the first, right sides together. Baste along one side, sewing with small running stitches through all layers. Finger-press open to the right side and add the next scrap of fabric. Continue in this manner until the entire foundation block is covered.

**Step 4**  The embroidery can be added to the individual blocks or after the blocks are joined. It is always easier to work on a smaller unit, but the embroidery must be worked over the joining seams when the quilt top is finished. Always remember, the embroidery is both decorative and necessary for strengthening the joining seams. I recommend using six-strand embroidery floss on a cotton quilt top, for its strength and extensive range of colors. Some of the more popular stitches are shown here.

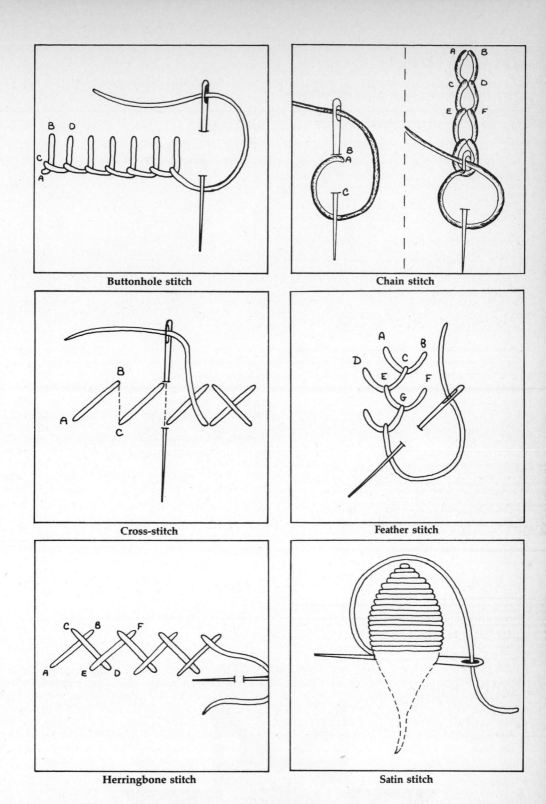

Buttonhole stitch

Chain stitch

Cross-stitch

Feather stitch

Herringbone stitch

Satin stitch

**Step 5**  Seam the blocks together in rows, then join the rows, being careful to align the blocks accurately.

**Step 6**  Add a solid border to frame the busy design you have created.

**Step 7**  When the quilt top is finished and all the embroidery completed, make the quilt sandwich. First, cut the backing 3" larger than the quilt top. Put the backing right side down on a large flat surface (most people use the floor). Center the batting, then add the quilt top. Pin the three layers together, smoothing the surface from the center outward. Be careful to line up the edges, making sure that the extra backing is even all around.

**Step 8**  The crazy quilt is usually not quilted because of the bulkiness of the many overlapped small pieces. However, it is necessary to secure the three layers by some method. I suggest one of the tying methods shown on page 82. Use six-strand embroidery floss or yarn to make the knots.

**Step 9**  A crazy quilt is often finished by using the backing as a self-binding. First, trim the excess backing to 1½" to 2" larger than the quilt top on all four sides. Wrap the backing forward over the quilt top and pin it in place. Fold the raw edge under ⅜" to ½" as you work, and blind-stitch it to the quilt top.

# DIAMONDS

Diamonds are used to form the star patterns.

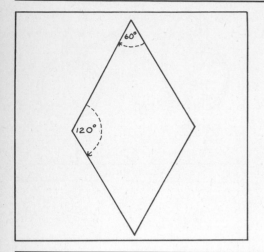

### DIAMOND 1

The six-pointed star is made using a diamond pattern with two angles of 60° and two angles of 120°.

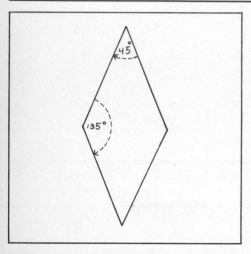

### DIAMOND 2

The eight-pointed star is made using a diamond pattern with two angles of 45° and two angles of 135°.

The following patterns are made by using one of the diamonds described above.

## FRAMED LONE STAR
**lone star**

This famous pattern is made by placing Diamond 2 in concentric circles radiating from the center, using a different color fabric for each circle. The same pattern without the dark frame is called the Lone Star.

## STARFISH BLOCK 1
**fish block**

This pattern is basically a six-pointed star (Diamond 1) centered over a larger six-pointed star with triangle tails placed on the outer tip of each point. Each fish is made in two tones of a different color.

## STARFISH BLOCK 2

This pattern is a simplified version of Starfish 1. It is placed on a hexagon background made of half diamonds.

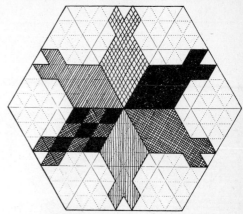

## HEXAGON STARS

These stars are made of six-pointed stars (Diamond 1) encircled with six diamonds to form a hexagon. The hexagons are joined with half diamonds to form a larger hexagon.

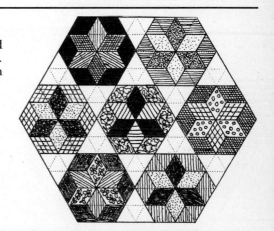

## COMPASS IN A HEXAGON

This is a split six-pointed diamond star (Diamond 1) placed over a larger six-pointed star and framed in a hexagon.

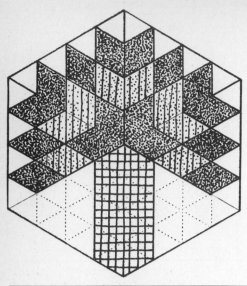

## FORBIDDEN FRUIT TREE IN A HEXAGON

This pattern is based on a six-pointed star (Diamond 1) and framed with half diamonds to form a hexagon.

## HHH THUNDERBIRD WITH HEXAGON FRAME

This pattern is worked in a combination of diamonds (Diamond 1) and half diamonds.

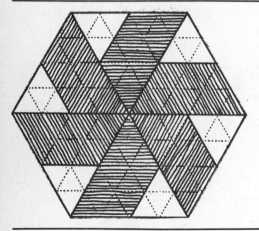

## WHIRLING TRIANGLES IN A HEXAGON

This pattern is based on a six-pointed star with half diamonds attached. It is framed with a contrasting-color half diamond to form the hexagon.

## WHIRLING TRIANGLES
**whirligig hexagon**

This is the reverse-color and joined variation of the Whirling Triangles in a Hexagon.

## TUMBLING BLOCKS

This historical pattern is made of diamonds (Diamond 1) placed to create this optical illusion.

## TUMBLING BLOCKS HEXAGON

Place the blocks made in the Tumbling Blocks pattern around a hexagon center separated by half diamonds and you have this framed hexagon.

## INNER-CITY BLOCK
### Y block

This block is constructed of diamonds (Diamond 1). Each color is made of three diamonds.

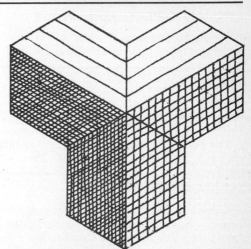

## INNER-CITY PATTERN 1
### city blocks, cornerstones

When placed as shown in the diagram, this pattern gives the illusion of an aerial picture of a city.

## INNER-CITY PATTERN 2
### city blocks, cornerstones

Each side of the "Y" blocks is worked in a different color fabric.

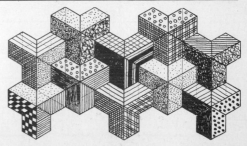

49

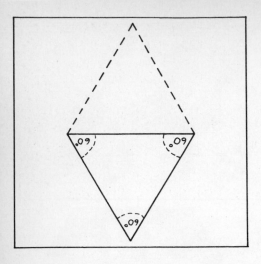

## HALF DIAMOND

The half diamond is an equilateral triangle with three equal sides and three equal angles (60°). This is half of Diamond 1 used to make the six-pointed star, and is the basic shape used in many of the patterns described above.

# EMBROIDERED QUILTING

## CREWEL

The crewel technique is occasionally used in quilt making. It was a popular form of working a few hundred years ago and had a revived interest in the 1960s and 1970s. Today, most crewel embroidery in quilt making is limited to crazy quilts (page 44).

## PERSIAN OR BRODERIE PERSE

Persian embroidery (also known as broderie perse) is the technique of appliquéing cutout pieces of a pictorial fabric (usually chintz) and embellishing them with embroidery.

## TURKEY RED

Turkey Red is the name given to a technique of embroidery popular for quilt work from the late 1800s to the early 1900s. Small transfer patterns are applied to white fabric blocks and embroidered in turkey red colored thread (hence the name). The embroidered blocks are joined to make a quilt.

The patterns are always small sentimental motifs, often depicting personal commemorations of events in the quilter's or recipient's life.

## TENERIFFE

Teneriffe embroidery, also known as Norwegian, Amish, snowflake, chicken scratching, and depression lace embroidery, gives the illusion of lace appliquéd on a dotted, gingham, or even-weave fabric. The lacy appearance makes this a popular form of decoration on crib quilts and nursery accessories.

Two stitches are needed to create this technique. The first is a double cross-stitch or Smyrna stitch. To work this stitch, start with a simple cross-stitch.

Then work a plus (+) over the cross-stitch.

The second is a straight stitch worked in the direction (horizontal or vertical) shown on your pattern chart. The symbol (o) is a circle formed by weaving the needle underneath the four straight stitches. To work, come up from the back and to the left of one of the straight stitches. Weave the needle under each straight stitch, going around twice (or doubling the thread and going around once).

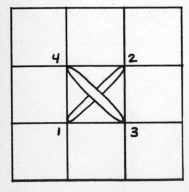
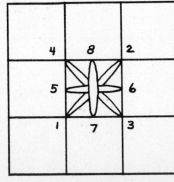

## To Work Teneriffe on Gingham

**Step 1** Choose a design and mark the center on both vertical and horizontal edges.

**Step 2** Determine the center of your fabric. **Note:** When working on gingham, be aware that the checks are rarely a true square. If it is rectangular, the appearance of the design will be altered and look wider and higher. Usually, a selvage at the top or bottom of the fabric will produce a design that appears wider than the chart; a selvage at the sides will produce a design that appears higher than the chart.

**Step 3** Use six-strand embroidery floss (see "Tools and Accessories," page 4, and suppliers, page vii) split into individual strands. On 14- to 16-count-to-the-inch gingham use one strand of floss, on 8-count use two strands, and on 4-count use three or four strands.

**Step 4** The symbol (X) on the chart is worked as a double cross-stitch or Smyrna stitch on the darkest square of the gingham.

**Step 5** The symbols ( I ) and ( – ) are the straight stitches and worked in the direction indicated on the chart on the medium-color square of the gingham fabric.

**Step 6** The symbol (o) is worked by weaving under the straight stitches as shown in the stitch diagrams.

**Step 7** One row of backstitch or one row of double cross-stitch in a darker color can be used to outline the motif if desired.

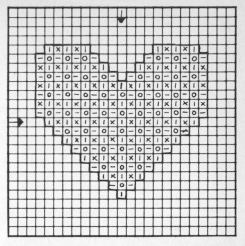

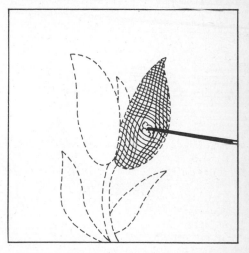

# ENGLISH PADDED QUILTING

This technique is often confused with Italian trapunto work (see page 81). In English padding, small bits of cotton or batting are stuffed from the back of the piece to create padded areas on the surface.

## To Work

**Step 1** Place the top fabric over the muslin backing, wrong sides together (inside). Baste.

**Step 2** Transfer the design and work the quilting in the normal manner, using very fine stitches. (See "Trapunto," page 81.)

**Step 3** Working from the back (muslin), carefully separate the threads where you want to add the padding. Use a yarn needle or fine steel crochet hook. Gently push very small pieces of batting into the hole you have just made.

**Step 4** After the area is stuffed to the desired thickness or level, carefully push the fabric threads back in place with the yarn needle or crochet hook. **Note:** If the backing material is too dense to allow the threads to be separated easily, make a small slit in the fabric, stuff, and sew the opening closed with a fine needle and thread.

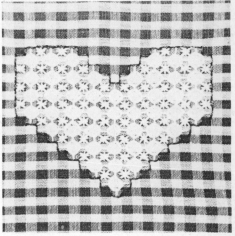

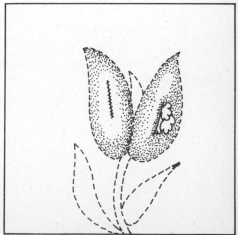

# ENGLISH PIECING

English piecing is the recommended method for joining pattern pieces that use hexagons (Grandmother's Flower Garden) or diamonds (Baby Blocks). The fabric is wrapped around a paper template to form the shape. The shapes are then joined to make the pattern.

Hexagons and diamonds can be joined by hand or machine without a paper template (American piecing method), but it is very difficult to match the corners or fit the angles together without forming small holes. English piecing usually eliminates this problem.

**Step 1** Make a template of the chosen shapes using cardboard or plastic. *Do not add any seam allowance.* This template will be used to make the paper shapes.

**Step 2** Make a second template of the chosen shape, *adding a ¼″ seam allowance all around.* This template will be used to mark and cut the fabric.

**Step 3** Trace and cut a number of the paper shapes, using the smaller template. Newsprint is often used for economy, but it is too soft and will dirty both the fabric and your hands. I recommend a stiffer paper, such as typing bond, old letters, or postal or greeting cards. They are cleaner and more durable and can be used several times if handled with care.

**Step 4** Using the larger template, trace and cut your fabric pieces.

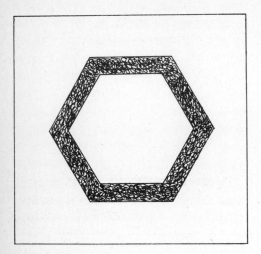

**Step 5** Holding the fabric with the wrong side facing you, place the paper shape in the center of the fabric piece. Pin the paper and fabric together.

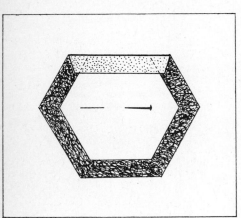

**Step 6** Fold the fabric seam allowance toward you over the paper and baste it in place with thread.

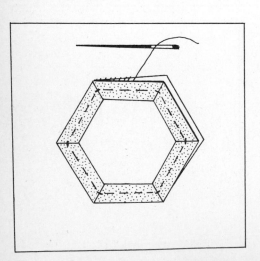

Forming sharp corners as you work, fold and baste on each side. Place a small tack stitch at each corner.

**Step 7**   To join, place the pieces right sides together and use small whipstitches through the fabric edges on the fold.

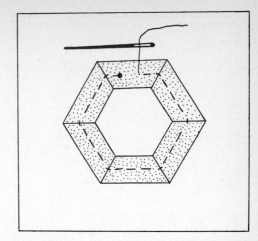

**Step 8**   Open and press each seam as you work for a smooth finished piece.

**Step 9**   As you complete a section and have pieces sewn around it on all sides, you can remove the basting thread and reuse the paper.

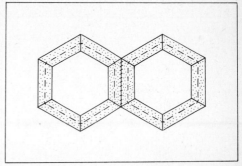

**Note:** There are examples of this method with the paper left in the finished quilt. This was not an error by the quilters, but rather a clever way to add warmth, known as poor man's insulation.

# HAWAIIAN QUILTING

Quilting was brought to the Hawaiian Islands in the early 1800s by missionaries from America. It didn't take long before a unique style, influenced by their own culture, love of color, and nature, evolved into the distinctive Hawaiian quilting we know today.

The designs are made as a giant free form appliquéd to a solid ground. Only two pieces of material are used to make the quilt top, with one color for the background and one for the appliqué.

Once a pattern is created it becomes the guarded personal property of the creator. Superstition and folklore guarantee a horrible fate to anyone who would dare to steal or copy another's pattern without permission. Even if permission is given, the copy must be altered in some way, such as by the addition of small openings or *pukas* somewhere in the design. Surprisingly, this tradition is followed in today's modern photocopy culture.

The subjects, though very stylized, are always taken from nature. The designs are always based on four or eight points and are traditionally square.

Hawaiian quilting patterns are cut from a single piece of fabric that has been folded in a precise manner to produce a perfectly symmetrical design. Always practice your cutting with a small sheet of paper before working with expensive large pieces of fabric. It will enable you to get the feel of the rhythmic lines and flowing forms created by this technique in a manageable scale or size.

## To Make a Pattern

**Step 1**   Place a sheet of square-cut paper on a flat surface. Fold in half and press along the fold line to crease sharply.

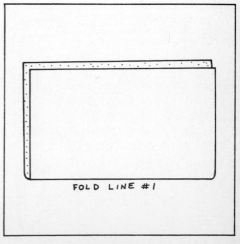

FOLD LINE #1

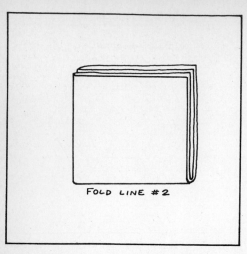

FOLD LINE #2

**Step 2** Fold in half again, from left to right, creasing sharply on the fold line as before. You now have a sheet of paper folded in quarters with a fold line on the left, two folds on the top, and open edges to the right and bottom.

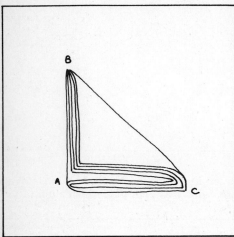

B

A    C

**Step 3** Fold A (upper right corner) to the left fold-line edge, making a triangle ABC. Crease sharply as before.

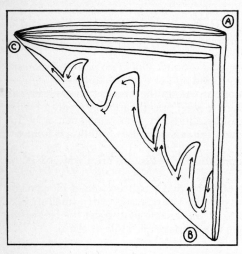

Ⓐ

Ⓒ

Ⓑ

**Step 4** Point B is the center and line BC the bias. Go to step 5 for a four-point pattern or step 6 for an eight-point pattern.

**Step 5** To design a four-point pattern, draw a continuous line from any imaginary point along the bottom half of line AB toward point B and along the bias line ending at point C. **Caution:** *Do not let the drawn line touch the center point or any of the folds.* This makes the pattern fall apart.

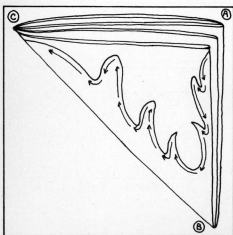

Ⓒ    Ⓐ

Ⓑ

**Step 6** To design an eight-point pattern, draw a continuous design line from point A toward point B, ending at point C. Note the caution in step 5.

**Step 7** Cut along the lines you have drawn. Be sure to cut through all eight thicknesses of the folded paper.

**Step 8** Unfold the paper. The pattern is now complete.

Try this a few times. The possibilities are infinite. When you have a pattern that you like, check the chart below to determine the size of your finished quilt. Remember, Hawaiian quilts are traditionally square. Many quilters have copied the Hawaiian style, elongated the design in one direction or added borders to make a rectangular quilt. This is Hawaiian style. I do not choose to anger the quilting gods in this manner.

| Type of Bed | Size in Inches | Squared Quilt Size* |
| --- | --- | --- |
| Crib | 27 × 52 | 40 × 40 |
| Twin | 39 × 75 | 84 × 84 |
| Double | 54 × 75 | 96 × 96 |
| Queen | 60 × 80 | 108 × 108 |
| King | 80 × 80 | 115 × 115 |

*This is an approximate size. The finished quilt may be made up to 6″ larger on all sides with little or no change in its look or fit. However, it must be square.

## To Make a Quilt Top

**Step 1** Prepare enough fabric of each color to make the entire quilt top in the size chosen from the above chart. If you cannot get a piece of material large enough to construct the quilt top without seaming, seam the fabric in three long strips; this way, the center or points won't fall on a seam. Be careful to cut each strip the same size to ensure that all the seams line up in the same place on each layer in the finished work. **Hint:** A large-width fabric can be cut from a 100% cotton sheet in your desired color. This can be a real timesaver.

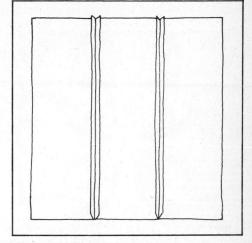

**Step 2** Wash and iron the prepared fabric. Take the fabric to be appliquéd and fold it exactly as you did the paper pattern in steps 1–4. Mark the points A, B, and C and the bias.

**Step 3** Place the folded fabric on a piece of wrapping paper that is larger than the folded fabric. Cut the paper to the exact size of the folded fabric. This will be used to cut the paper pattern. **Note:** Some quilters and teachers suggest the use of newspaper for this step. I never allow a student to touch newspaper when handling fabric. It will make your hands very dirty and the fabric often becomes unsalvageable.

**Step 4** To enlarge the original paper pattern, first mark the large piece of wrapping paper on the center (point B), bias, and points A and C. Next, accurately mark the design freehand on the large paper (or see "Enlarging and Reducing Patterns," page 18). When the pattern is drawn on the large paper, cut it out.

**Step 5** Place the cutout paper pattern on the folded fabric and pin it carefully through all eight layers.

**Step 6** Cut on the pattern line through all the layers.

**Step 7** Remove the pins and pattern and unfold the fabric. Gently place it on the other prepared top piece of fabric. If necessary, line up any seams to match exactly.

**Step 8** Starting at the center and working out toward the points, carefully pin the appliqué to the top layer. Do not pull or stretch the appliqué.

Step 9 Starting at the center, baste each section (horizontal, vertical, and diagonal). If it is perfectly centered, baste around the perimeter of the appliqué, working about ½" in from the edges.

Step 10 Rolling the edges of the appliqué under about ⅛", blindstitch around the entire piece. When all the edges are sewn, remove the basting stitches.

Step 11 Assemble the appliqué top, batting, and backing in the usual manner.

### To Quilt

Hawaiian quilting is worked in a special way. The technique used is called outline, echo, or wave quilting and is placed in lines about ½" apart. Use a quilting thread that closely matches the fabric. It is a tedious, time-consuming process.

### To Finish the Hawaiian Quilt

Traditionally, these quilts are bound around the outside edges with strips of fabric 2" to 2½" wide. The corners may be mitered or lapped. Stitch the binding to the back, turn to the front, and blindstitch in place.

# HEXAGONS

The hexagon is a six-sided geometric shape. Hexagons can be joined into rings or circles to form a medallion or into rows to create a mosaic pattern.

The traditional Grandmother's Flower Garden pattern is made by placing rings of hexagons around a center hexagon to form the flower. The flowers are often surrounded by a circle of green fabric hexagons to symbolize leaves or grass. The final circle is made of a solid, usually white, fabric to represent the paths.

## THE HEXAGON PATTERN

The hexagon pattern shape is easily made using a compass and a piece of paper.

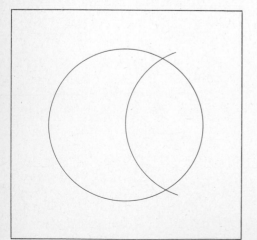

Step 1 Using the compass, make a circle on the paper the *exact* size you want your finished hexagon shape to be. The distance between the compass point and the pencil point is always the length of the radius or, more simply, half of the finished size of the circle. For example, to make a 2" circle, set the points of the compass 1" apart. Do not change your compass setting after the circle is made.

Step 2 Put the point of the compass on any spot on the circumference and describe an arc where the pencil point crosses the circumference.

**Step 3** Put the point of the compass on the point where the arc you just made crosses the circumference and make another arc.

**Step 4** Continue around the circle, repeating step 3 until you have six points on the circumference.

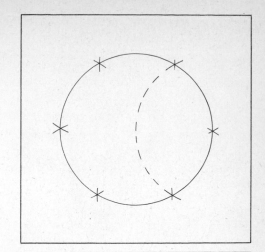

**Step 5** Using a straight edge or ruler, join the points with a straight line around the circle. The hexagon is now formed.

**Step 6** Make the hexagon template from this pattern. Remember to add a ¼″ seam allowance when cutting the fabric.

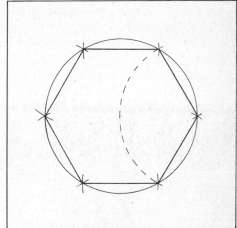

There are many hexagon patterns based on Grandmother's Flower Garden. Most of these begin with a simple flower pattern.

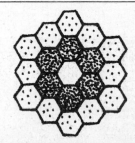

## HEXAGON FLOWERS
**hexagon garden**

## GRANDMOTHER'S FLOWER GARDEN 1
**flower garden, flower patch**

Add a path, join the flowers, and you have the simple Grandmother's Flower Garden.

## GRANDMOTHER'S FLOWER GARDEN 2
### flower garden

Add a few rows to the flowers and you have a more complex variation.

## GRANDMOTHER'S FLOWER GARDEN 3
### flower garden with leaves, interlocked hexagon stars

Call the addition leaves (green print or solid) or call them points (any solid color) and you have a flower with leaves or an allover star pattern.

## MOSAIC TILE PATTERN
### tile pattern

Elongate the hexagon flower and use three colors (solid or print).

## LONE FLOWER QUILT
### hexagon trip around the world

Add as many rows to the center flower as you require to make the finished size.

## FLOWER

Add a stem and leaves to make the flower into a realistic picture.

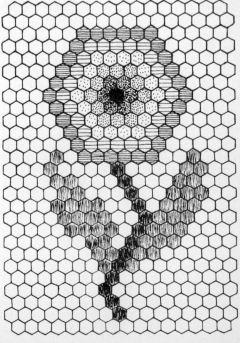

## FLOWER BASKET
### hexagon flower basket, hexagon bouquet

Add a basket to the basic flowers.

## FLOWERPOT
### hexagon potted flowers

Add a flowerpot to the flowers.

## VASE OF FLOWERS

Add some green leaves and a vase to the flowers.

## GRANDMOTHER'S FLOWER CARTWHEEL
**grandmother's flower garden**

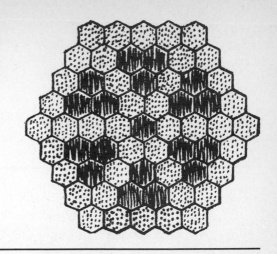

## TILE PATTERN
**hexagon flower garden, hexagon mosaic**

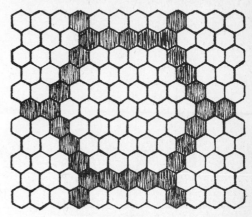

## DIAMOND PATTERN

The hexagons are placed to form a diamond shape (see diagram). This is the basis for the diamond patterns.

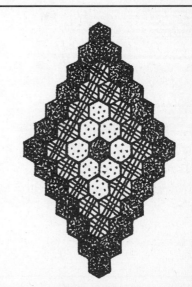

## DIAMOND MINE 1

Add a path to the diamond shape to make this allover pattern.

61

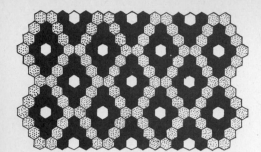

## DIAMOND MINE 2
### diamond mosaic

Make a startling allover diamond pattern by using only two colors and a path.

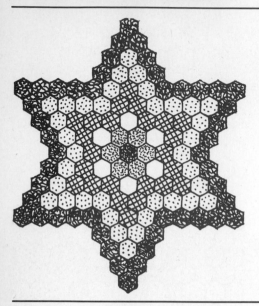

## HEXAGON STAR

This pattern is worked in the same manner as Grandmother's Flower Garden. Place the hexagons as shown in the diagram and you have made a star.

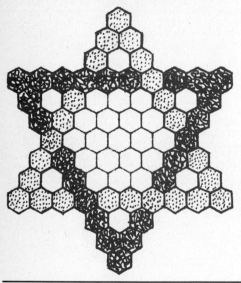

## INTERLOCKED STAR PATTERN
### woven star

Work each triangle of hexagons in a different color.

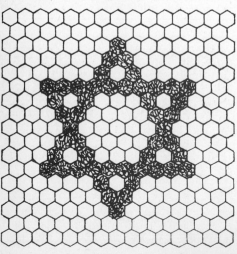

## STAR OF DAVID

Change to one color and you have a different pattern.

# HEXAGON BORDER PATTERNS

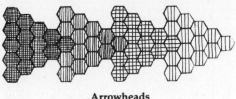

Arrowheads

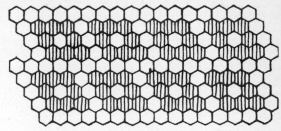

Hexagon Diamonds (Diamond Chain or Chains)

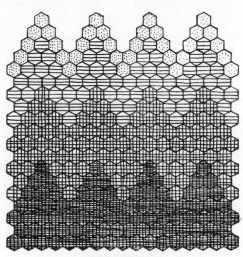

Hexagon Waves 1

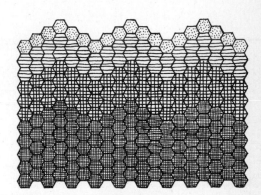

Hexagon Waves 2

---

# INDIAN PATCHWORK

The Seminole Indians of Florida developed a brightly colored form of strip quilting that was inserted in clothing fabric as an embellishment.

Long strips of fabric of different widths are stitched together by machine, then cut and resewn to make border patterns in their own unique style. The patterns have become so popular with quilters that you will find adaptations used in making quilts and other household furnishings.

## To Work

Step 1    Cut strips of fabric on the grain, in widths varying from ¾" to 3".
Step 2    Right sides together, stitch along the long edge, leaving at least ¼" for the seam allowance.
Step 3    Repeat with three or four strips, pressing the seams to one side after each strip has been sewn.

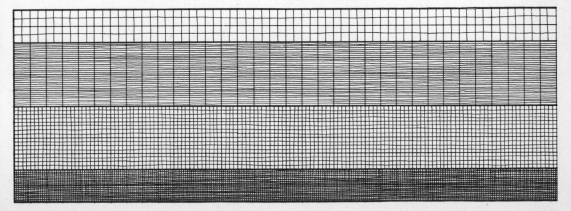

**Step 4** When the desired number of strips have been joined and pressed, cut them into strips as shown in the diagram. **Note:** Remember to leave a ¼" seam allowance when determining the width of these strips.

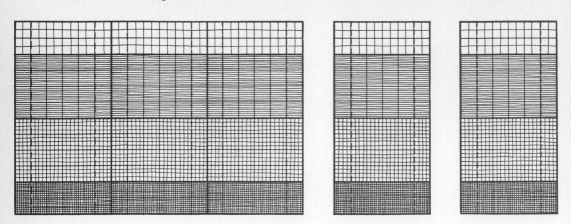

**Step 5** Join these strips as shown in the following pattern examples. **Note:** You can insert one or more solid strips, offset one or more strips, or stagger, reverse, or cut on the bias.

## Finishing

The finished patchwork strips must be lined when used in the Indian patchwork manner as a clothing embellishment.

## PATTERN EXAMPLES

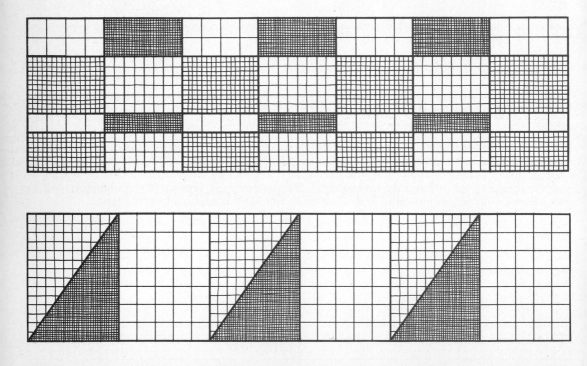

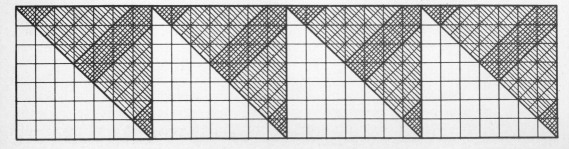

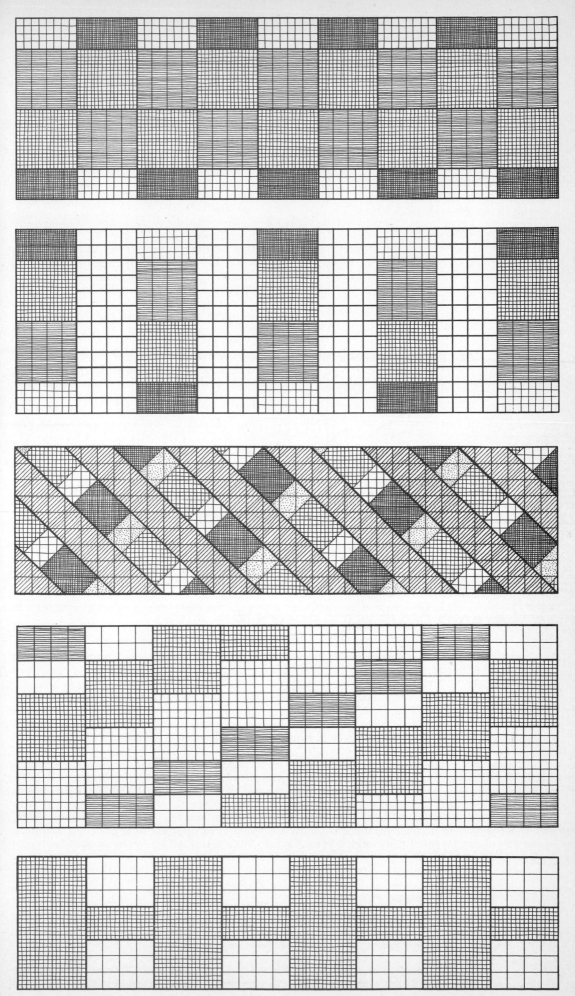

65

# JOINING QUILTED BLOCKS

It is often necessary to join individual quilted blocks to form a quilt top or large piece of quilted fabric. Sampler quilts, lap quilts, and many group projects must be joined in this manner.

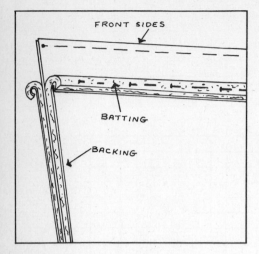

After you have determined the *set* of the quilt top:

**Step 1** Place the two blocks to be joined right sides facing.

**Step 2** Fold the batting and backing to the back and pin in place so that it is out of the way.

**Step 3** Pin or baste the two *front* pieces together. Make certain to line up the edges and corners.

**Step 4** Stitch across the two front pieces of fabric by hand or machine.

**Step 5** Sew all the blocks together in a row in the same manner. Thumb-press the seams in one direction as you work.

**Step 6** Place the row of joined blocks front side down on a flat surface. Remove the pins from the batting and backing. Now, trim the batting so that it butts (not overlaps) the joined blocks.

**Step 7** Gently pull the backing of one block over the batting of the next block. Turn under a ¼" seam allowance on the second block and place it *over* the backing of the first block. Slip-stitch in place, forming a lapped seam. Repeat until all the blocks are joined into rows.

**Step 8** Join the rows of blocks together in the same manner.

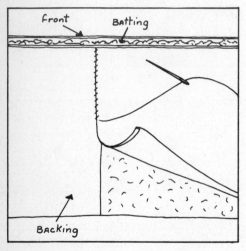

# MOLA AND REVERSE APPLIQUÉ

On the island of San Blas, off the coast of Panama, the Cuna Indians still make a traditional form of quilting handed down from mother to daughter, called Mola. In the native Cuna language, this word means "clothes."

It is often said that the first traditional mola designs were based on the tribal art of body painting. The molas' design formulas are usually derived from nature, with stylized flowers, animals, and all kinds of creatures associated with water dominating these colorful works. Although the first molas are attributed to these Indians of San Blas, fine examples of mola are also identified with the northern part of South America.

The basic mola technique is a reverse appliqué with three to eight layers of different-colored fabrics stacked together like a sandwich. The top layer is traditionally red and the bottom layer traditionally black. Bright greens, reds, yellows, pinks, blues, oranges, and white are the usual filler colors in this sandwich of fabrics. The design is formed by cutting through these layers of fabric, beginning with the top, to expose the filler colors. Each layer is turned under and blindstitched (hemmed) as the pattern develops. To understand the art of mola you must think opposite of appliqué. Appliqué is worked by *adding* layers of fabric on top of each other. Mola is worked by *cutting away and remvoing* layers of fabric.

### To Work a Mola (Reverse Appliqué)

**Step 1** To begin, plan a simple design. Try to determine a sequence for layering the fabric.

**Step 2** The fabric must be made of cotton or percale. Synthetic or mixed-content fabrics are often slippery, heavyweights provide too much bulk, and loosely woven fabrics stretch uncontrollably.

**Step 3** Place the fabrics on top of each other in the sequence required for the finished mola design. Each piece must be cut to the same size. Trace the design on the top piece of fabric, using a pen with disappearing or water-soluble ink. For a very complex design that will be worked over a long period of time, use a soft pencil to transfer the design.

**Step 4** Baste all the layers together along the outer edges.

**Step 5** Using sharp-pointed scissors, beginning with the top layer, carefully cut to the second layer. *Always leave a ¼" seam allowance.* Clip the curves to the seam line for ease in turning.

**Step 6** Turn the ¼" seam allowance under and sew to the back through *all* the layers with tiny blind stitches. The thread used should match the fabric being sewn at each level.

**Step 7** Continue in sequence, cutting and stitching each layer until the design is completed. *Never cut the bottom layer of fabric.*

**Step 8** When a different or accent color is needed for only one or two places, insert the piece of fabric (cut slightly larger than the opening). Sew it in place by stitching through the layer of fabric above it and all the layers under it.

Mola is used traditionally for making blouses and other clothing embellishments. It requires many hours of planning, cutting, and stitching to create a large wall hanging or quilt top, but is well worth the effort. **Hint:** Consider using the mola technique as a medallion set into a pieced quilt top or one block of a sampler quilt.

The menorah pictured in this photograph was worked using reverse appliqué and mola techniques.

## MENORAH

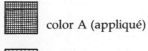

color A (appliqué)

color B
(reverse appliqué)

color C
(reverse appliqué)

color D
(reverse appliqué)

color E
(reverse appliqué)

color F (candle flame—
may be appliqué or
embroidered with thread)

color G (background—
dark color)

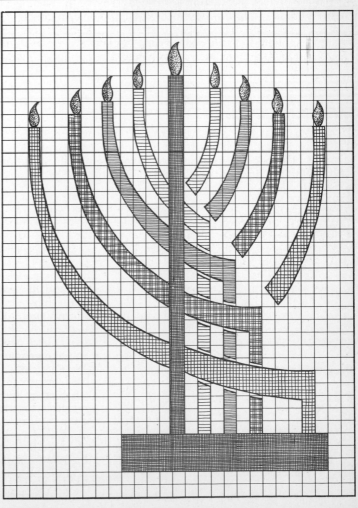

# PAINTED QUILT BLOCK

You can easily paint or stencil quilt patterns on the quilt top instead of piecing or appliquéing it. Filler or batting and a fabric backing complete the traditional quilt sandwich. The design is outline-quilted by hand.

The design or pattern can be a classic quilting pattern, a stencil pattern, or even a tracing or adaptation of a fabric design. Use your imagination.

Draw a full-scale pattern for the quilt block (see "Enlarging and Reducing Patterns," page 18). Using any of the transfer methods outlined in "Tools and Accessories" (page 4), transfer the pattern to the fabric.

The fabric should be tightly woven, smooth-surfaced, and washable. Using fabric paint (available at needlework and crafts supply stores) or acrylic paint (from an art supply store) as directed by the paint manufacturer, paint the design on the fabric. (Some of these paints must be heat-set or ironed, so be sure to read the instructions.) When the painting is complete, let it dry thoroughly.

Place an unpainted square of the size of your painted square on a flat surface. Smooth two layers of batting over the fabric and trim away any of it that extends beyond the seam lines. Put the painted square, right side up, over the batting.

Using long basting stitches through all layers of the quilt sandwich, carefully divide the block into quarters, basting a straight line from top to bottom and another from side to side. Then tack through all layers at each corner. The block is easier to quilt if tacked to a set of stretcher bars or placed in a quilting hoop. (See "Tools and Accessories," page 4.)

To quilt, start in the center of the block about ¼" away from the painted design and work small quilting stitches outlining all main areas of the design. Pull the stitches tightly to give a raised look to the pattern. When the quilting is finished, remove the basting stitches.

This method can be used to create a quilt top on a single piece of fabric, but then it becomes bulky, unmanageable, and nonportable. There is also the danger of making a painting error or blotch in one area and spoiling the entire top. When working with paint, I feel more comfortable creating small blocks and joining them later, as with pieced or appliquéd blocks.

# PAPER LINERS

The early quilters often lined their quilt pieces with paper, and hexagonal quilts were usually made this way. The paper helped hold the shape firmly in place during the construction, and, since it was often left in the finished quilt, also added warmth. (See "English Piecing," page 52.)

# PENTAGONS

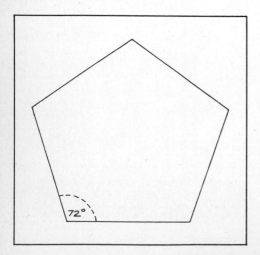

The pentagon is a geometric shape with five equal sides and five equal angles each measuring 72°. Unlike the hexagon or diamond, it cannot be used as a pattern joined to another pentagon to make a larger flat piece of fabric, as it will not lie flat. However, when twelve pentagons are joined together they form a ball-like geometric shape called a dodecahedron.

I have included this shape for everyone who made a baby or crib quilt and, using the scraps and the English piecing method (see page 52), joined twelve pentagons together, stuffed the dodecahedron with batting, and made a matching infant toy ball. Many quilters add a bell. One showed me a very old sample with some beans placed in a ring-size cardboard box buried in the center of the stuffing. This was probably one of the earliest methods used to make baby rattles.

# POSTAGE STAMP AND CHARTED QUILTING

This method of quilting was first used as a way to use scraps of material to create a larger piece of fabric or quilt top. The name "postage stamp" refers to the size of each piece of fabric. Some are as small as an ordinary postage stamp. These pieces are joined in a random or planned manner. Cross-stitch and needlepoint charts are an excellent source for charted quilting patterns.

Many quilters regard this type of work as the ultimate challenge. A twin-size quilt top measuring 72" × 90" will require assembling 6,480 1" pieces of fabric. A less ambitious quilt using 2" squares would use 1,620 pieces of fabric.

Every quilter should try this technique at least once. It is very gratifying to finish a work of these proportions and, I must add, a very humbling experience for even the most experienced quilter.

I have selected three sample charts as examples. The Christmas Tree pattern can be used as a seasonal wall hanging; it measures 24 units high × 20 units wide. It is a good choice for a first project, giving the quilter enough detail to keep it challenging and small enough to be finished in a reasonable time. It is attractive and colorful.

## CHRISTMAS TREE
### To Work

**Step 1**  Look at the chart. It will measure 20" × 24" using 1" squares of fabric, 40" × 48" using 2" squares, etc. Remember that piecing smaller squares requires more skill and dexterity.

**Step 2**  Select your fabric, using the legend as a guide for choosing color.

**Step 3**  Cut the fabric into squares, adding a ¼" seam allowance on all four sides.

**Step 4**  Right sides facing, using a small running stitch or by machine, seam the squares together in strips or rows. When a number of rows have been completed, join the rows in the same way.

**Step 5**  Assemble the quilt sandwich.

**Step 6**  Quilt the surface as desired.

**Step 7**  Add a border or finish with a bias binding. (See page 262.)

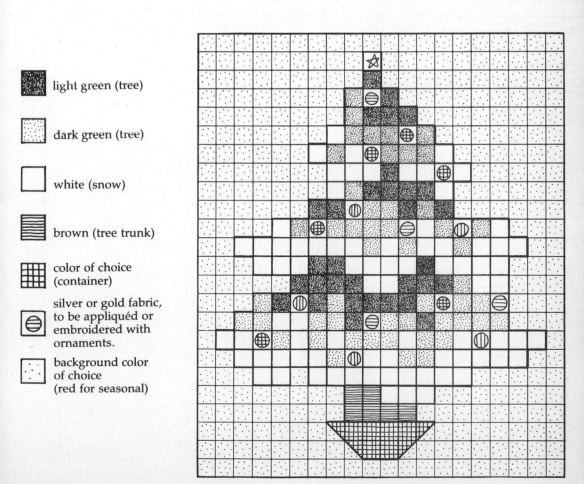

light green (tree)

dark green (tree)

white (snow)

brown (tree trunk)

color of choice
(container)

silver or gold fabric,
to be appliquéd or
embroidered with
ornaments.

background color
of choice
(red for seasonal)

# TOY SOLDIER

This is another good first project. It measures 15 units wide × 37 units high. One panel will make a very colorful wall hanging for a child's room or den. Worked in 2″ squares, it can be used as the center panel for a twin-bed-size quilt.

**Note:** For beginners I recommend that you try Quilters Secret™ for this project. It will give you a good head start. (See "Tools and Accessories," page 4.)

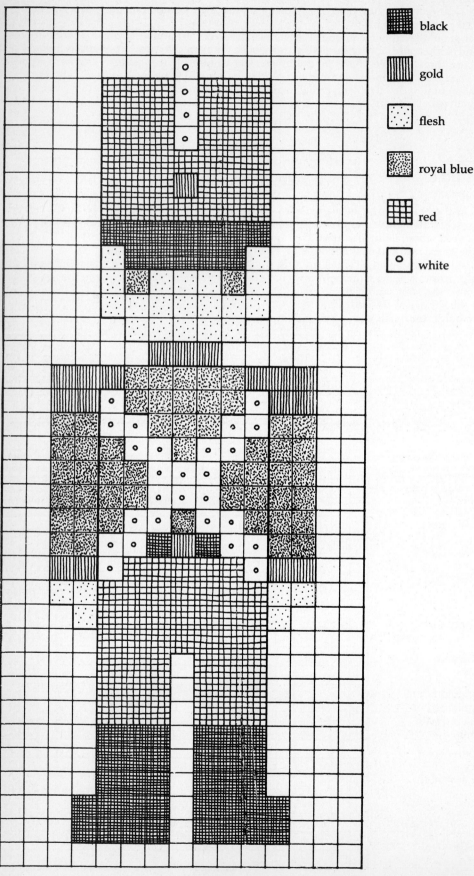

| | |
|---|---|
| ▓ | black |
| ▥ | gold |
| ⬚ | flesh |
| ▦ | royal blue |
| ▦ | red |
| ▢ | white |

## THE FARM

Here is an example of the "challenge" quilt. It measures 40 units wide × 60 units high and can be made into a beautiful quilt or wall hanging.

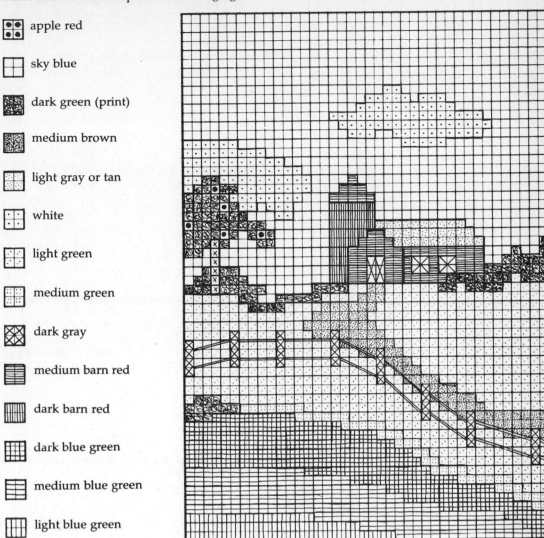

|  |  |
|--------|-------|
| apple red |
| sky blue |
| dark green (print) |
| medium brown |
| light gray or tan |
| white |
| light green |
| medium green |
| dark gray |
| medium barn red |
| dark barn red |
| dark blue green |
| medium blue green |
| light blue green |
| brown |

# PRESTUFFED QUILTING

Prestuffed quilting is made of individual modular units that are ultimately joined together to form a larger piece. They can be squares, triangles, or rhomboids just as long as they match at the joining points. This technique works into a most attractive piece using charted patterns found in cross-stitch books. Many pieced patchwork patterns also work up beautifully with this technique.

## Method I

**Step 1** Cut two pieces of fabric (one for the front and one for the back) to the size desired plus a ¼" seam allowance on all four sides.

**Step 2** Placing right sides together, seam by hand or machine around three of the sides plus part of the fourth. Clip the corners for turning.

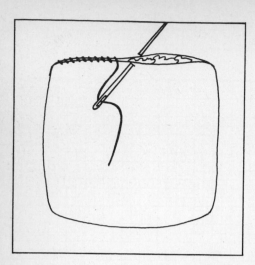

**Step 3** Turn the piece right side out and press.
**Step 4** Stuff with a piece of batting cut to the same size. For a thicker, more fluffy module, use two or three pieces of batting.
**Step 5** After stuffing to the desired puffiness, turn in the seam of the open side and slip-stitch together.
**Step 6** Join the modules with slip stitches.

**Note:** With careful charting, a different pattern design can be placed on each side of the quilt.

## Method II

**Step 1** Cut two *different*-sized pieces of fabric, one for the front (top) and one for the backing. The piece for the backing is cut to the desired finished size plus ¼" on each side. The top piece is cut 1½" larger, to allow for the puff stuffing. For example, if the finished piece is to measure 4" × 4", cut the backing to 4½" × 4 ½" and the top piece to 6" × 6".
**Step 2** Put the two pieces together, wrong sides facing, and pin, taking two evenly spaced tucks on each of three sides.

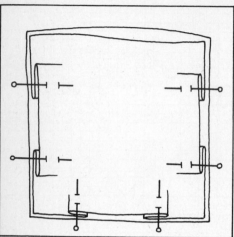

**Step 3** Sew around the three pinned sides ¼" in from the edge.
**Step 4** *Softly* stuff through the open side.

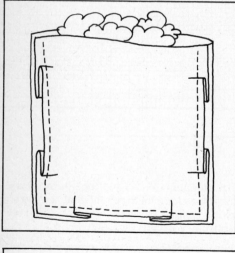

**Step 5** Make two tucks on the open side and sew across.
**Step 6** Repeat for each module.
**Step 7** When you have a number of completed modules, place them right sides together. To join, sew on the seam line.

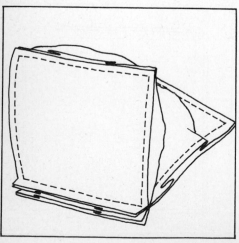

**Step 8** Join all modules together, row by row. Then join the rows in the same way.

**Step 9** For a finished look, attach a backing piece of fabric. Use bias binding to finish the edges. Tie the quilt. (See page 82.)

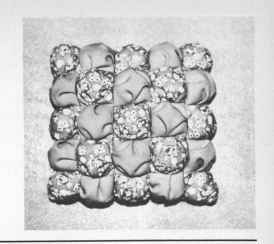

# QUILTER'S KNOT

The quilter's knot is known as the secret knot, Asian knot, silk-thread knot, foolproof knot, and little wonder knot. By any name, it is small and firm and slips securely into the batting or filler layer of the quilt sandwich.

## To Make the Quilter's Knot

**Step 1** Thread the needle with thread about 18" long.

**Step 2** Holding the threaded eye of the needle between the thumb and index finger of the right hand, bring the tail of the thread over the needle.

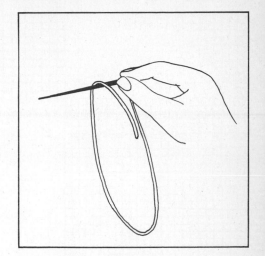

**Step 3** Secure the tail of the thread with the thumb of the right hand against the eye of the needle while winding the thread around the needle two to four times with the left hand.

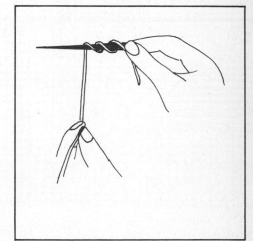

**Step 4** With the right hand, pull the wrapped coils of thread over the eye and down the length of the thread to the end until the knot tightens.

**Step 5** Trim the tail if necessary.

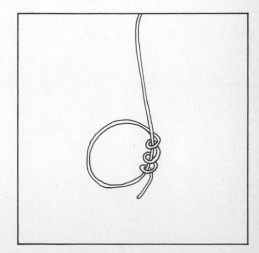

**Note:** Left-handed quilters can substitute the left hand for the right hand in these instructions. No other reversal is necessary.

# QUILTING STITCHES

## OUTLINE QUILTING

The simplest quilting to master is traditional outline quilting. Running stitches are worked ¼" to ⅜" inside the seam line of each shape. This secures the layers and gives a puffy texture to the surface of the quilt.

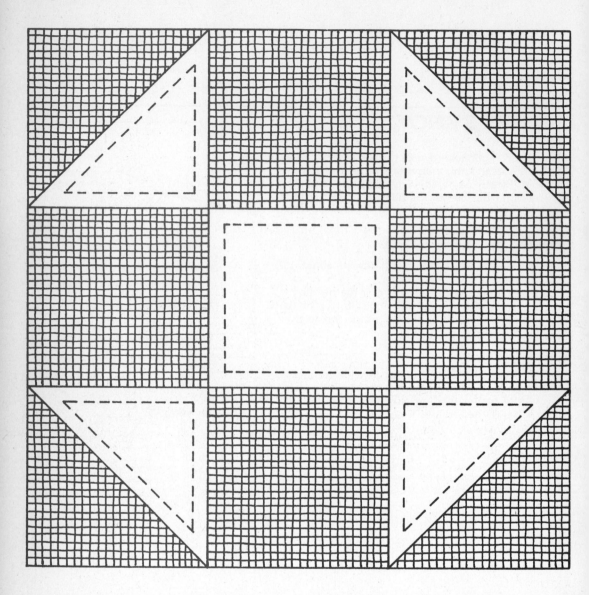

## ECHO OR OUTLINE PATTERNS

A pictorial pattern looks best with parallel lines that radiate around and follow the outline of the form. This technique is also called echo outline. Remember, closely placed quilted lines will make the center form puff out, while widely spaced lines will make the background appear puffy.

# STRAIGHT ALLOVER PATTERNS

Repeated straight-line patterns and diagonal, horizontal, and vertical channels all fall into this broad category. The lines are evenly spaced and can be marked with pencil (not recommended, as it can leave a permanent smudgy line), chalk line, dressmaker's carbon and wheel, disappearing-ink marker, a soap sliver on dark fabrics, and, my favorite, masking tape. The tape can be purchased in widths of ¼", ½", ¾", 1", etc. Just press the tape in place lightly on the quilt surface and stitch along the edge. Move the tape over one width and sew the next line. Continue in this manner until all the lines are sewn.

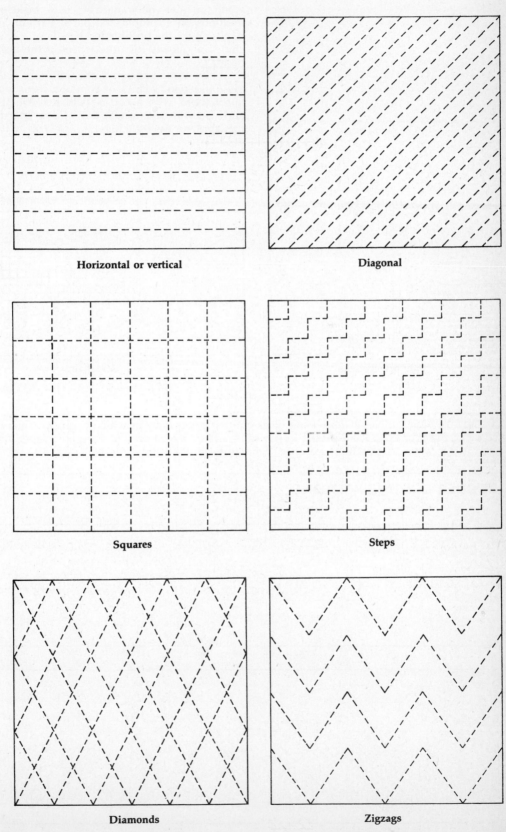

| Horizontal or vertical | Diagonal |
|:---:|:---:|
| Squares | Steps |
| Diamonds | Zigzags |

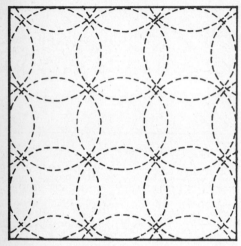

**Clamshell**

## CURVED ALLOVER PATTERNS

Curved patterns can be made with a string and pencil, compass, or, most traditionally, the "teacup" method. Familiar household objects like a teacup, drinking glass, dish, or pot lid were used to mark circular designs for quilting. This works to make a chain of circles, interlocked circles, clamshells, or an original design of your own.

You can easily make a perforated pattern from the finished drawing by punching the paper with a pin along the lines you want to stitch. To make even perforations on a complicated paper pattern, place the paper under the unthreaded needle of a sewing machine and slowly turn the wheel of the machine by hand.

To transfer the design to the quilt top, you can apply dressmaker's chalk or common cornstarch to the perforations with a cotton ball. Remove the paper and you will have a neat line of dots transferred to the fabric for easy stitching.

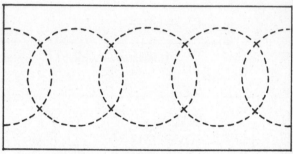

**Circle chain**

**Interlocked circles**

The following samples of border and block quilting patterns are provided to give you an example of some of the more popular patterns in use today. They are all drafted on graph paper and can be enlarged to a working-pattern size. (See "Enlarging and Reducing Patterns," page 18.)

## BORDER QUILTING PATTERNS

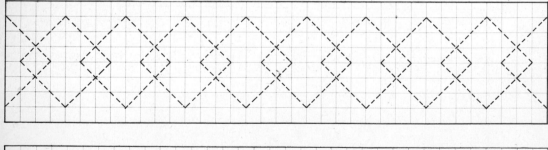

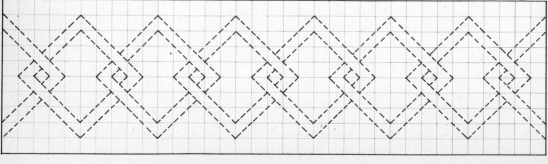

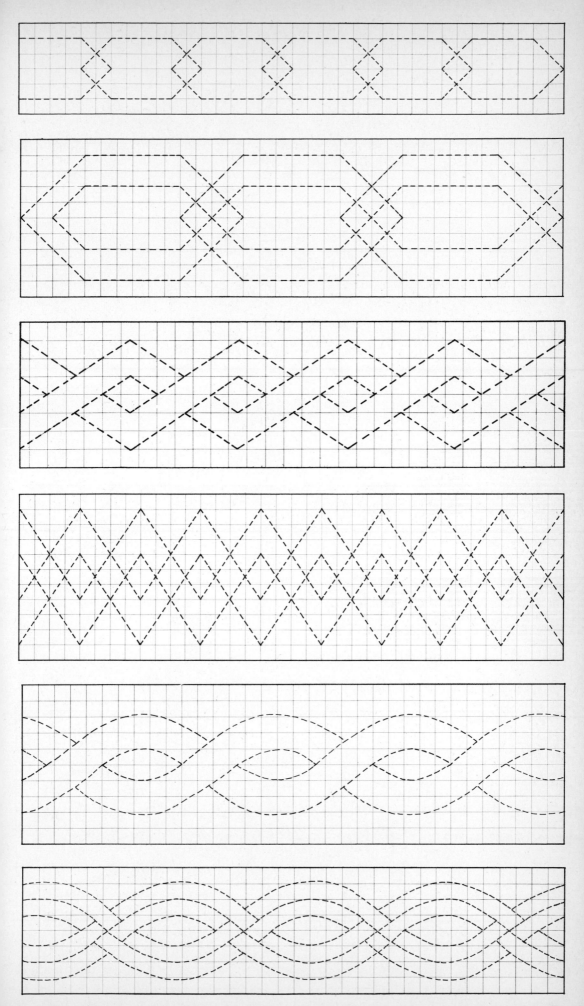

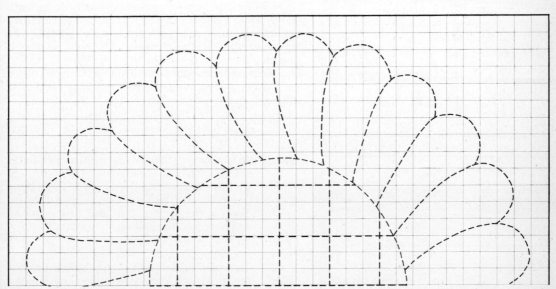

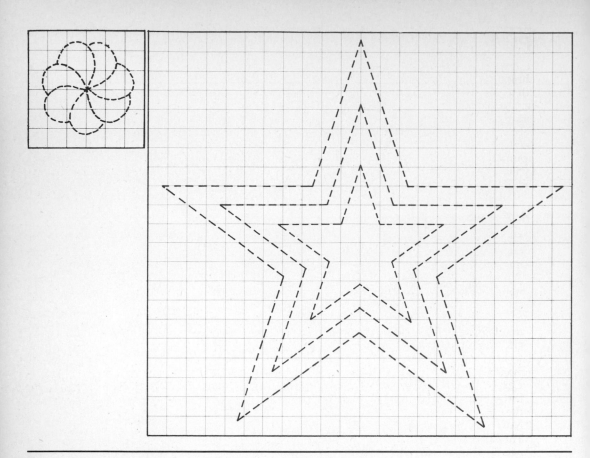

## QUILTING BY HAND

**Step 1** Place the prepared marked layers to be quilted in a hoop or on stretcher strips.

**Step 2** Cut the quilting thread about 18" long and place in a quilting needle (size 8 or 10 is recommended). Knot one end of the thread.

**Step 3** Insert the needle in the backing layer and through the batting and quilt top. Tug gently on the thread so that the knot passes through the backing layer and becomes buried in the batting.

**Step 4** Sew on the marked line with a running stitch. Make the stitches small and close together. Try to space them evenly so that they are of equal length on both sides of the quilt. Five to ten stitches would be considered adequate, although purists try to work twelve or more stitches to the inch. Unless you plan to enter your quilt in a juried show or rank yourself as an expert, don't get too upset if the best you can work is seven or eight stitches to the inch.

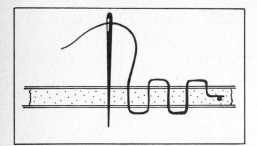

Work toward your body, putting one hand beneath the work to guide the needle and ensure that all three layers are caught with each stitch. **Caution:** Take care to avoid stabbing your finger. My only advice is, practice.

Start by working one stitch at a time. Then try three or four at a time until the best working rhythm is found.

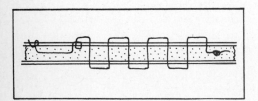

**Step 5** To end off (method I), make one or two backstitches. Then make one long stitch through the top and batting only. Finish by making one more tiny backstitch and clip the thread close to the surface. The end of the thread will sink into the batting.

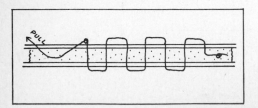

To end off (method II), stop before the last stitch. Make a knot close to the surface of the fabric. Work the last stitch, bringing the needle up to the surface 1" to 2" away. Pull the thread with enough pressure to move the knot through the top into the batting layer. Cut the thread close to the surface.

# TRAPUNTO

This technique is also called Italian quilting or corded quilting. The design is raised or puffed from the back with a piece of heavy yarn or cord, or stuffed with batting placed between lines or channels of stitching.

To work trapunto quilting, a fabric sandwich is made by placing a top layer of tightly woven white cotton fabric on a backing of loosely woven white fabric or muslin. Usually, the filler is eliminated (even low-loft), since the trapunto effect is created by stuffing individual areas only. Traditional or pure trapunto uses cord or heavy yarn to create the raised effect. English padded work (see page 51) uses tiny fluffs of cotton or batting materials pushed through the backing into stitched areas to create the raised effect. Modern trapunto combines these techniques and misnames it Italian trapunto.

## To Work Trapunto or Corded Quilting

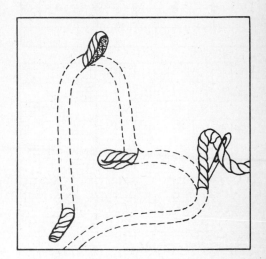

**Step 1** Place the quilt top fabric over the muslin backing, wrong sides together (inside). Baste.

**Step 2** Traditionally, the design is marked on the wrong side or backing, but if you feel more comfortable working from the front, you can mark the design on the front fabric with the new water-soluble or disappearing-ink markers. *Remember to make your design channels about ¼" wide, to allow room for the cord to be inserted later.*

**Step 3** Carefully work very fine running stitches through both layers of fabric on the lines of the drawn design.

**Step 4** Now you *must* work from the back only. Thread a large-eye embroidery or tapestry needle with white yarn or cord. Insert the needle through the loosely woven backing fabric into the channel by pushing the threads apart to form a small hole. *Be careful not to let the needle pierce the front fabric.* Push the needle along the channel between the two stitched lines until a curve or angle prevents further progress. Then bring the needle up through the backing and reinsert it to continue working the design. Each time you remove the needle and reinsert it, leave a very small loop of yarn or cord showing on the back. This will keep the cord from shifting or puckering the design if the cord shrinks from atmospheric changes or laundering.

**Step 5** To end off a length of cord or yarn, bring it up through the backing fabric and cut it off.

The following photographs show traditional trapunto and English padding worked in combination. Most trapunto work is done in this manner today.

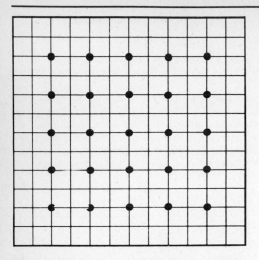

# TYING

The layers of a quilt must be secured in some way to prevent shifting. To avoid shifting, a technique called tying has been developed. A series of decorative knots or tufts, made of yarn, embroidery floss, or string, are arranged in a simple pattern on the surface of the quilt.

## To Make a Knot

**Step 1**  To begin, assemble the quilt sandwich (backing, batting, and quilt top) in the usual manner. Using a yardstick to measure, mark the quilt top on the right side in a grid or other pattern. Place the dots 2″ to 8″ apart. **Note:** You can tie patchwork blocks without marking the top by placing a knot or tuft at the center and four corners of each block.

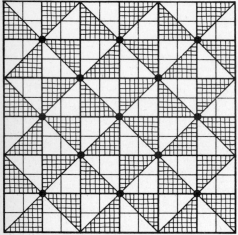

**Step 2**  Pin and baste the quilt top, batting, and backing together, smoothing out any wrinkles as you work.

**Step 3**  To make the knots at the points marked on the quilt top, thread an embroidery needle with yarn or floss in a matching or contrasting color. Depending on the desired effect and the thickness of the yarn or floss, thread the needle with one or two strands.

**Step 4**  Starting at the center of the quilt and working toward the edges, put the needle from front to back through all layers of the quilt. Leave a 2″ to 3″ tail dangling on the surface. Put the needle about ⅛″ from the entry point from the back to the front.

**Step 5**  Tie a square knot: right over left, then left over right.
Tug firmly on the two ends and trim to about 2″.

**Step 6**  Repeat steps 4 and 5 for each knot.

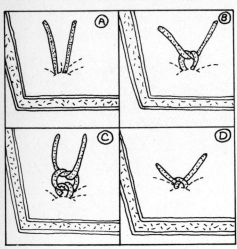

## To Make a Tuft

A tuft is fluffier and more decorative than a knot. Use a large-eye embroidery needle and thread it with three to six strands of yarn or thread. Make the knot as above in steps 4 and 5. You will have many strands of yarn above the knot at the surface of the quilt. Clip these strands about ¼″ to ⅜″ above the knot to make the puffy tuft.

# WHITEWORK

This is the technique of placing fine stitches in white thread on white fabric. The design work is similar to trapunto, but without the high-relief effect. It is, most simply, painting with a needle and thread, and requires a high degree of technical proficiency.

Traditionally, the design was drawn on the backing of the quilt sandwich (top, *flat-loft* filler, and backing, basted together), but today water-soluble and disappearing-ink markers (see "Tools and Accessories," page 4) enable us to place the design on the top. This gives more control to the stitcher and therefore makes the technique a reasonable choice for the ambitious intermediate quilter.

The design is traditionally pictorial, but any line drawing will work well in whitework. The sample shown below is part of a wedding quilt made for my daughter. Each block represented some interest or event in the lives of the bride and groom. This design is an adaptation of the seal from the college where they met. It was worked in the whitework method as follows:

**Step 1** Draw the chosen design, enlarging or reducing it to the desired finished size using any of the methods described in "Enlarging and Reducing Patterns" (page 18).

**Step 2** Transfer the design to the fabric with a water-soluble marker.

**Step 3** Make the quilt sandwich; marked fabric on top, low-loft batting in the middle, backing on the bottom; baste through all layers.

**Step 4** Place the work in a quilting hoop or frame. I find stretcher bars (see "Tools and Accessories," page 4) ideal for keeping the fabric tight and smooth for this work.

**Step 5** Using the smallest stitches you can manage, quilt on every line drawn on the fabric. Solid areas are best represented by crosshatch, channel, or diagonal quilting.

# YO-YO QUILTING

A yo-yo (also known as a Suffolk puff) is a small circular piece of fabric that is gathered and sewn to other yo-yos to form a larger fabric. This fabric can then be used as a coverlet, clothing, baby quilt, or carriage cover. The yo-yo can be lined with a small circle of batting covered with a circle of fabric.

These little circle puffs can also be strung together with string or elastic to create a wiggly snake or clown doll toy.

## To Make a Yo-Yo

**Step 1** Make a circle template from cardboard or a sheet of plastic. (You can use a cup, saucer, or compass to draw the circle.) The diameter of the circle template should measure twice the diameter of the finished yo-yo plus a ¼" seam allowance. To make a 2" yo-yo, cut the circle template 4¼" in diameter.

**Step 2** Put the template circle on the wrong side of the fabric, mark around, and cut out.

**Step 3** Turn the ¼" seam allowance to the back and sew around the circle with small running stitches.

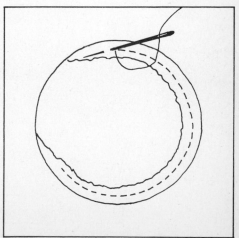

**Step 4** Carefully pull up the thread, gathering the edge as you work.
**Step 5** Backstitch in place a few times to end off.
**Step 6** Repeat steps 2 to 5 for each yo-yo. The gathered side is the right side. Make a number of yo-yos.

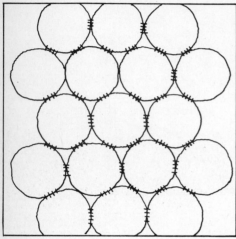

**Step 7** Join the yo-yos from the back (smooth side) with small slip stitches on four sides.

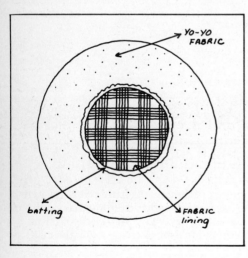

## To Line a Yo-Yo

**Step 1** Cut a circle template slightly smaller than the finished size of the yo-yo.
**Step 2** Using this template, cut one circle of batting and one circle of lining fabric.
**Step 3** Follow the directions for making a yo-yo, steps 1 to 3.
**Step 4** Put the circle of batting on the wrong side of the fabric, in the center of the yo-yo. Add the circle of lining fabric, right side up.
**Step 5** Work steps 4 to 7 of To Make a Yo-Yo.
**Note:** The joined yo-yos can be left as an openwork fabric or lined with a backing (on the smooth side) to create a solid fabric.

# Patchwork Patterns

The patterns shown on the following pages are arranged in alphabetical order. Most are known by various names. This is common when patterns or names are passed, changing slightly, from quilter to quilter and generation to generation or are transported to another part of the country. All efforts have been made to list as many names as could be found for each pattern. I have tried to verify as many of these as possible and be as accurate as I could when working with what was essentially an orally transmitted subject.

All patterns in this chapter are drafted on graph paper so that a working full-size pattern or template (see "Templates," page 259, and "Enlarging and Reducing Patterns," page 18) can be made from each.

I have also included a color legend for each pattern to help the quilter determine suggested light, medium, and dark areas for fabric choice. I did not indicate any specific colors, only tonal choices for any desired color.

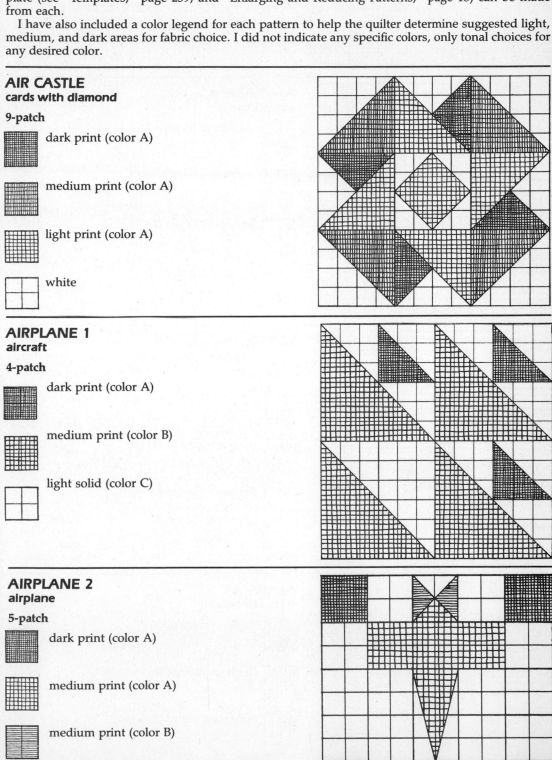

## AIR CASTLE
**cards with diamond**

**9-patch**

dark print (color A)

medium print (color A)

light print (color A)

white

## AIRPLANE 1
**aircraft**

**4-patch**

dark print (color A)

medium print (color B)

light solid (color C)

## AIRPLANE 2
**airplane**

**5-patch**

dark print (color A)

medium print (color A)

medium print (color B)

light solid (color C)

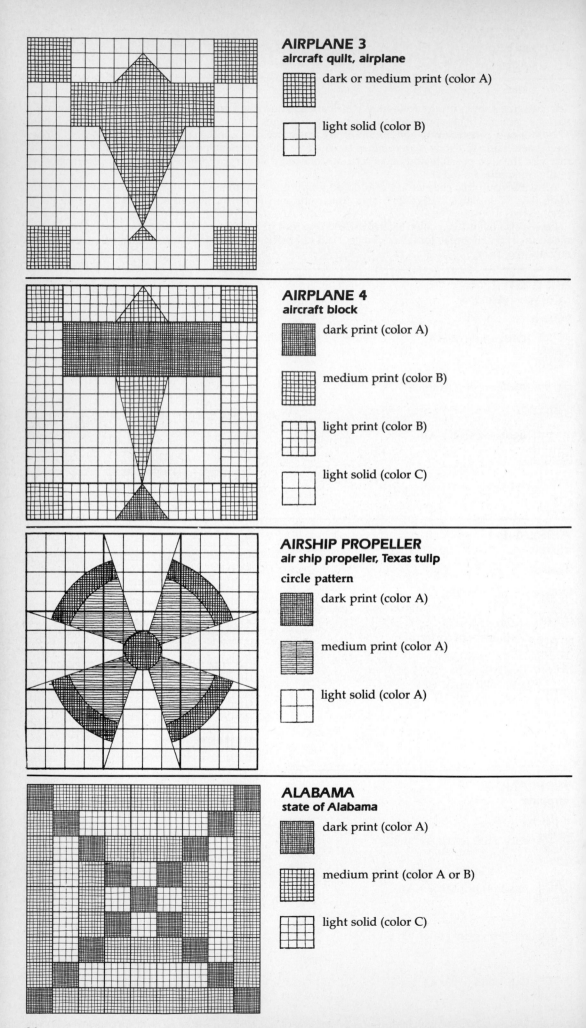

## AIRPLANE 3
### aircraft quilt, airplane

dark or medium print (color A)

light solid (color B)

## AIRPLANE 4
### aircraft block

dark print (color A)

medium print (color B)

light print (color B)

light solid (color C)

## AIRSHIP PROPELLER
### air ship propeller, Texas tulip
### circle pattern

dark print (color A)

medium print (color A)

light solid (color A)

## ALABAMA
### state of Alabama

dark print (color A)

medium print (color A or B)

light solid (color C)

## ALABAMA STAR BEAUTY
**Alabama beauty**

**4-patch circle**

dark print (color A)

medium print (color B)

light solid (color C)

## ALASKA TERRITORY
**Alaska**

**5-patch**

dark print (color A)

medium print (color B)

light solid (color C)

## ALBUM 1

**9-patch**

dark print (color A)

medium print (color B)

medium print (color A)

light solid (color B)

## ALBUM 2

**9-patch**

dark print (color A)

dark solid (color A)

medium print (color B)

light solid

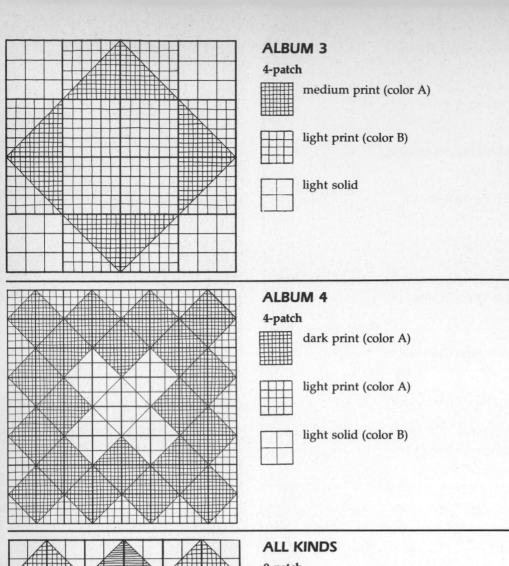

## ALBUM 3

**4-patch**

▦ medium print (color A)

▦ light print (color B)

▯ light solid

## ALBUM 4

**4-patch**

▦ dark print (color A)

▦ light print (color A)

▯ light solid (color B)

## ALL KINDS

**9-patch**

▦ dark print (color A)

▦ medium print (color B)

▯ light solid (color A or C)

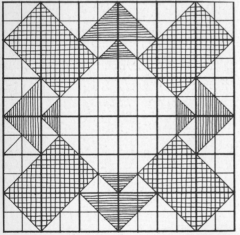

## AMISH BASKET
**basket**

**4-patch**

▦ dark solid

▯ medium light solid

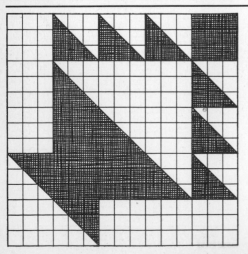

## ANNAPOLIS PATCH
**Annapolis star, Annapolis**

4-patch

◼ dark print or solid (color A)

▦ medium print (color A)

▦ light print (color B)

☐ light or white solid

## ANVIL 1
**anvil I, the anvil**

4-patch

▦ dark print or solid (color A)

▦ medium print or solid (color B)

☐ light solid or white

## ANVIL 2
**the anvil**

4-patch

▦ dark print (color A)

▦ light print or solid (color B)

☐ light solid or white (color C)

## ARBOR WINDOW
**the arbor window**

9-patch

▦ dark print (color A)

▦ medium print (color B)

☐ light solid or white

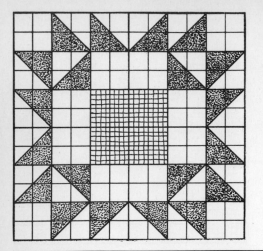

## ARIZONA 1
**State of Arizona**

**4-patch**

 dark print or solid (color A)

 medium print (color B)

 light solid or white

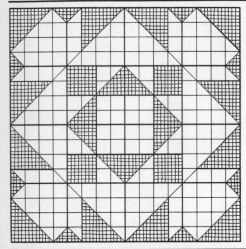

## ARIZONA 2

**4-patch**

 medium print (color A)

 light print or solid (color B)

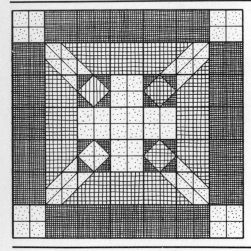

## ARKANSAS

**4-patch**

 dark print (color A)

 medium print (color B)

 light print or solid (color C)

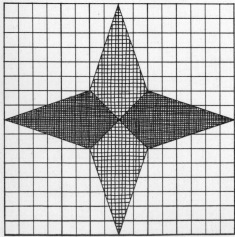

## ARKANSAS SNOWFLAKE 1
**four point, kite, Job's troubles**

**4-patch**

 dark print (color A)

 medium print (color B)

 light solid (color C)

## ARKANSAS SNOWFLAKE 2
**four-point, kite, Job's trouble**

**9-patch**

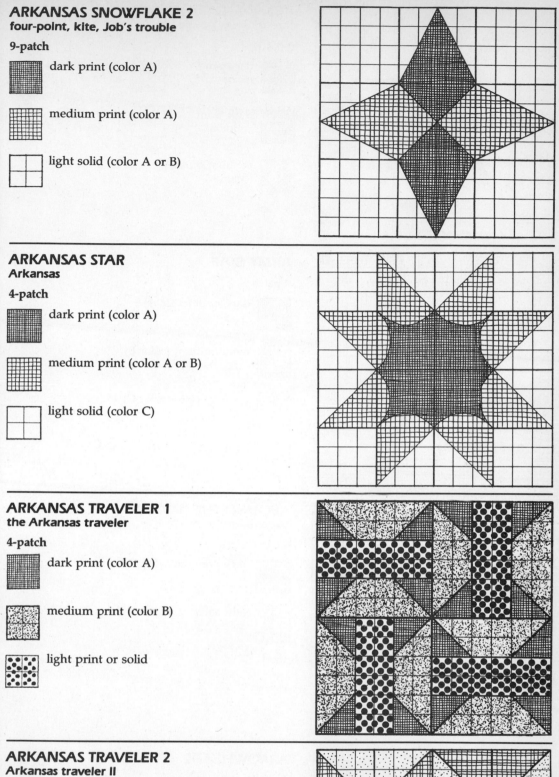

□ dark print (color A)

□ medium print (color A)

□ light solid (color A or B)

## ARKANSAS STAR
**Arkansas**

**4-patch**

□ dark print (color A)

□ medium print (color A or B)

□ light solid (color C)

## ARKANSAS TRAVELER 1
**the Arkansas traveler**

**4-patch**

□ dark print (color A)

□ medium print (color B)

□ light print or solid

## ARKANSAS TRAVELER 2
**Arkansas traveler II**

**4-patch**

□ dark solid (color A)

□ medium print (color A or B)

□ light solid (color A or B)

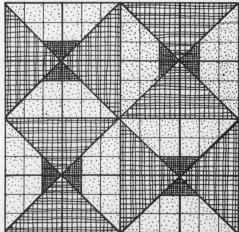

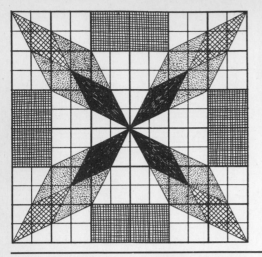

## ARKANSAS TRAVELER 3
### the Arkansas Traveler I

**9-patch**

 dark print
(color A)

 medium print
(color B)

 dark print
(color B)

 light solid
(Color A or B)

 medium print
(color A)

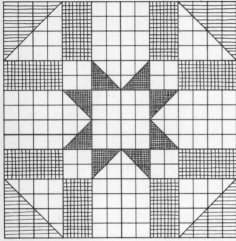

## ARMY STAR

**4-patch**

 dark print (color A)

 medium print (color B)

 medium print (color C)

 light solid or white

## AROUND THE WORLD
### a round world

**4-patch circle**

 dark print (color A)

 light solid or white

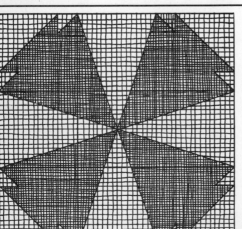

## ARROWHEADS

**4-patch**

 dark print (color A)

 medium light print (color B)

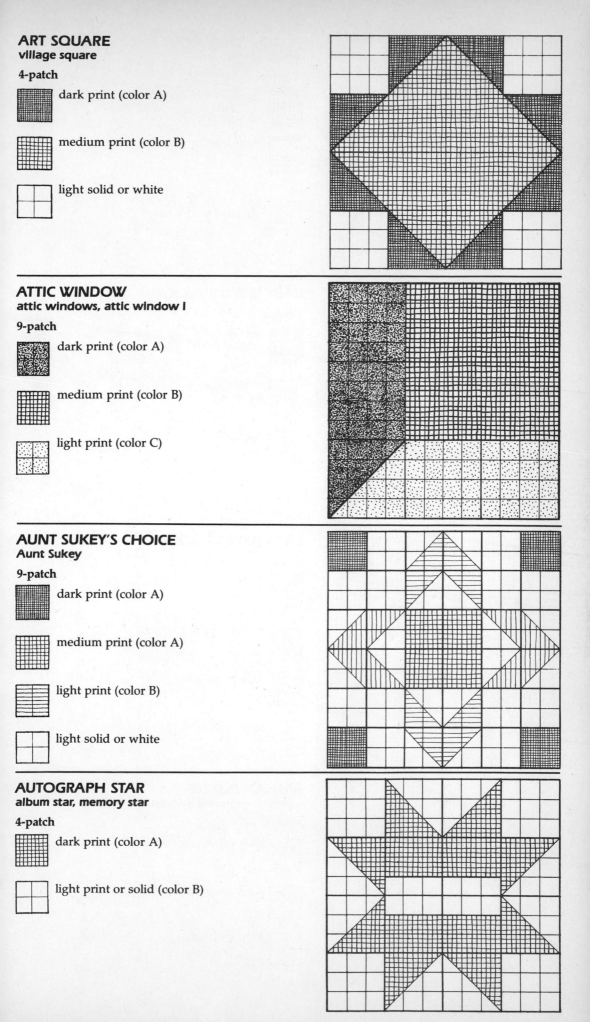

## ART SQUARE
### village square

4-patch

| | |
|---|---|
| | dark print (color A) |
| | medium print (color B) |
| | light solid or white |

## ATTIC WINDOW
### attic windows, attic window I

9-patch

| | |
|---|---|
| | dark print (color A) |
| | medium print (color B) |
| | light print (color C) |

## AUNT SUKEY'S CHOICE
### Aunt Sukey

9-patch

| | |
|---|---|
| | dark print (color A) |
| | medium print (color A) |
| | light print (color B) |
| | light solid or white |

## AUTOGRAPH STAR
### album star, memory star

4-patch

| | |
|---|---|
| | dark print (color A) |
| | light print or solid (color B) |

93

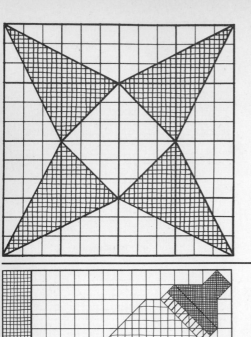

## A WORLD WITHOUT END
world without end

**4-patch**

 dark print (color A)

 light solid or white

---

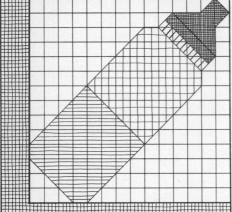

## BABY BOTTLE BLOCK

**1-patch**

 tan (nipple)

 medium print (color B)

 print (bottle contents)

medium solid (color A)

light solid (color A)

---

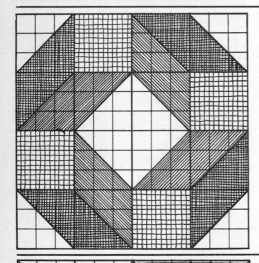

## BACHELOR'S PUZZLE

**4-patch**

 dark print (color A)

 medium print (color A)

 light print (color A)

 light solid or white

---

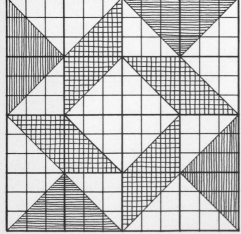

## BALKAN PUZZLE
windblown square, windblown reverse

**4-patch**

 dark print (color A)

 medium print (color A)

 light solid or white

## BANDSTAND
**bandstand square, trees in the park**

4-patch

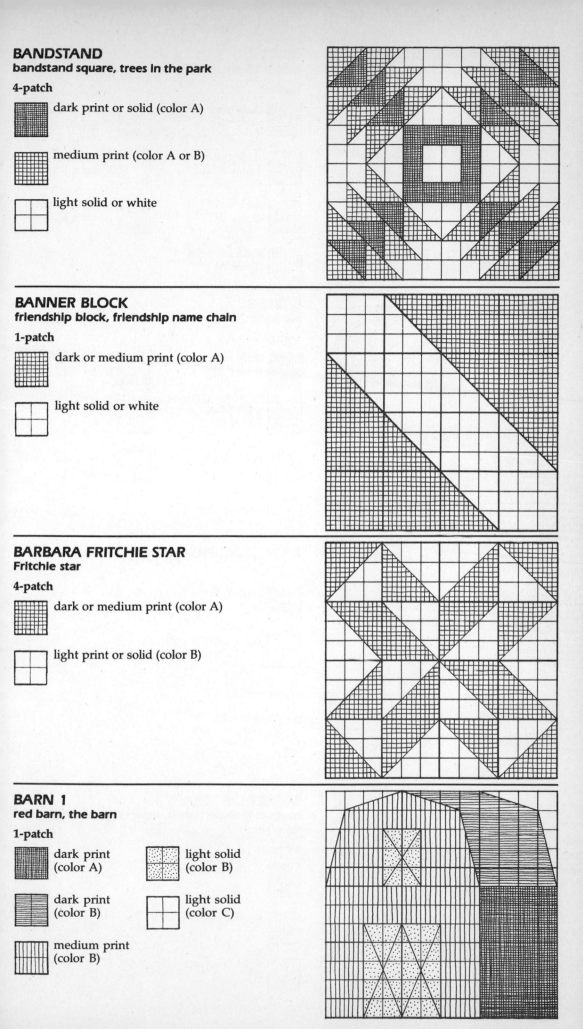

dark print or solid (color A)

medium print (color A or B)

light solid or white

## BANNER BLOCK
**friendship block, friendship name chain**

1-patch

dark or medium print (color A)

light solid or white

## BARBARA FRITCHIE STAR
**Fritchie star**

4-patch

dark or medium print (color A)

light print or solid (color B)

## BARN 1
**red barn, the barn**

1-patch

dark print
(color A)

light solid
(color B)

dark print
(color B)

light solid
(color C)

medium print
(color B)

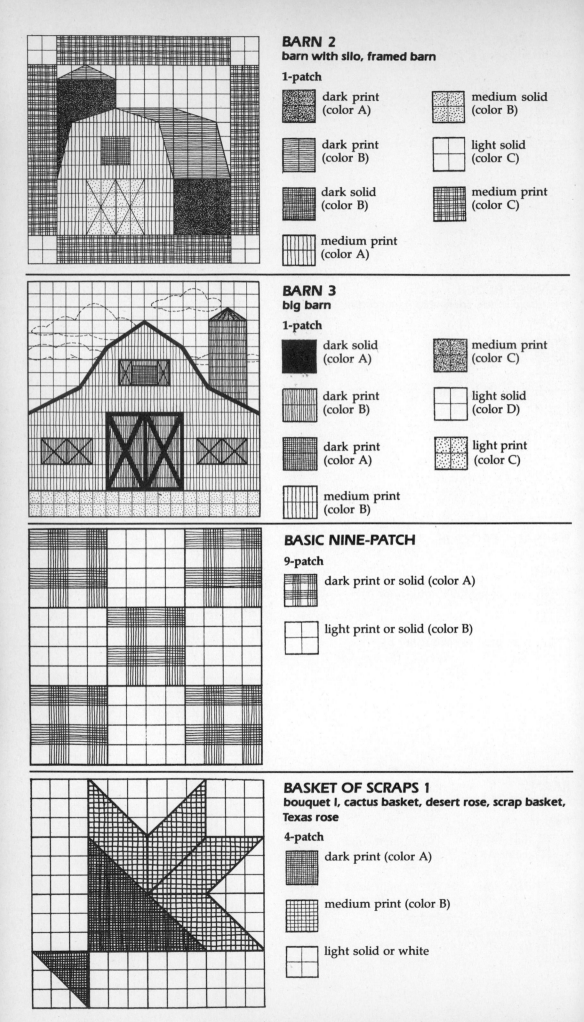

## BARN 2
**barn with silo, framed barn**

**1-patch**

dark print (color A)

medium solid (color B)

dark print (color B)

light solid (color C)

dark solid (color B)

medium print (color C)

medium print (color A)

## BARN 3
**big barn**

**1-patch**

dark solid (color A)

medium print (color C)

dark print (color B)

light solid (color D)

dark print (color A)

light print (color C)

medium print (color B)

## BASIC NINE-PATCH

**9-patch**

dark print or solid (color A)

light print or solid (color B)

## BASKET OF SCRAPS 1
**bouquet I, cactus basket, desert rose, scrap basket, Texas rose**

**4-patch**

dark print (color A)

medium print (color B)

light solid or white

## BASKET OF SCRAPS 2
**bouquet, basket of scraps, cactus basket, desert rose**

**4-patch**

dark print (color A)

medium print (color B)

medium print (color C)

medium print (color D)

medium print (color E)

light solid or white

## BASKETWEAVE 1
**basket weave**

**1–2-patch**

dark print (color A)

medium print (color A or B)

light print (color A or C)

## BASKETWEAVE 2
**basket weave, twist**

**9-patch**

dark print (color A)

medium print (color B)

light solid or white

## BAT, THE
**dove, the dove**

**4-patch**

dark print (color A)

light solid or white

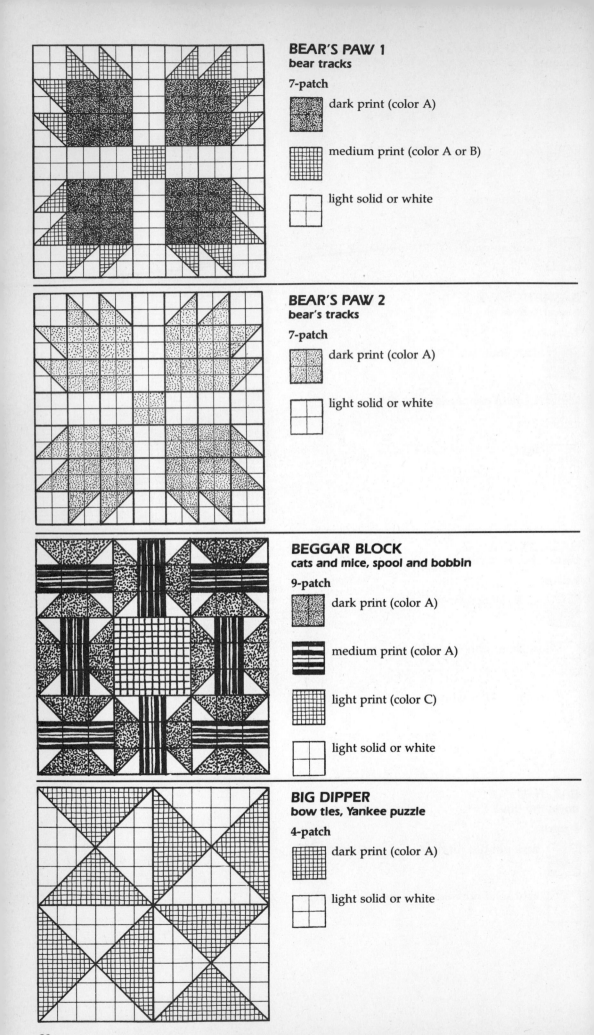

### BEAR'S PAW 1
**bear tracks**

7-patch

dark print (color A)

medium print (color A or B)

light solid or white

### BEAR'S PAW 2
**bear's tracks**

7-patch

dark print (color A)

light solid or white

### BEGGAR BLOCK
**cats and mice, spool and bobbin**

9-patch

dark print (color A)

medium print (color A)

light print (color C)

light solid or white

### BIG DIPPER
**bow ties, Yankee puzzle**

4-patch

dark print (color A)

light solid or white

## BIRDS IN THE AIR 1
**birds in air**

**4-patch**

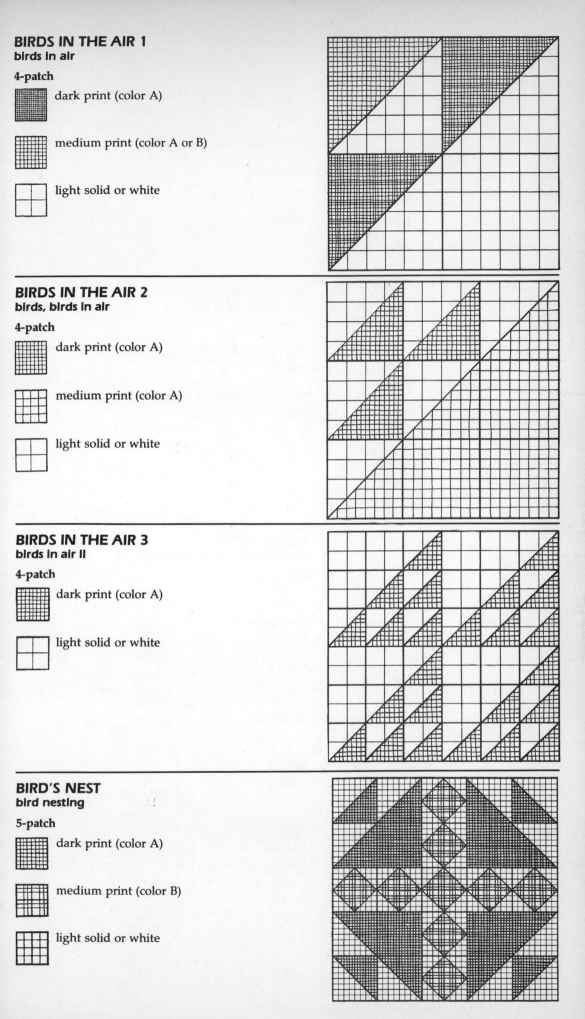

dark print (color A)

medium print (color A or B)

light solid or white

## BIRDS IN THE AIR 2
**birds, birds in air**

**4-patch**

dark print (color A)

medium print (color A)

light solid or white

## BIRDS IN THE AIR 3
**birds in air II**

**4-patch**

dark print (color A)

light solid or white

## BIRD'S NEST
**bird nesting**

**5-patch**

dark print (color A)

medium print (color B)

light solid or white

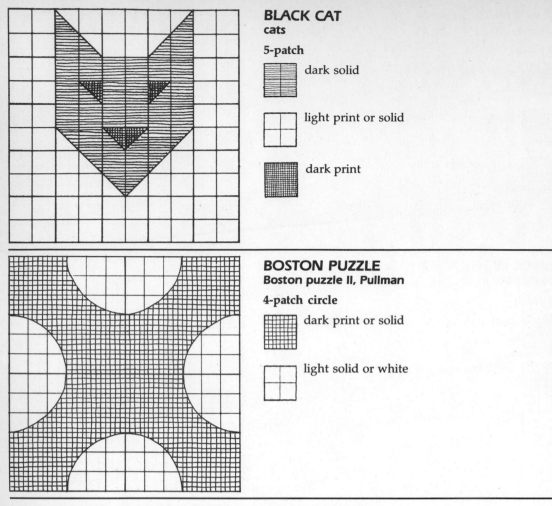

## BLACK CAT
cats

**5-patch**

dark solid

light print or solid

dark print

## BOSTON PUZZLE
**Boston puzzle II, Pullman**

**4-patch circle**

dark print or solid

light solid or white

## BOUQUET STAR
**galactica star, star bouquet**

**4-patch**

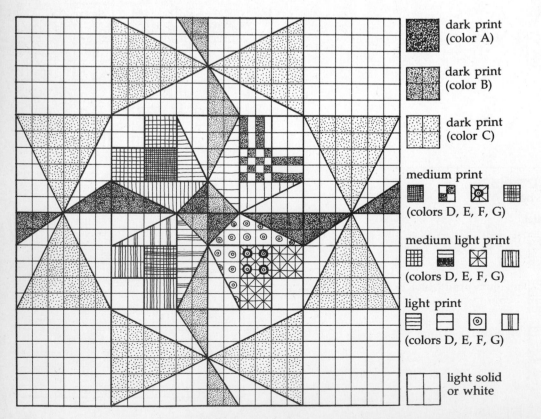

dark print
(color A)

dark print
(color B)

dark print
(color C)

medium print

(colors D, E, F, G)

medium light print

(colors D, E, F, G)

light print

(colors D, E, F, G)

light solid
or white

## BOW
**bow tie**

9-patch

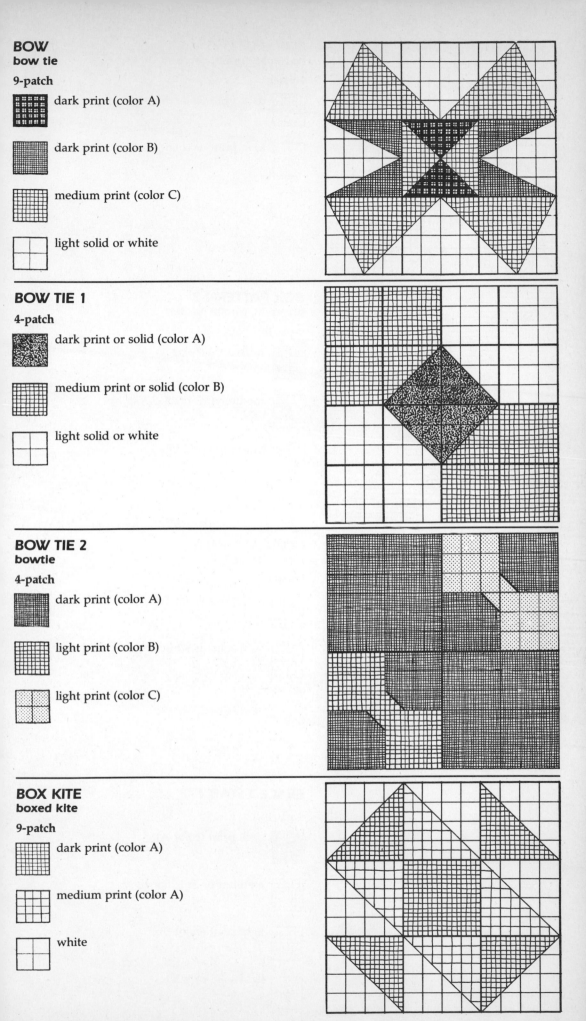

dark print (color A)

dark print (color B)

medium print (color C)

light solid or white

## BOW TIE 1

4-patch

dark print or solid (color A)

medium print or solid (color B)

light solid or white

## BOW TIE 2
**bowtie**

4-patch

dark print (color A)

light print (color B)

light print (color C)

## BOX KITE
**boxed kite**

9-patch

dark print (color A)

medium print (color A)

white

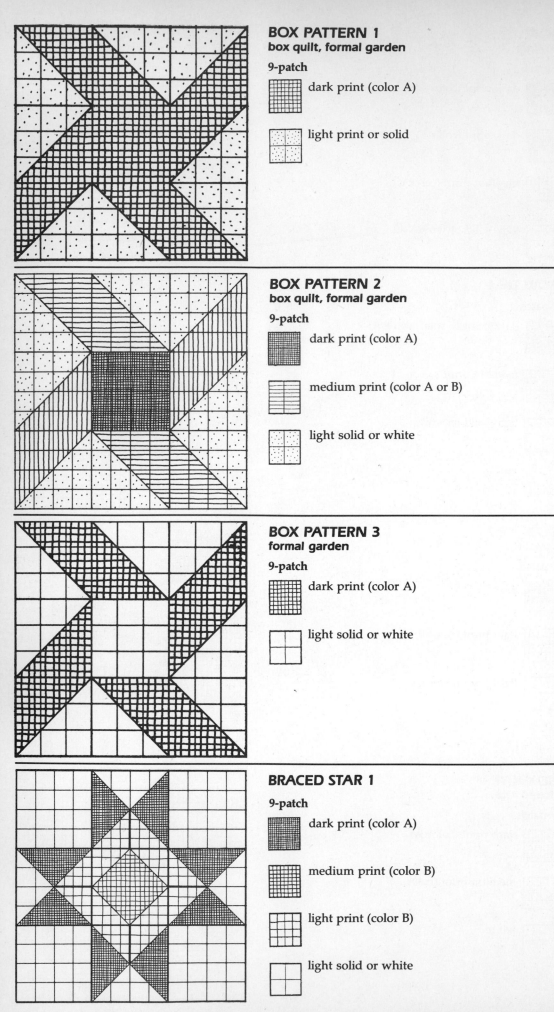

**BOX PATTERN 1**
**box quilt, formal garden**

9-patch

dark print (color A)

light print or solid

**BOX PATTERN 2**
**box quilt, formal garden**

9-patch

dark print (color A)

medium print (color A or B)

light solid or white

**BOX PATTERN 3**
**formal garden**

9-patch

dark print (color A)

light solid or white

**BRACED STAR 1**

9-patch

dark print (color A)

medium print (color B)

light print (color B)

light solid or white

## BRACED STAR 2

**9-patch**

| | | | |
|---|---|---|---|
| ▦ | dark print (color A) | ▦ | medium print (color D) |
| ▦ | dark print (color B) | ▦ | light print (color D) |
| ▦ | dark print (color C) | ▦ | light solid or white |
| ▦ | dark print (color D) | | |

## BRACED STAR 3

**9-patch**

| | |
|---|---|
| ▦ | dark print or solid (color A) |
| ▦ | medium solid (color B) |
| ▢ | light solid or white |
| ▦ | inside frame is made from scraps of medium and light prints |

## BREECHES

**circle**

| | |
|---|---|
| ■ | dark print (color A) |
| ▢ | light solid or white |

## BRIDAL PATH
**bride's path**

**4-patch**

| | |
|---|---|
| ▦ | dark print (color A) |
| ▦ | medium print (color A) |
| ▢ | light solid or white |

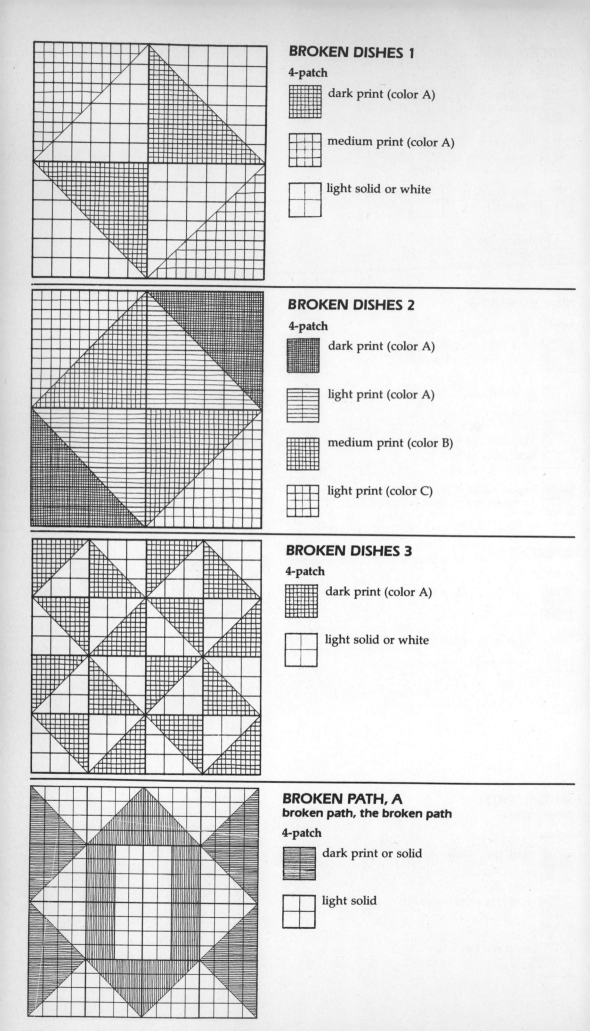

**BROKEN DISHES 1**

4-patch

dark print (color A)

medium print (color A)

light solid or white

**BROKEN DISHES 2**

4-patch

dark print (color A)

light print (color A)

medium print (color B)

light print (color C)

**BROKEN DISHES 3**

4-patch

dark print (color A)

light solid or white

**BROKEN PATH, A**
broken path, the broken path

4-patch

dark print or solid

light solid

104

## BUDDED STAR
**budding star, star with flower buds**

### 4-patch

dark print (color A)

light print (color A)

medium print (color B)

light solid or white

## BULL'S-EYE
**doe and darts**

### 5-patch

dark print (color A)

medium print (color A or B)

light solid or white

## BUTTERFLY

### 9-patch

dark solid (color A)

dark print (color B)

medium print (color B)

light print (color B)

light solid or white

## BUTTERFLY SQUARED

### 4-patch

dark solid (color A)

dark print (color B)

medium print (color B)

light print (color B)

medium print (color C)

light solid or white

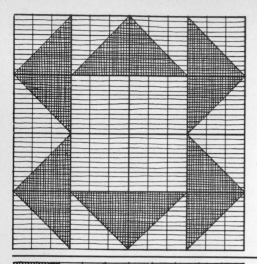

## BUZZARD ROOST
**buzzard's roost**

4-patch

 dark print (color A)

 light solid or white

## CAKE STAND 1

5-patch

 dark print or solid (color A)

 medium print or solid (color B)

 light solid or white

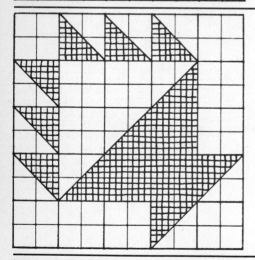

## CAKE STAND 2

5-patch

 dark print or solid (color A)

 light solid or white

## CALICO PATCH
**colonial patch, country colonial patch**

7-patch

 each square equals a different color print or solid fabric

106

## CALIFORNIA
**California state**

9-patch

dark print (color A)

medium print (color A)

medium print (color B)

light print or solid (color C)

## CANE PATTERN
**basketweave and octagon, twist and octagon**

9-patch

dark print (color A)

medium print (color B)

light solid or white

## CARD TRICKS
**interlaced squares**

9-patch

dark print (color A)

medium print (color B)

light solid or white

## CASTLES IN THE AIR
**castles-in-air**

9-patch

dark print (color A)

medium print (color A)

light print (color A)

light solid or white

107

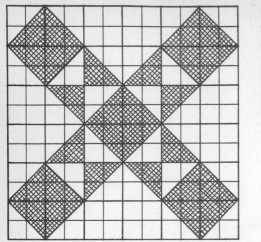

## CAT AND MICE
### cat and mouse

**9-patch**

 dark print

light solid or white

---

## CHAINED HEARTS AND STRIPES
### sweetheart chain

**1–2-patch**

 dark solid (color A)

each square represents a different color fabric

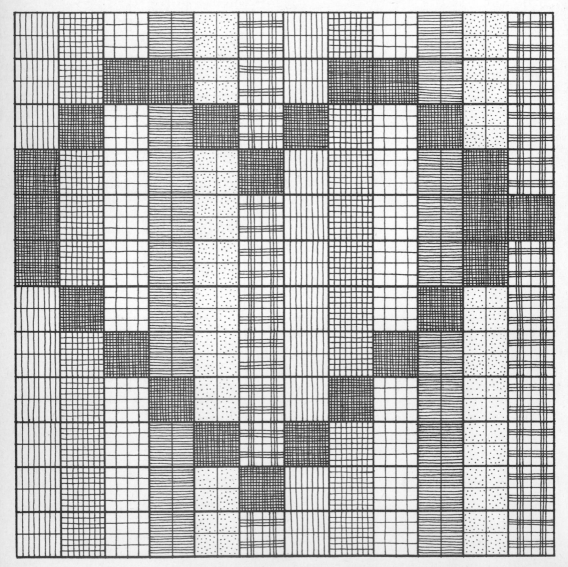

## CHAIN OF DIAMONDS
**diamond chain**

### 4-patch

 dark solid (color A)

medium print (color A or B)

light solid or white

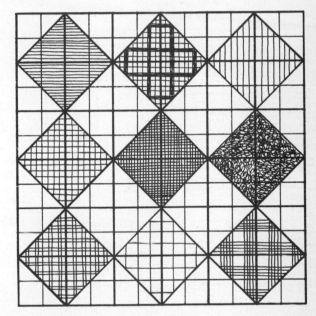

## CHECKERBOARD
**diamond checkerboard, scrap diamonds**

### 9-patch

light solid or white

 each diamond represents a different scrap of fabric

## CHEVRON SQUARES
**chevron**

### 4-patch

dark print (color A)

light print (color A or B)

dark solid (color C)

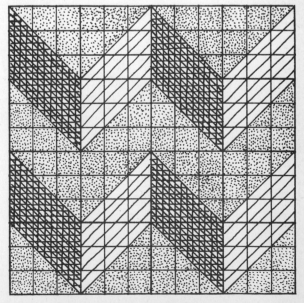

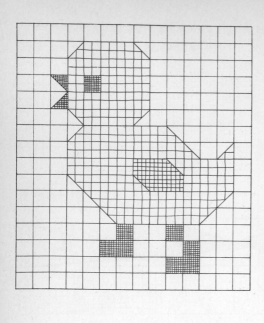

## CHICK 1
### Chicken Little

**1–2-patch**

**Note:** This pattern works up very nicely as a border pattern on a child's quilt.

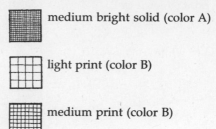

medium bright solid (color A)

light print (color B)

medium print (color B)

light solid or white

## CHICK 2

**1–2-patch**

dark solid (color A)

light print (color B)

medium print (color B)

light solid or white

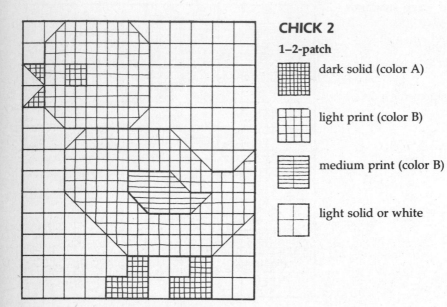

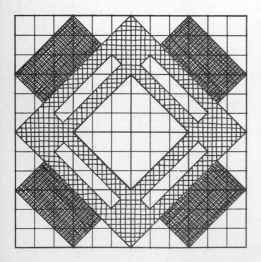

## CHILDREN OF ISRAEL
### Israel, child of Israel

**4-patch**

dark print or solid (color A)

medium print or solid (color B)

light solid or white

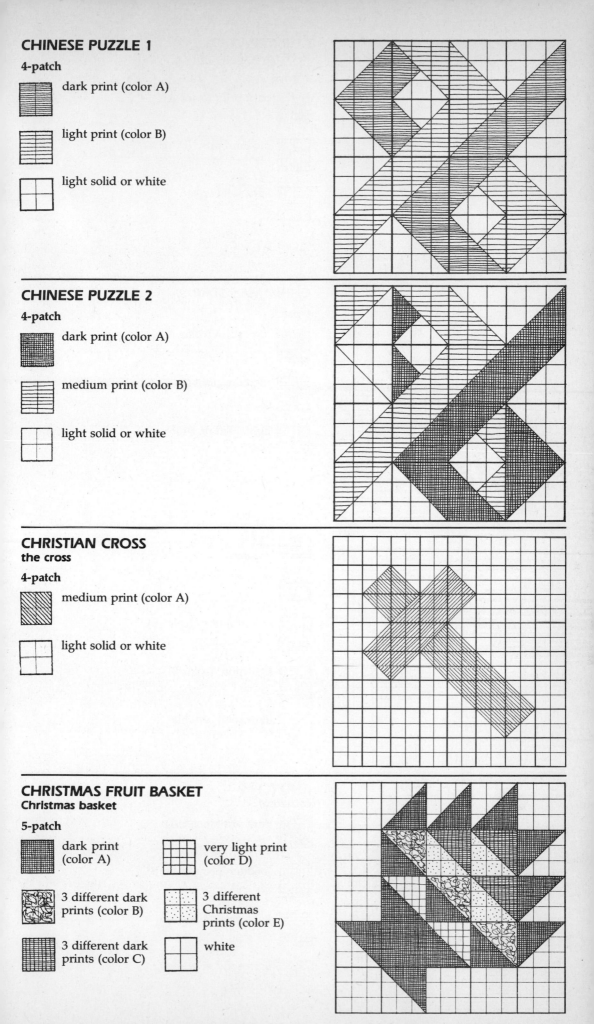

# CHINESE PUZZLE 1

**4-patch**

- dark print (color A)
- light print (color B)
- light solid or white

# CHINESE PUZZLE 2

**4-patch**

- dark print (color A)
- medium print (color B)
- light solid or white

# CHRISTIAN CROSS
**the cross**

**4-patch**

- medium print (color A)
- light solid or white

# CHRISTMAS FRUIT BASKET
**Christmas basket**

**5-patch**

- dark print (color A)
- 3 different dark prints (color B)
- 3 different dark prints (color C)
- very light print (color D)
- 3 different Christmas prints (color E)
- white

111

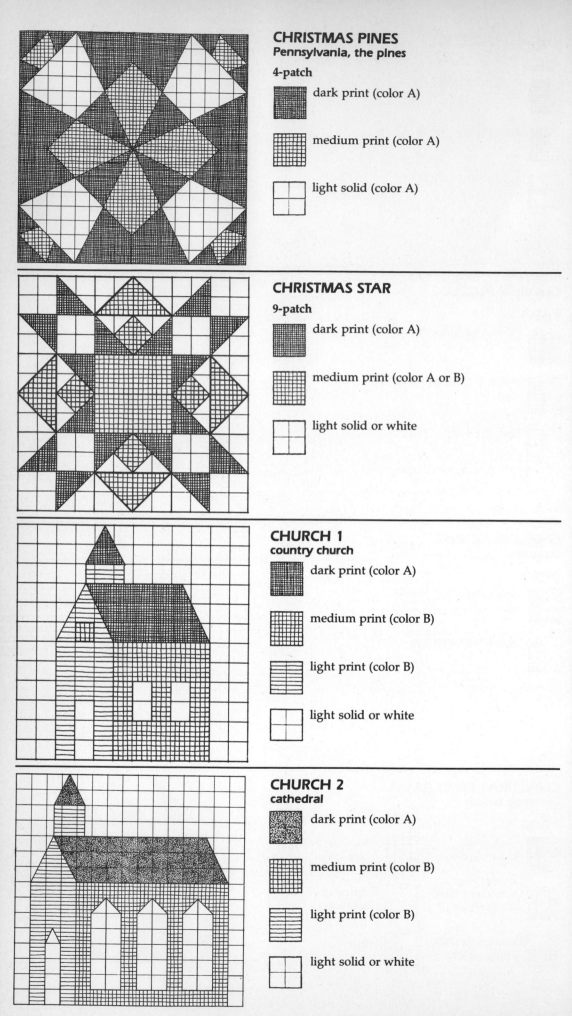

## CHRISTMAS PINES
**Pennsylvania, the pines**

4-patch

■ dark print (color A)

▦ medium print (color A)

□ light solid (color A)

## CHRISTMAS STAR

9-patch

■ dark print (color A)

▦ medium print (color A or B)

□ light solid or white

## CHURCH 1
**country church**

■ dark print (color A)

▦ medium print (color B)

▤ light print (color B)

□ light solid or white

## CHURCH 2
**cathedral**

▨ dark print (color A)

▦ medium print (color B)

▤ light print (color B)

□ light solid or white

# CHURN DASH 1

**5-patch**

dark print (color A)

medium print (color B)

light solid or white

# CHURN DASH 2

**9-patch**

dark print (color A)

medium print (color B)

light solid or white

# CIRCLE IN A CIRCLE
### circle within a circle

**circle**

dark print (color A)

medium print (color A)

light solid or white

# CIRCLE IN A SQUARE
### circle in a frame

**4-patch circle**

dark print (color A)

medium print (color B)

light solid (color B) or white

113

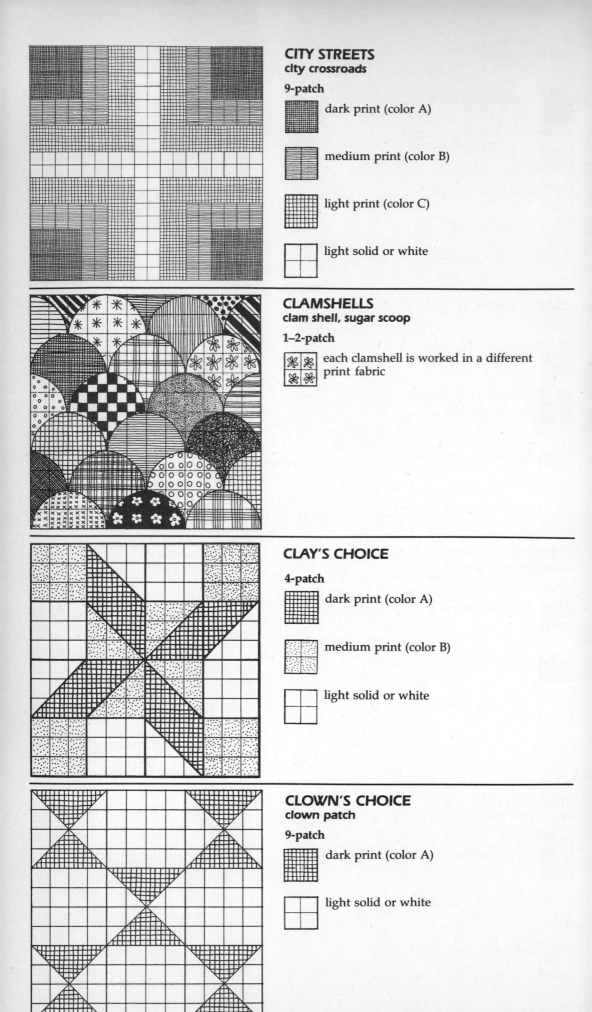

## CITY STREETS
**city crossroads**

**9-patch**

- dark print (color A)
- medium print (color B)
- light print (color C)
- light solid or white

## CLAMSHELLS
**clam shell, sugar scoop**

**1–2-patch**

- each clamshell is worked in a different print fabric

## CLAY'S CHOICE

**4-patch**

- dark print (color A)
- medium print (color B)
- light solid or white

## CLOWN'S CHOICE
**clown patch**

**9-patch**

- dark print (color A)
- light solid or white

## COFFIN STAR
### coffin, coffin block

**4-patch**

dark print or solid (usually black)

light solid or white

## COLONIAL ROSE GARDEN
### colonial rose

**9-patch circle**

dark print (color A)

medium print (color B)

light solid or white

## COMET
### Halley's comet, the comet

**5-patch**

dark print (color A)

medium print (color B)

light print (color C)

## COMPASS
### simple compass, the compass block

**4-patch circle**

medium print (color A)

light solid or white

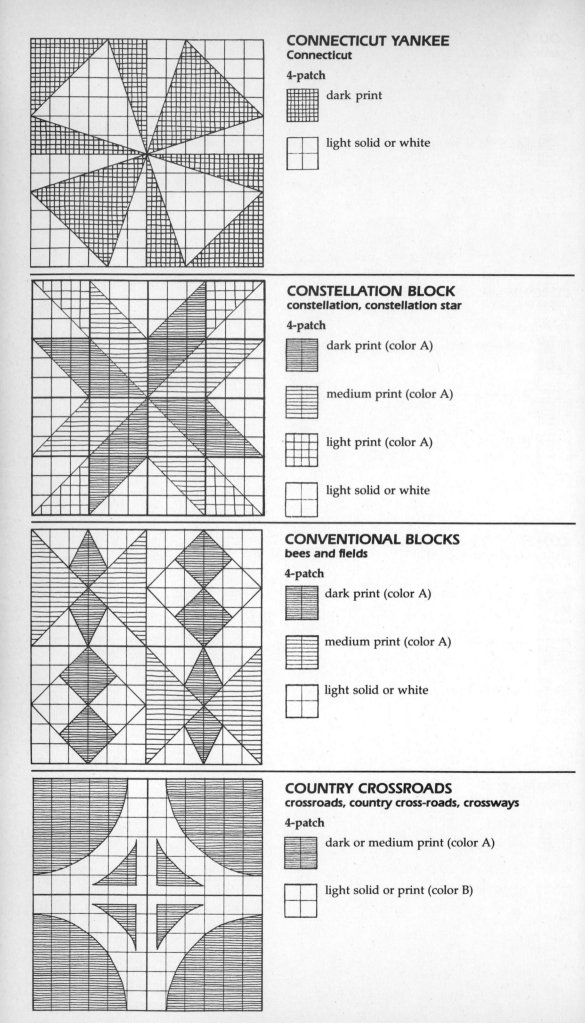

## CONNECTICUT YANKEE
**Connecticut**

4-patch

dark print

light solid or white

## CONSTELLATION BLOCK
**constellation, constellation star**

4-patch

dark print (color A)

medium print (color A)

light print (color A)

light solid or white

## CONVENTIONAL BLOCKS
**bees and fields**

4-patch

dark print (color A)

medium print (color A)

light solid or white

## COUNTRY CROSSROADS
**crossroads, country cross-roads, crossways**

4-patch

dark or medium print (color A)

light solid or print (color B)

## COUNTRY ROADS
### country crossroads

**7-patch**

dark print (color A)

medium print (color B)

light solid or white

## CRAB CLAWS
### wrenches

**9-patch**

dark print (color A)

medium print (color B)

white

## CRAZY ANN 1

**5-patch**

dark print (color A)

medium print (color A)

medium print (color B)

light solid or white

medium print (color C)

## CRAZY ANN 2

**5-patch**

dark print (color A)

light print (color A)

light solid or white

117

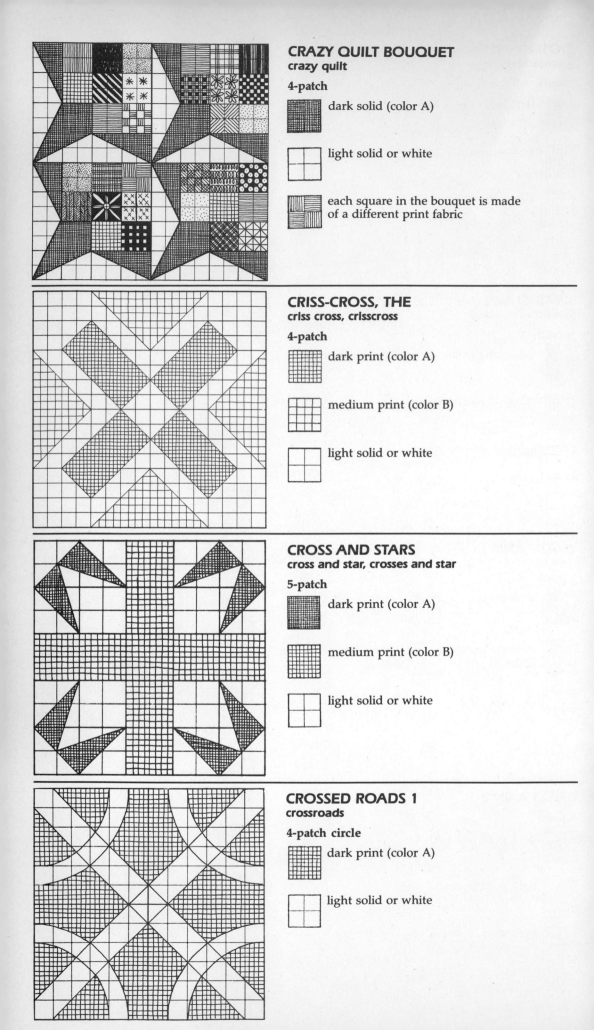

## CRAZY QUILT BOUQUET
**crazy quilt**

**4-patch**

dark solid (color A)

light solid or white

each square in the bouquet is made of a different print fabric

## CRISS-CROSS, THE
**criss cross, crisscross**

**4-patch**

dark print (color A)

medium print (color B)

light solid or white

## CROSS AND STARS
**cross and star, crosses and star**

**5-patch**

dark print (color A)

medium print (color B)

light solid or white

## CROSSED ROADS 1
**crossroads**

**4-patch circle**

dark print (color A)

light solid or white

## CROSSED ROADS 2
**crossroads**

4-patch

dark print (color A)

medium print (color B)

light print (color C)

light solid or white

## CROSSED ROADS TO OKLAHOMA
**roads to Oklahoma**

4-patch

dark print (color A)

medium print (color B)

light print (color B)

white

## CROSS ON A CROSS
**cross on cross**

4-patch

dark print (color A)

medium print (color B)

light solid or white

## CROSS WITHIN THE CROSS
**cross within a cross**

4-patch

dark print (color A)

medium print (color B)

light solid or white

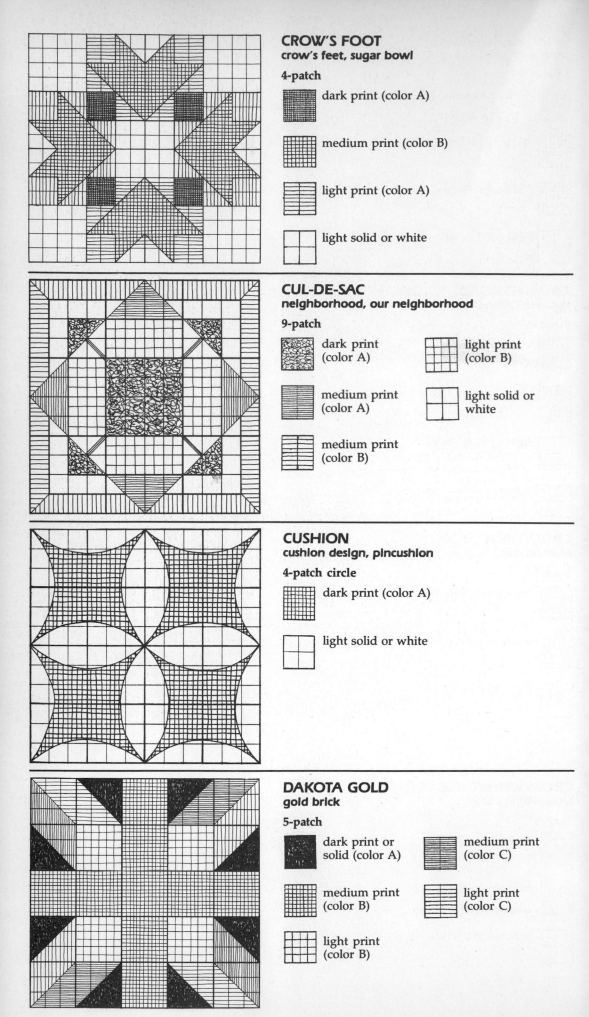

## CROW'S FOOT
**crow's feet, sugar bowl**

**4-patch**

dark print (color A)

medium print (color B)

light print (color A)

light solid or white

## CUL-DE-SAC
**neighborhood, our neighborhood**

**9-patch**

dark print (color A)

medium print (color A)

medium print (color B)

light print (color B)

light solid or white

## CUSHION
**cushion design, pincushion**

**4-patch circle**

dark print (color A)

light solid or white

## DAKOTA GOLD
**gold brick**

**5-patch**

dark print or solid (color A)

medium print (color B)

light print (color B)

medium print (color C)

light print (color C)

## DAVID AND GOLIATH

**5-patch**

dark print (color A)

medium print (color B)

light solid or white

## DELAWARE

**Delaware state**

**9-patch**

dark print (color A)

medium print or solid (color B)

light solid or white

## DESERT ROSE BASKET

**cactus basket, desert rose, Texas rose**

**9-patch**

dark print or solid (color A)

light print (color A)

medium print (color B)

light print or white

medium print (color C)

## DEVIL CLAWS

**bright stars, cross plains, Idaho beauty, lily block, sweet gum**

**4-patch**

dark print (color A)

medium print (color B)

light solid or white

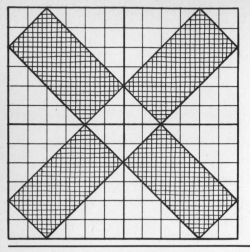

### DEVIL'S PUZZLE
**fly foot**

**4-patch**

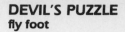 dark print (color A)

light solid or white

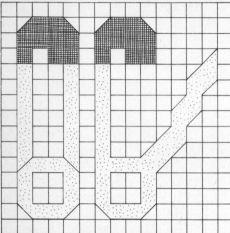

### DIAPER PINS

**1–2-patch**

medium print (color A)

light print (color B)

light solid or white

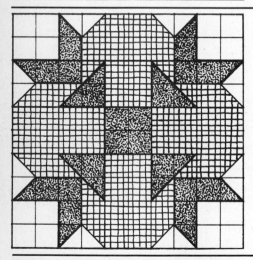

### DOE AND DARTS

**5-patch**

dark print (color A)

medium print (color B)

light solid or white

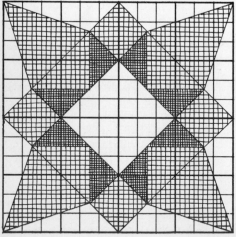

### DOGTOOTH VIOLET
**dog-tooth violet**

**4-patch**

dark print (color A)

medium print (color B)

light solid or white

## DOMINO 1

**5-patch**

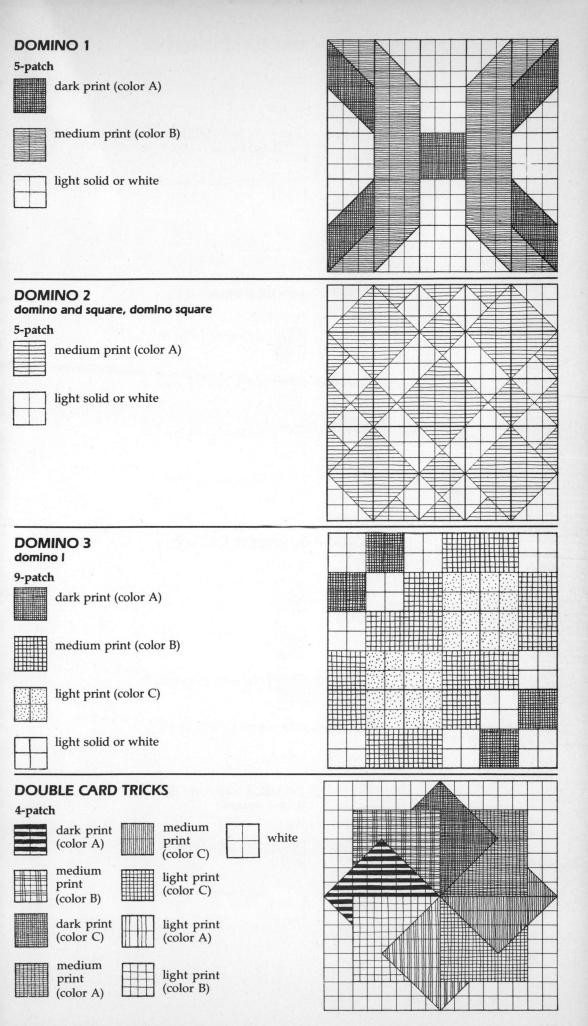

dark print (color A)

medium print (color B)

light solid or white

## DOMINO 2
**domino and square, domino square**

**5-patch**

medium print (color A)

light solid or white

## DOMINO 3
**domino I**

**9-patch**

dark print (color A)

medium print (color B)

light print (color C)

light solid or white

## DOUBLE CARD TRICKS

**4-patch**

dark print (color A)

medium print (color C)

white

medium print (color B)

light print (color C)

dark print (color C)

light print (color A)

medium print (color A)

light print (color B)

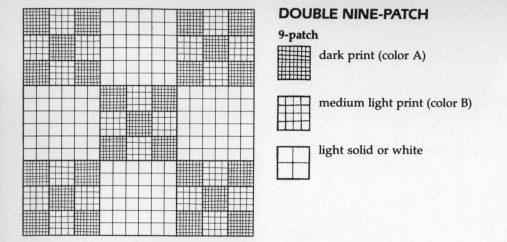

## DOUBLE NINE-PATCH

**9-patch**

dark print (color A)

medium light print (color B)

light solid or white

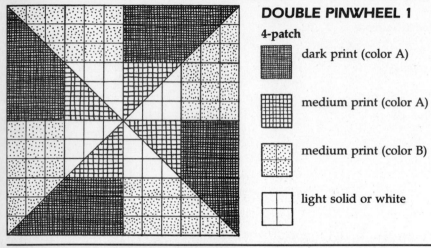

## DOUBLE PINWHEEL 1

**4-patch**

dark print (color A)

medium print (color A)

medium print (color B)

light solid or white

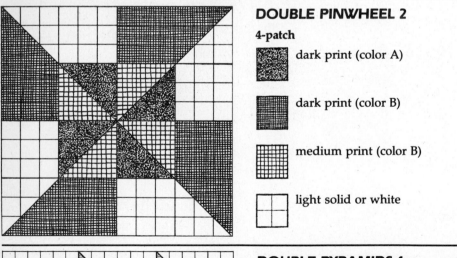

## DOUBLE PINWHEEL 2

**4-patch**

dark print (color A)

dark print (color B)

medium print (color B)

light solid or white

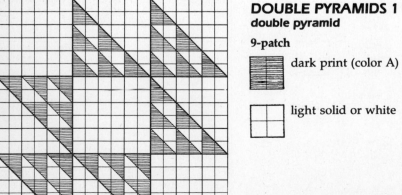

## DOUBLE PYRAMIDS 1
**double pyramid**

**9-patch**

dark print (color A)

light solid or white

## DOUBLE PYRAMIDS 2

**9-patch**

dark print (color A)

light solid or white

## DOUBLE T
**eight-pointed star**

**4-patch**

dark print (color A)

medium print (color B)

light print (color B)

light solid or white

## DOUBLE TULIP

**4-patch**

dark print (color A)

medium print (color B)

light solid or white

## DOUBLE X–1
**double-X**

**4-patch**

medium print (color A)

light solid or white

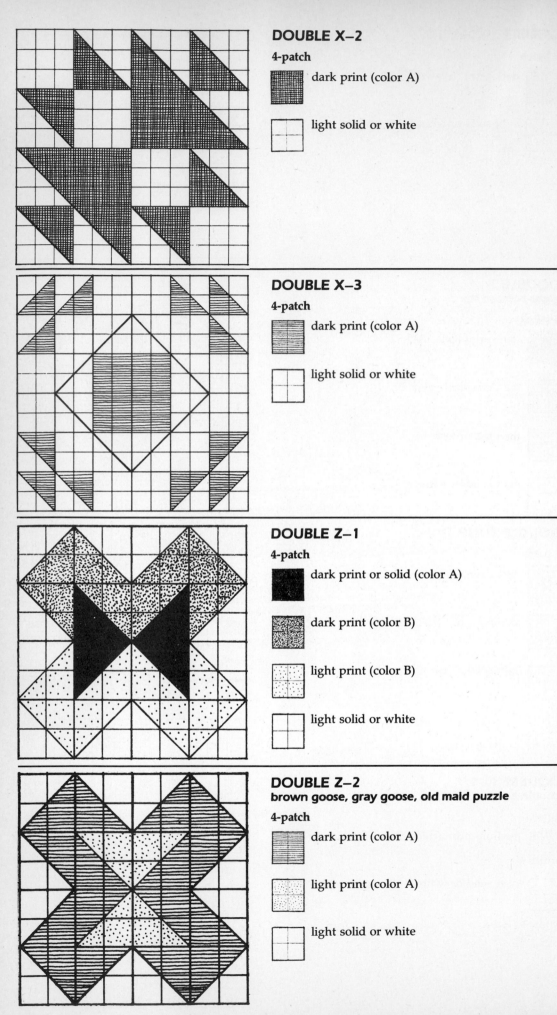

### DOUBLE X–2
4-patch

▨ dark print (color A)

☐ light solid or white

### DOUBLE X–3
4-patch

▨ dark print (color A)

☐ light solid or white

### DOUBLE Z–1
4-patch

■ dark print or solid (color A)

▨ dark print (color B)

☐ light print (color B)

☐ light solid or white

### DOUBLE Z–2
**brown goose, gray goose, old maid puzzle**
4-patch

▨ dark print (color A)

☐ light print (color A)

☐ light solid or white

## DOVE IN A WINDOW
### dove in the window

**4-patch**

▨ dark print (color A)

▨ medium print (color B)

☐ light solid or white

## DOVE IN WINDOW 1
### dove in a window

**7-patch**

▨ dark print (color A)

▤ dark print (color B)

▨ medium print (color C)

☐ light solid or white

## DOVE IN WINDOW 2

**4-patch**

▤ dark print

☐ white

## DOVER
### Dover block, Dover quilt block

**9-patch**

▥ dark print (color A)

▦ light print (color B)

☐ light solid or white

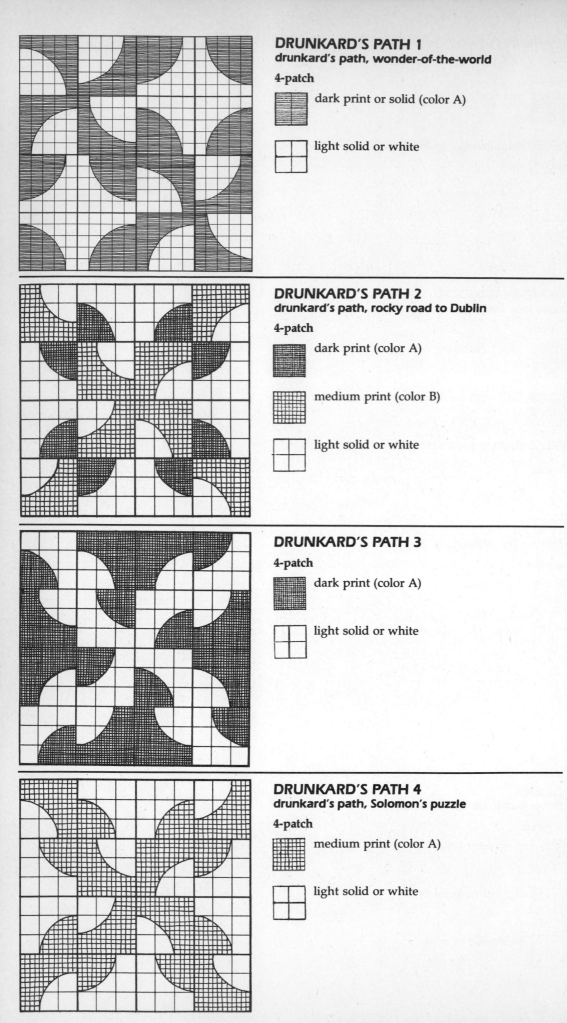

## DRUNKARD'S PATH 1
**drunkard's path, wonder-of-the-world**

**4-patch**

dark print or solid (color A)

light solid or white

## DRUNKARD'S PATH 2
**drunkard's path, rocky road to Dublin**

**4-patch**

dark print (color A)

medium print (color B)

light solid or white

## DRUNKARD'S PATH 3

**4-patch**

dark print (color A)

light solid or white

## DRUNKARD'S PATH 4
**drunkard's path, Solomon's puzzle**

**4-patch**

medium print (color A)

light solid or white

## DRUNKARD'S PATH 5
### dirty windows, snowy windows

**4-patch**

light solid or white

quarter circles made of scraps of medium prints

## DRUNKARD'S PATH 6

**4-patch**

dark print

light solid or white

## DUCK AND DUCKLINGS

**5-patch**

medium print (color A)

light solid or white

## DUCK BLOCK

**1-patch**

dark print (color A)

light print (color D)

medium print (color B)

light solid or white

dark solid (color C)

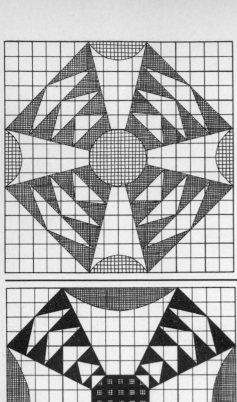

## DUSTY MILLER 1

**4-patch circle**

 dark print (color A)

 medium print (color B)

 light solid or white

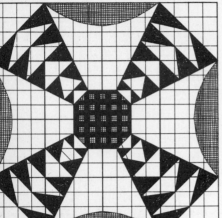

## DUSTY MILLER 2

**4-patch circle**

 dark print (color A)

 dark print (color B)

 medium print (color C)

 light solid or white

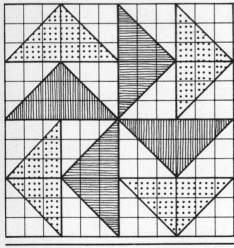

## DUTCHMAN PUZZLE

**Dutchman's puzzle, mosaic**

**4-patch**

 dark print (color A)

 medium print (color B)

 light solid or white

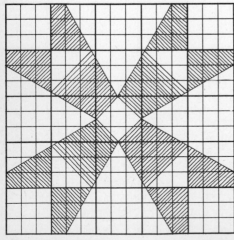

## DUTCH MILL 1

**5-patch**

 medium print (color A)

 light solid or white

## DUTCH MILL 2

**4-patch**

dark print or solid (color A)

medium print (color B)

light solid or white

## ECONOMY 1

*economy*

**4-patch**

dark print (color A)

light print (color B)

light solid or white

## ECONOMY 2

**4-patch**

medium print (color A)

light solid or white

## ECONOMY 3

**4-patch**

dark print or solid (color A)

light print (color B)

white

131

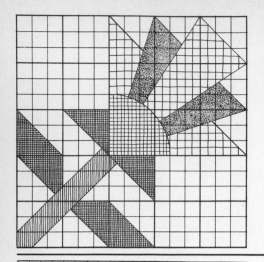

## EGYPTIAN LOTUS FLOWER
### lotus flower, Nile flower

**5-patch**

 dark print (color A)

 dark print (color B)

 medium print (color A)

 medium light print (color B)

 light print (color A)

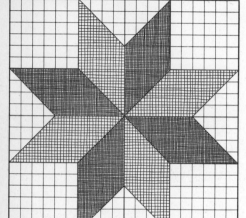

## EIGHT-POINT STAR 1
### 8-pointed star

**4-patch**

 dark print (color A)

 light print (color A)

 light solid or white

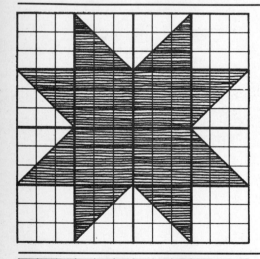

## EIGHT-POINT STAR 2
### 8-pointed star

**4-patch**

 dark print (color A)

 light solid or white

## ELECTRIC FANS
### fan blades

**4-patch**

 dark print (color A)

light solid or white

132

# ELEPHANT PATCH

| | |
|---|---|
| dark print (color A) | dark solid scrap (eye) |
| light print (color B) | light solid or white |
| light print or solid (color B) | |

---

# ENGLISH IVY
**tree, pine variation I**

**4-patch**

dark print (color A)

dark print (color B)

medium print (color B)

light solid or white

---

# EVENING STAR
**economy star**

**4-patch**

dark print (color A)

light solid or white

---

# EVENING STAR—MORNING STAR
**stars and squares, rising star, rising star and square**

**4-patch**

dark print (color A)

medium print (color B)

light solid or white

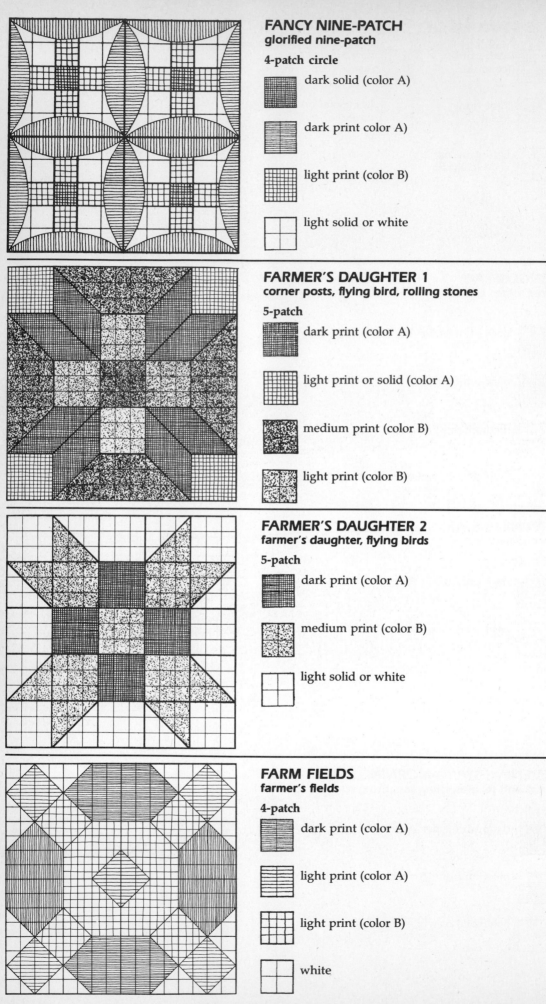

**FANCY NINE-PATCH**
glorified nine-patch

4-patch circle

dark solid (color A)

dark print color A)

light print (color B)

light solid or white

**FARMER'S DAUGHTER 1**
corner posts, flying bird, rolling stones

5-patch

dark print (color A)

light print or solid (color A)

medium print (color B)

light print (color B)

**FARMER'S DAUGHTER 2**
farmer's daughter, flying birds

5-patch

dark print (color A)

medium print (color B)

light solid or white

**FARM FIELDS**
farmer's fields

4-patch

dark print (color A)

light print (color A)

light print (color B)

white

## FEATHER STAR AND SQUARE
**feathery star with square**

**4-patch**

dark print (color A)

light print (color B)

light solid or white

## FENCE RAIL 1
**fence rail, fence rail III**

**1–2-patch**

dark print (color A)

medium dark print (color A or B)

medium print (color A or C)

light print (color A or D)

## FENCE RAIL 2
**fence rails, fence rail I**

**1–2-patch**

dark print (color A)

medium print (color B)

light solid or white

## FIFTY-FOUR FORTY OR FIGHT 1
**54–40 or fight**

**9-patch**

dark print (color A)

medium print (color B)

light solid or white

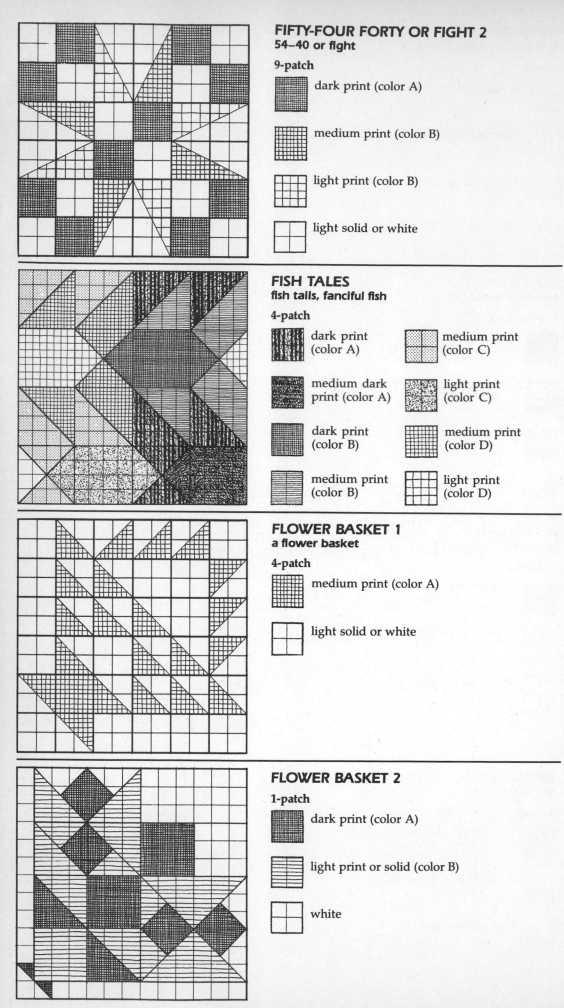

## FIFTY-FOUR FORTY OR FIGHT 2
**54–40 or fight**

9-patch

▦ dark print (color A)

▦ medium print (color B)

▦ light print (color B)

▢ light solid or white

## FISH TALES
**fish tails, fanciful fish**

4-patch

▦ dark print (color A)

▦ medium dark print (color A)

▦ dark print (color B)

▦ medium print (color B)

▦ medium print (color C)

▦ light print (color C)

▦ medium print (color D)

▦ light print (color D)

## FLOWER BASKET 1
**a flower basket**

4-patch

▦ medium print (color A)

▢ light solid or white

## FLOWER BASKET 2

1-patch

▦ dark print (color A)

▦ light print or solid (color B)

▢ white

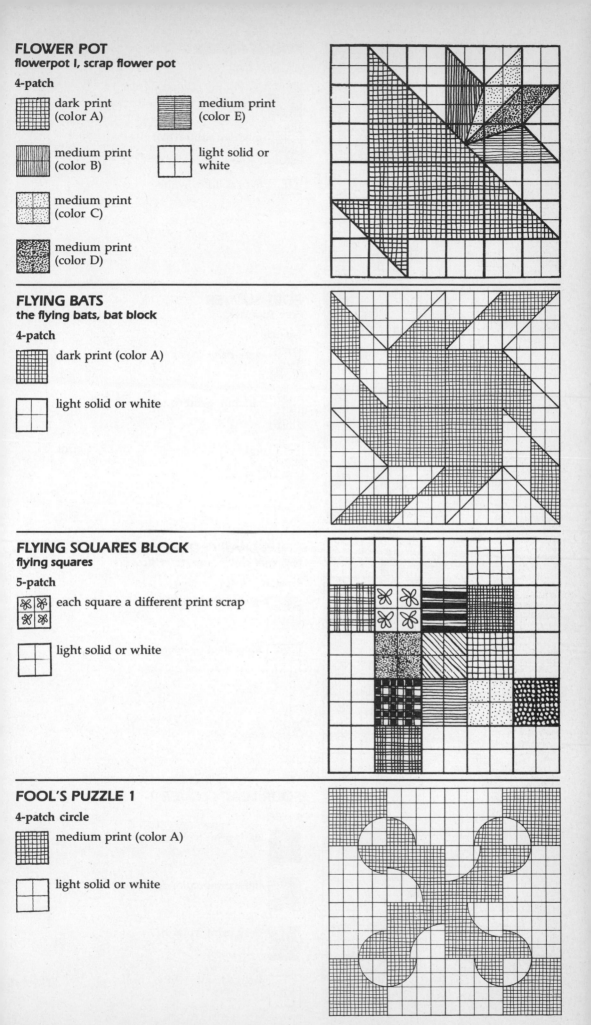

## FLOWER POT
**flowerpot I, scrap flower pot**

**4-patch**

| | dark print (color A) | | medium print (color E) |
|---|---|---|---|

| | medium print (color B) | | light solid or white |
|---|---|---|---|

| | medium print (color C) |
|---|---|

| | medium print (color D) |
|---|---|

## FLYING BATS
**the flying bats, bat block**

**4-patch**

| | dark print (color A) |
|---|---|

| | light solid or white |
|---|---|

## FLYING SQUARES BLOCK
**flying squares**

**5-patch**

| | each square a different print scrap |
|---|---|

| | light solid or white |
|---|---|

## FOOL'S PUZZLE 1
**4-patch circle**

| | medium print (color A) |
|---|---|

| | light solid or white |
|---|---|

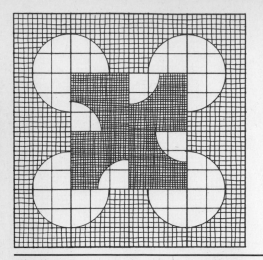

## FOOL'S PUZZLE 2
**4-patch circle**

 dark print (color A)

 medium print (color B)

 light solid or white

## FORT SUMTER
**Fort Sumpter**

**4-patch**

 dark print (color A)

 medium print (color B)

 light print (color A)

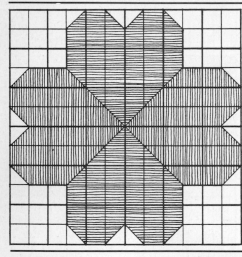

## FOUR LEAF CLOVER
**four-leaf clover, hearts 'n' flowers**

**4-patch**

 dark print (color A)

 light solid or white

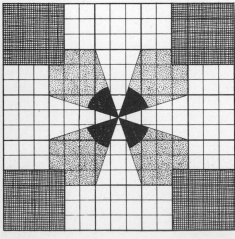

## FOUR LEAF CLOVER 2
**5-patch**

 dark print (color A)

 light print (color A)

 dark print (color B)

 light solid or white

## FOUR PATCH
**basic 4-patch**

**4-patch**

dark print or solid (color A)

light print or solid (color B)

## FOUR PATCH CHAINS
**fancy 4-patch, four patch, four patch chain**

**4-patch**

dark print (color A)

medium print (color A or B)

light solid or white

## FOUR POINTS
**Fort Sumpter**

**4-patch**

dark print (color A)

medium print (color B)

light solid or white

## FOUR T SQUARE

**9-patch**

dark print

light solid or white

139

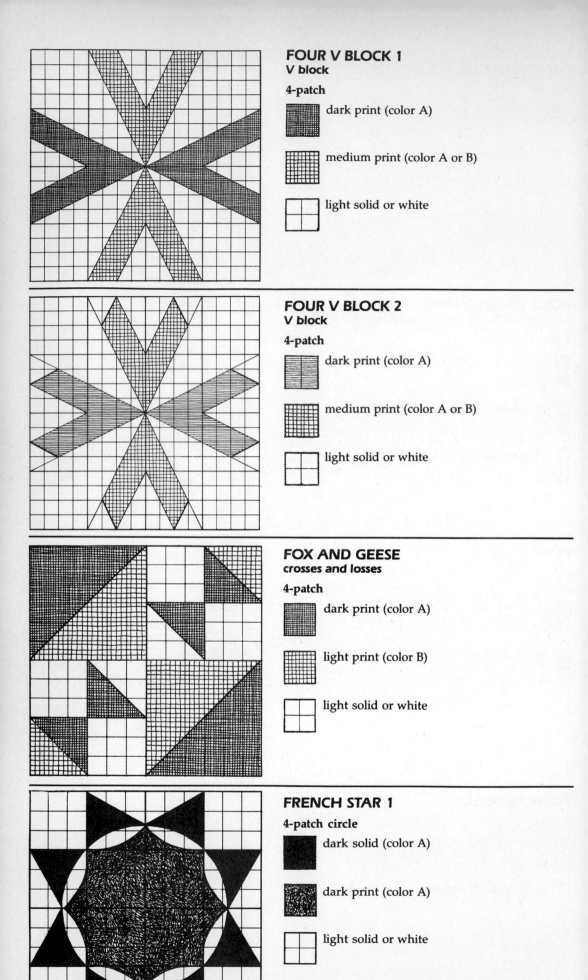

## FOUR V BLOCK 1
**V block**

4-patch

dark print (color A)

medium print (color A or B)

light solid or white

## FOUR V BLOCK 2
**V block**

4-patch

dark print (color A)

medium print (color A or B)

light solid or white

## FOX AND GEESE
**crosses and losses**

4-patch

dark print (color A)

light print (color B)

light solid or white

## FRENCH STAR 1
**4-patch circle**

dark solid (color A)

dark print (color A)

light solid or white

# FRENCH STAR 2

## 4-patch circle

■ dark solid (color A)

▦ light print (color B)

▨ medium print (color A)

⊞ light solid or white

▩ dark print (color B)

---

# FRIDAY THE THIRTEENTH
**Friday the 13th**

## 4-patch

▦ dark print (color A)

▦ medium print (color B)

⊞ light print (color B)

---

# FRUIT BASKET 1

## 5-patch

▦ medium print (color A)

▦ medium print (color B)

⊞ light solid or white

---

# FRUIT BASKET 2

## 5-patch

▦ medium print (color A)

▦ dark print (color B)

□ white

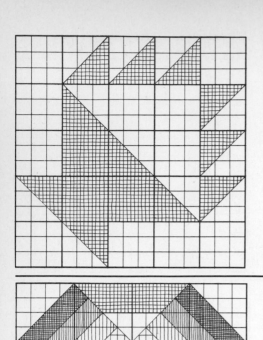

## FRUIT BASKET 3

**5-patch**

| | |
|---|---|
| dark print (color A) | |
| light solid or white | |

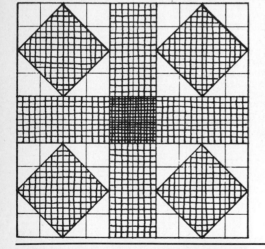

## GARDEN GAZEBO

**4-patch**

| | |
|---|---|
| dark print (color A) | medium dark print (color B) |
| medium print (color A) | medium print (color B) |
| light print (color A) | light print (color B) |
| dark print (color B) | medium print (color C) |
| | light solid (color C) |

## GARDEN OF EDEN
**economy**

**5-patch**

| | |
|---|---|
| dark print (color A) | |
| medium print (color B) | |
| light solid (color A or white) | |

## GARDEN PATH
*formal garden*

**4-patch**

| | |
|---|---|
| dark print (color A) | medium print (color B) |
| medium print (color A) | light print (color B) |
| light print (color A) | white |
| dark print (color B) | |

## GENTLEMAN'S FANCY
gentlemen's fancy

9-patch

▦ dark print (color A)

▦ medium print (color B)

▦ light print (color B)

▢ white

## GENTLEMEN'S FANCY
bachelor puzzle, gentleman's fancy, Mexican block, young man's fancy

5-patch

▦ medium print (color A)

▢ light solid or white

## GEORGETOWN
Georgetown circle

4-patch

▦ dark print (color A)

▦ light print (color B)

▦ medium print (color A)

▢ white

▦ light print (color A)

## GEORGIA
state of Georgia

5-patch

▦ dark print (color A)

▦ medium print (color B)

▢ light solid or white

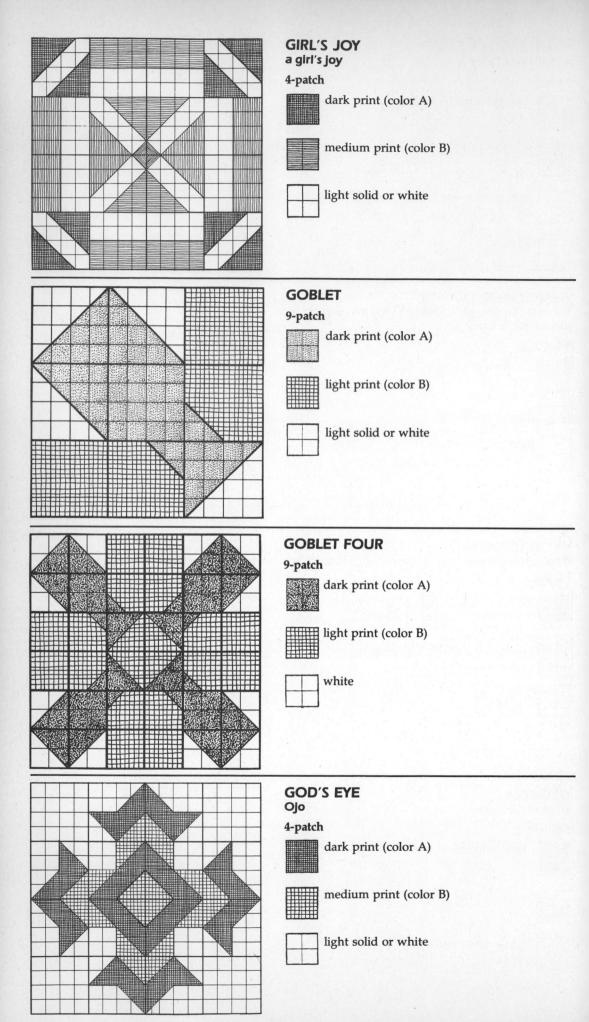

**GIRL'S JOY**
a girl's joy

4-patch

▨ dark print (color A)

▤ medium print (color B)

☐ light solid or white

**GOBLET**

9-patch

▦ dark print (color A)

▦ light print (color B)

☐ light solid or white

**GOBLET FOUR**

9-patch

▨ dark print (color A)

▦ light print (color B)

☐ white

**GOD'S EYE**
Ojo

4-patch

▨ dark print (color A)

▦ medium print (color B)

☐ light solid or white

144

# GOOD LUCK AND NINE
## good-luck block

**4-patch**

dark print (color A)

light solid or white

# GOOSE IN THE POND
## Mexican block, young man's fancy

**5-patch**

dark print (color A)

medium print (color B)

light solid or white

# GRANDMOTHER'S BASKET
## grandmother basket

**4-patch**

dark print (color A)

medium light print (color B)

light solid or white

# GRANDMOTHER'S CROSS
## grandma's cross

**5-patch**

dark print (color A)

light print (color A or B)

white

### GRANDMOTHER'S DREAM

**4-patch**

 dark print (color A)

 medium print or solid (color B)

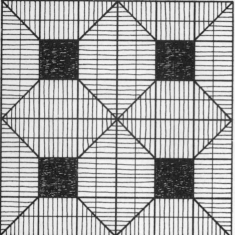

### GRANDMOTHER'S OWN 1

**4-patch**

 dark print (color A)

 light print (color B)

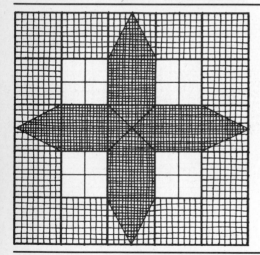

### GRANDMOTHER'S OWN 2

**5-patch**

 dark print (color A)

 medium print (color A or B)

 light solid or white

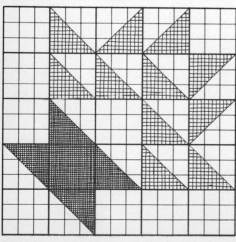

### GRAPE BASKET 1

**5-patch**

 dark print (color A)

 medium print (color B)

 light solid or white

# GRAPE BASKET 2

**5-patch**

dark print (color A)

medium print (color B)

light solid or white

# GRECIAN DESIGN 1
**Grecian block**

**9-patch**

dark print (color A)

light solid or white

# GRECIAN DESIGN 2
**Grecian, Grecian pattern**

**9-patch**

dark print (color A)

medium print (color A or B)

light solid or white

# GRECIAN SQUARE
**Greek square**

**4-patch circle**

dark print (color A)

light print (color B)

white

147

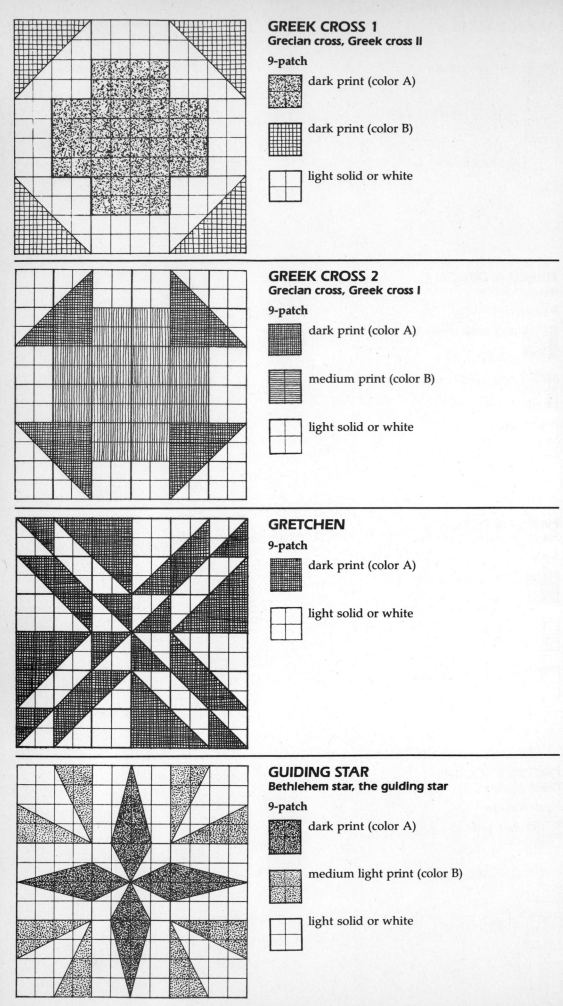

## GREEK CROSS 1
### Grecian cross, Greek cross II
9-patch

dark print (color A)

dark print (color B)

light solid or white

## GREEK CROSS 2
### Grecian cross, Greek cross I
9-patch

dark print (color A)

medium print (color B)

light solid or white

## GRETCHEN
9-patch

dark print (color A)

light solid or white

## GUIDING STAR
### Bethlehem star, the guiding star
9-patch

dark print (color A)

medium light print (color B)

light solid or white

148

## HANDS ALL ROUND
**hand all around**

5-patch

▨ dark print (color A)

☐ light solid or white

## HANDY-ANDY
**handy Andy**

4-patch

▨ dark print (color A)

▨ medium print or solid (color B)

☐ white

## HARTFORD
**Hartford block, hope of Hartford**

5-patch

▨ dark print (color A)

▨ medium print (color B)

☐ light solid or white

## HENS AND CHICKENS
**hen and chickens, hens and chicks**

7-patch

▨ dark print (color A)

▨ medium print (color A)

▨ light print (color B)

☐ light solid or white

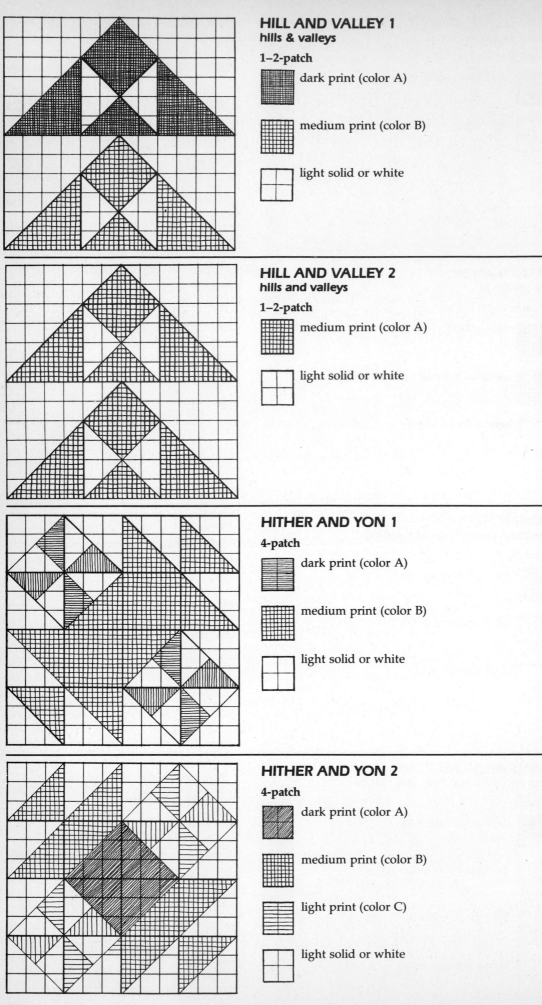

## HILL AND VALLEY 1
**hills & valleys**

**1–2-patch**

dark print (color A)

medium print (color B)

light solid or white

## HILL AND VALLEY 2
**hills and valleys**

**1–2-patch**

medium print (color A)

light solid or white

## HITHER AND YON 1

**4-patch**

dark print (color A)

medium print (color B)

light solid or white

## HITHER AND YON 2

**4-patch**

dark print (color A)

medium print (color B)

light print (color C)

light solid or white

**1–2-patch**

## HOLE IN THE BARN DOOR
**Amish hole in barn door**

**4-patch**

dark print or solid

light solid

## HOME MAKER, THE
**homemaker, home maker**

**4-patch circle**

dark print or solid (color A)

medium print (color )

light solid or white

## HOME TREASURES
**home treasure**

**4-patch**

dark print (color A)

light print (color A)

light solid or white

## HONEY BEE

**4-patch**

dark print or solid (color A)

medium print (color B)

light print (color B)

light solid or white

151

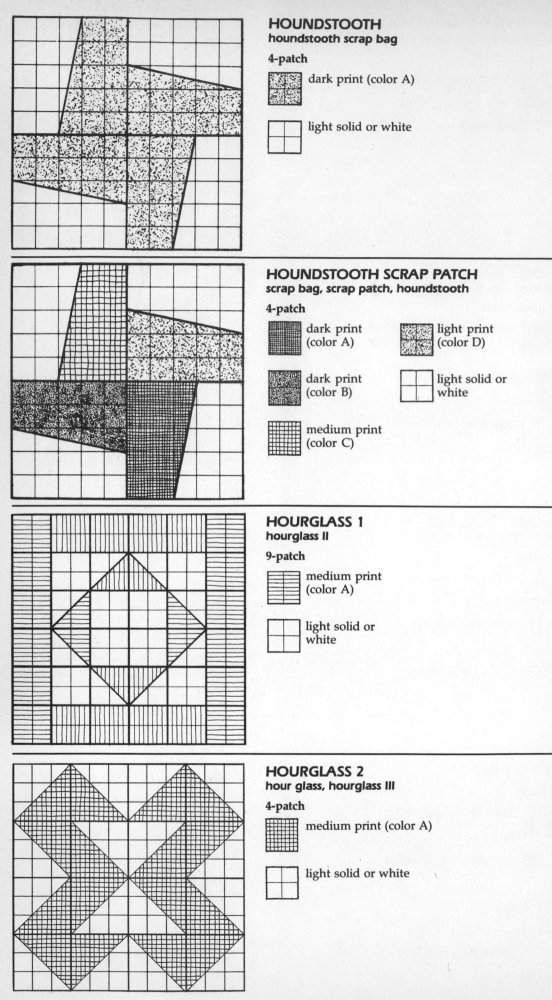

## HOUNDSTOOTH
**houndstooth scrap bag**

**4-patch**

dark print (color A)

light solid or white

## HOUNDSTOOTH SCRAP PATCH
**scrap bag, scrap patch, houndstooth**

**4-patch**

dark print
(color A)

dark print
(color B)

medium print
(color C)

light print
(color D)

light solid or
white

## HOURGLASS 1
**hourglass II**

**9-patch**

medium print
(color A)

light solid or
white

## HOURGLASS 2
**hour glass, hourglass III**

**4-patch**

medium print (color A)

light solid or white

152

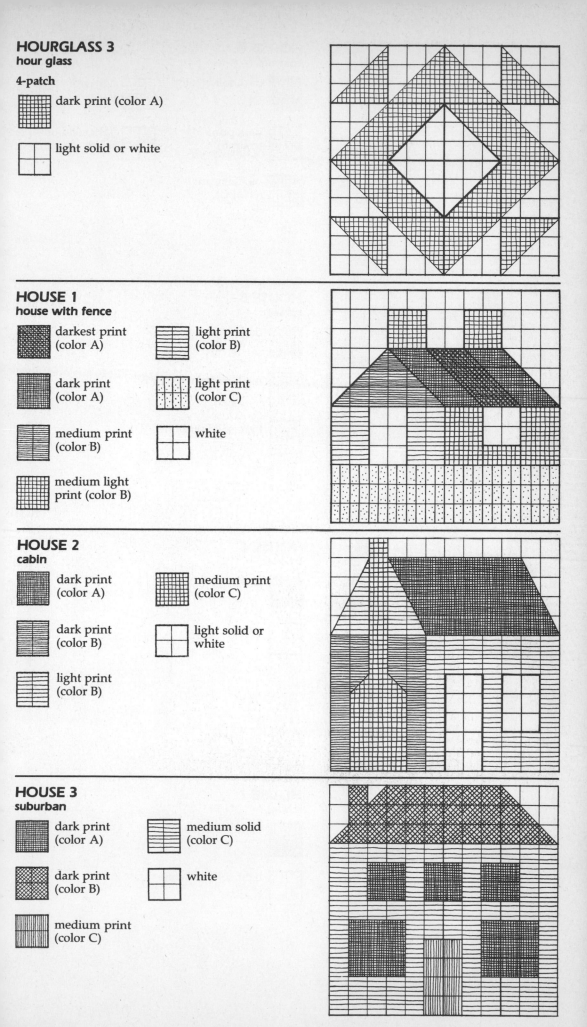

## HOURGLASS 3
### hour glass

**4-patch**

dark print (color A)

light solid or white

## HOUSE 1
### house with fence

darkest print (color A)

dark print (color A)

medium print (color B)

medium light print (color B)

light print (color B)

light print (color C)

white

## HOUSE 2
### cabin

dark print (color A)

dark print (color B)

light print (color B)

medium print (color C)

light solid or white

## HOUSE 3
### suburban

dark print (color A)

dark print (color B)

medium print (color C)

medium solid (color C)

white

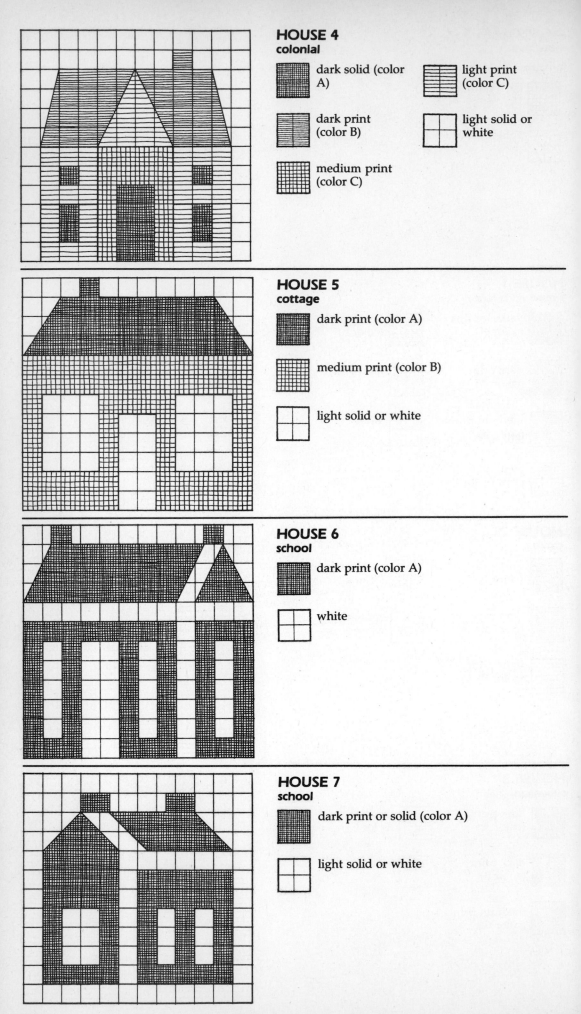

## HOUSE 4
### colonial

- dark solid (color A)
- dark print (color B)
- medium print (color C)
- light print (color C)
- light solid or white

## HOUSE 5
### cottage

- dark print (color A)
- medium print (color B)
- light solid or white

## HOUSE 6
### school

- dark print (color A)
- white

## HOUSE 7
### school

- dark print or solid (color A)
- light solid or white

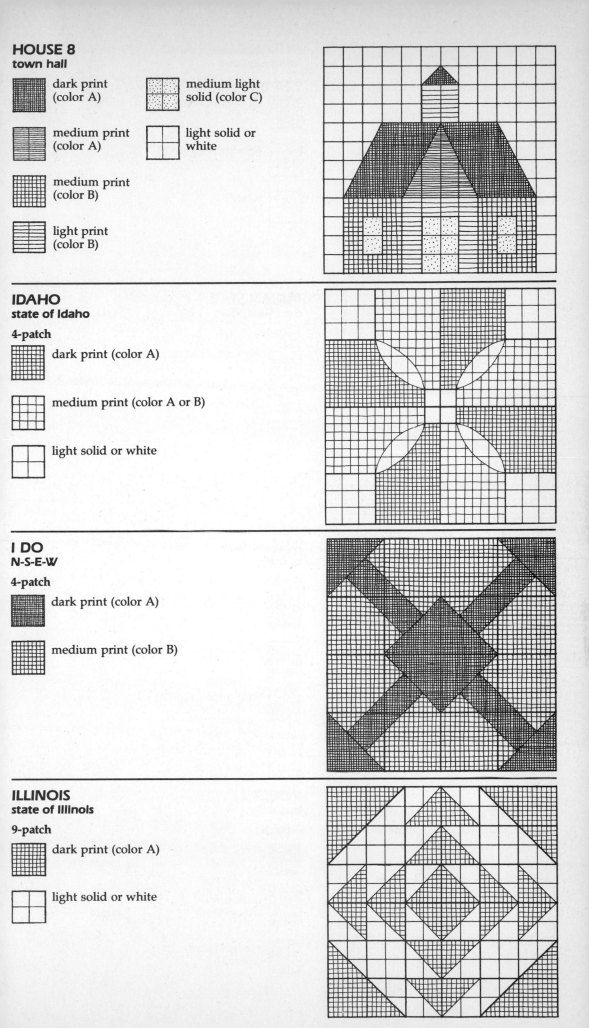

## HOUSE 8
### town hall

- dark print (color A)
- medium print (color A)
- medium print (color B)
- light print (color B)
- medium light solid (color C)
- light solid or white

## IDAHO
### state of Idaho

**4-patch**

- dark print (color A)
- medium print (color A or B)
- light solid or white

## I DO
### N-S-E-W

**4-patch**

- dark print (color A)
- medium print (color B)

## ILLINOIS
### state of Illinois

**9-patch**

- dark print (color A)
- light solid or white

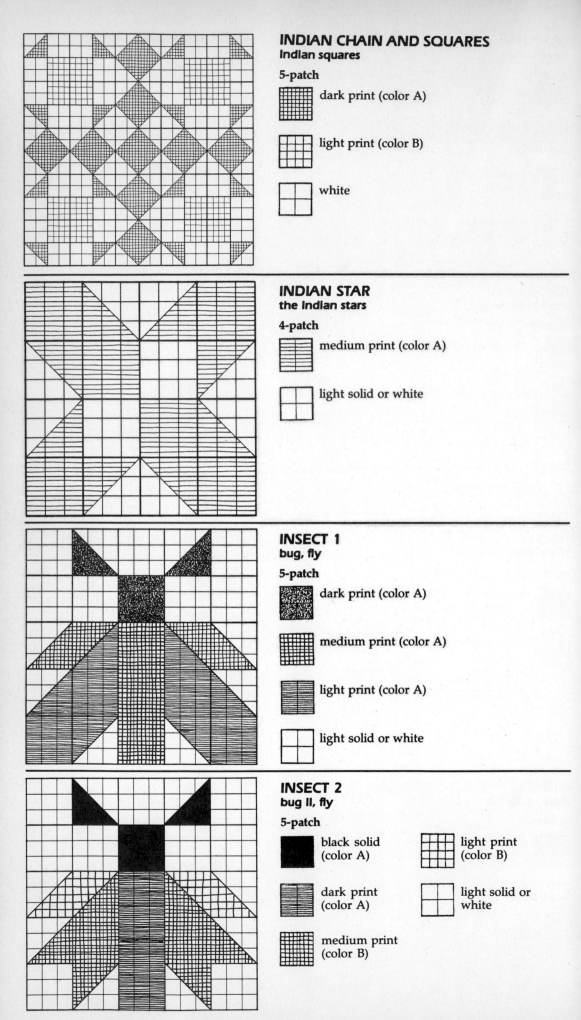

## INDIAN CHAIN AND SQUARES
**Indian squares**

5-patch

dark print (color A)

light print (color B)

white

## INDIAN STAR
**the Indian stars**

4-patch

medium print (color A)

light solid or white

## INSECT 1
**bug, fly**

5-patch

dark print (color A)

medium print (color A)

light print (color A)

light solid or white

## INSECT 2
**bug II, fly**

5-patch

black solid (color A)

dark print (color A)

medium print (color B)

light print (color B)

light solid or white

## INSECT 3
**bug, fantasy bug**

**5-patch**

- ■ dark solid (color A)
- ▦ dark print (color B)
- ▦ medium print (color B)
- ▢ light solid or white

## INSECT 4
**bug, blackbug**

**5-patch**

- ▦ black solid
- ▢ light solid or print

## INTERLACED STAR
**laced star, star path, starry path**

**4-patch**

- ▦ dark print
- ▦ medium dark print
- ▦ medium print
- ▦ light print
- ▢ light solid or white

## INTERLOCKED SQUARES
**interlaced squares, interlocking squares**

**4-patch**

- ▦ dark print (color A)
- ▦ medium print (color B)
- ▢ light solid or white

157

# INTERNATIONAL SIGNAL FLAGS
## code flags

The following legend is used for all letters of the alphabet signal code flags.

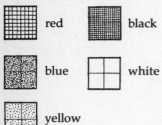

red    black

blue   white

yellow

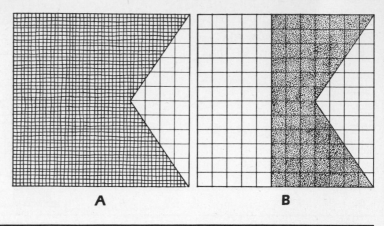

A          B

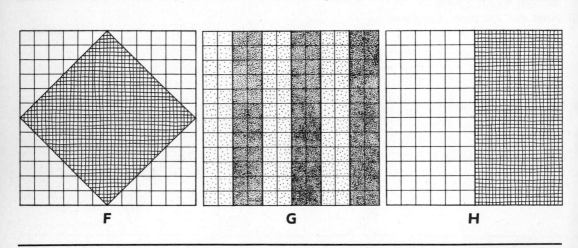

C          D          E

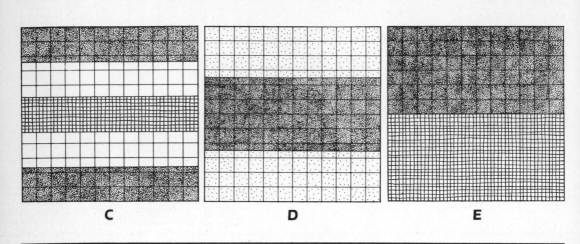

F          G          H

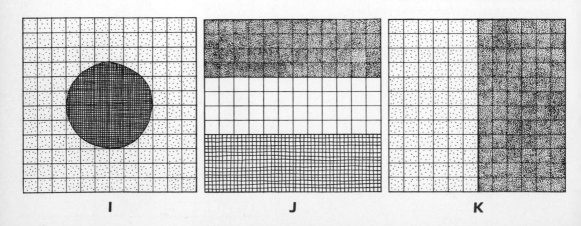

I          J          K

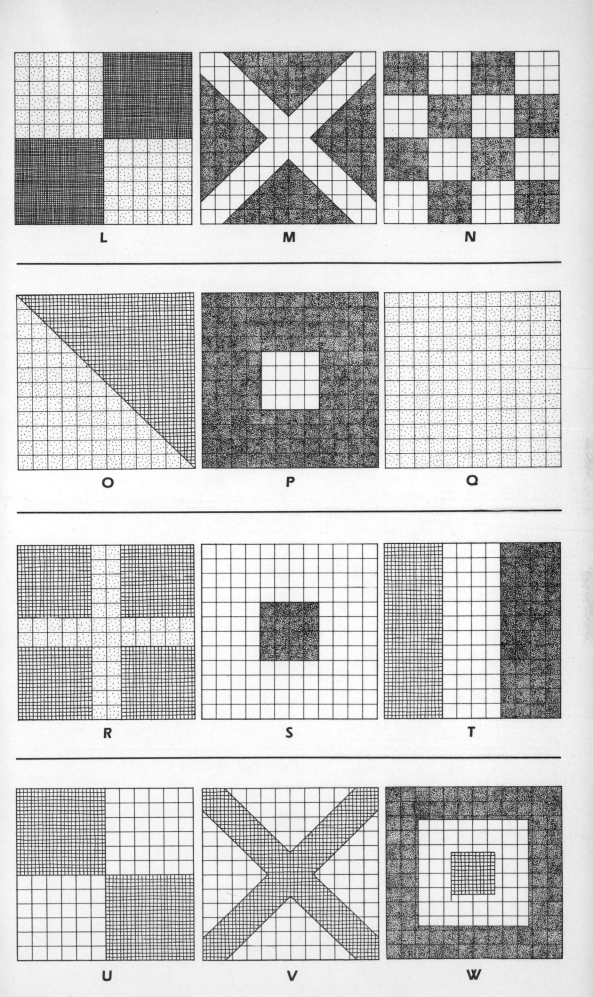

L       M       N

O       P       Q

R       S       T

U       V       W

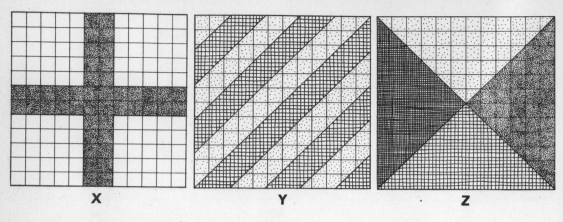

X          Y          Z

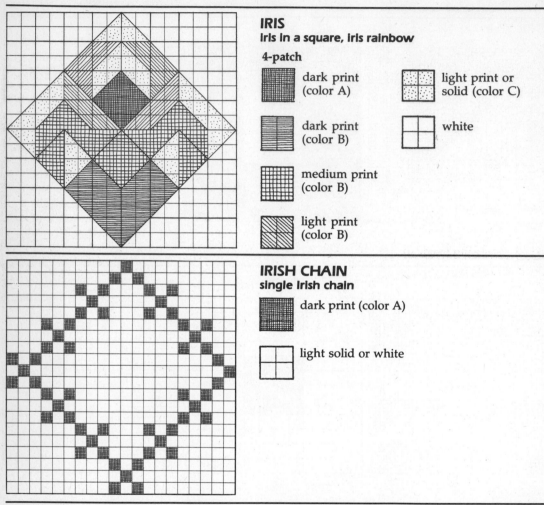

## IRIS
**iris in a square, iris rainbow**

**4-patch**

dark print
(color A)

light print or
solid (color C)

dark print
(color B)

white

medium print
(color B)

light print
(color B)

## IRISH CHAIN
**single irish chain**

dark print (color A)

light solid or white

## JACK IN THE BOX 1

**5-patch**

dark print (color A)

light print (color A)

medium print (color B)

light solid or white

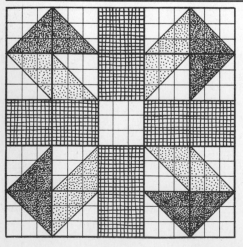

160

## JACK IN THE BOX 2

**5-patch**

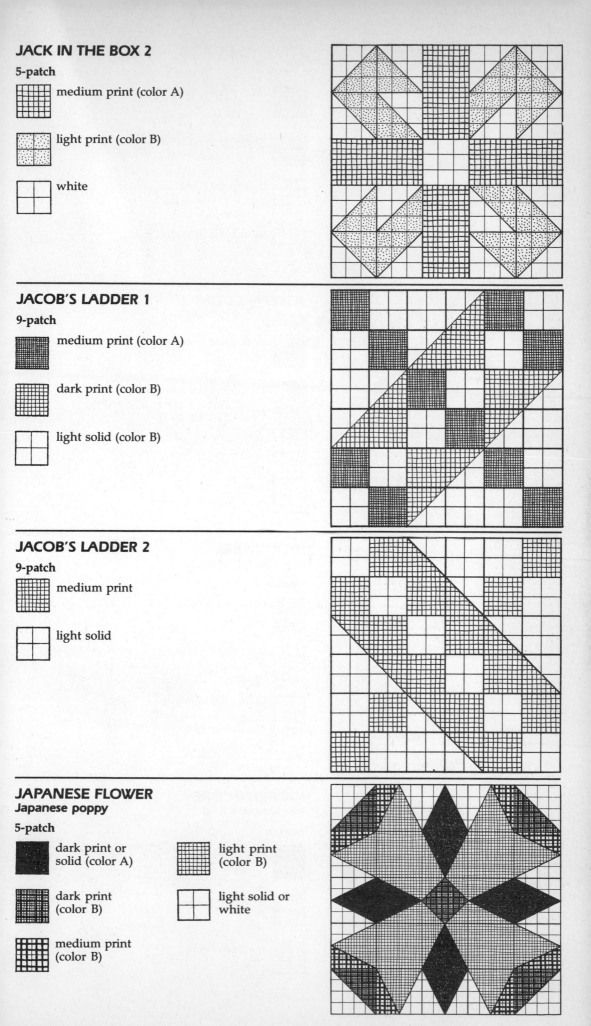

medium print (color A)

light print (color B)

white

## JACOB'S LADDER 1

**9-patch**

medium print (color A)

dark print (color B)

light solid (color B)

## JACOB'S LADDER 2

**9-patch**

medium print

light solid

## JAPANESE FLOWER
**Japanese poppy**

**5-patch**

dark print or solid (color A)

light print (color B)

dark print (color B)

light solid or white

medium print (color B)

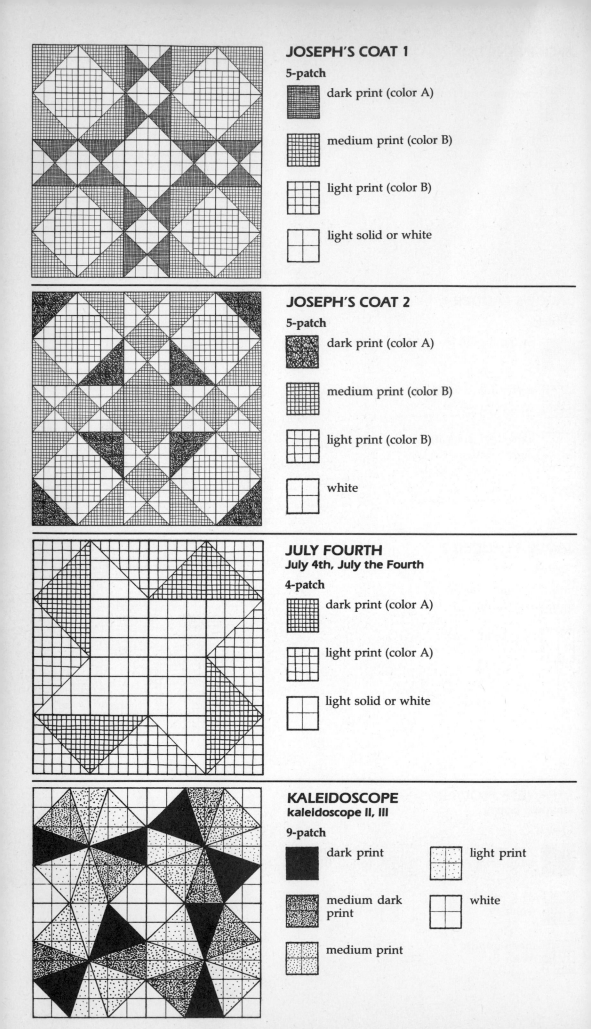

## JOSEPH'S COAT 1

**5-patch**

- dark print (color A)
- medium print (color B)
- light print (color B)
- light solid or white

## JOSEPH'S COAT 2

**5-patch**

- dark print (color A)
- medium print (color B)
- light print (color B)
- white

## JULY FOURTH
### July 4th, July the Fourth

**4-patch**

- dark print (color A)
- light print (color A)
- light solid or white

## KALEIDOSCOPE
### kaleidoscope II, III

**9-patch**

- dark print
- medium dark print
- medium print
- light print
- white

# KANSAS DUGOUT
**Kansas dug-out**

**4-patch**

dark print (color A)

medium print (color B)

light solid or white

# KANSAS TROUBLES
**Indian war dance**

**4-patch**

dark print (color A)

medium print (color A)

light print (color A or B)

white

# KENTUCKY CHAIN
**framed X**

**4-patch**

dark print (color A)

medium print (color B)

light solid or white

# KING'S CROSS
**king's X**

**4-patch**

dark print (color A)

medium print or solid (color A)

light solid or white

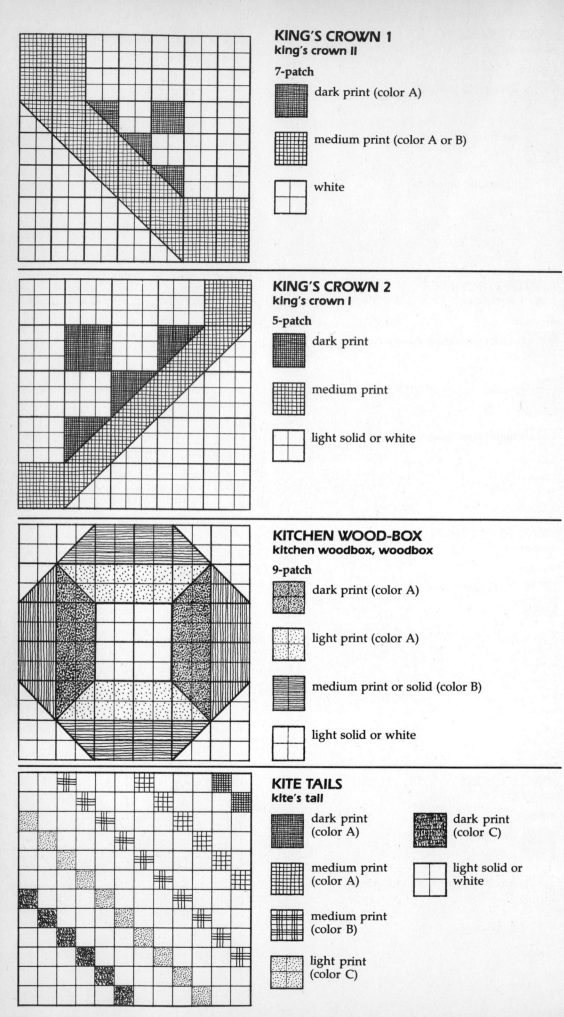

## KING'S CROWN 1
### king's crown II
**7-patch**

- dark print (color A)
- medium print (color A or B)
- white

## KING'S CROWN 2
### king's crown I
**5-patch**

- dark print
- medium print
- light solid or white

## KITCHEN WOOD-BOX
### kitchen woodbox, woodbox
**9-patch**

- dark print (color A)
- light print (color A)
- medium print or solid (color B)
- light solid or white

## KITE TAILS
### kite's tail

- dark print (color A)
- medium print (color A)
- medium print (color B)
- light print (color C)
- dark print (color C)
- light solid or white

# LADIES' DELIGHT

5-patch

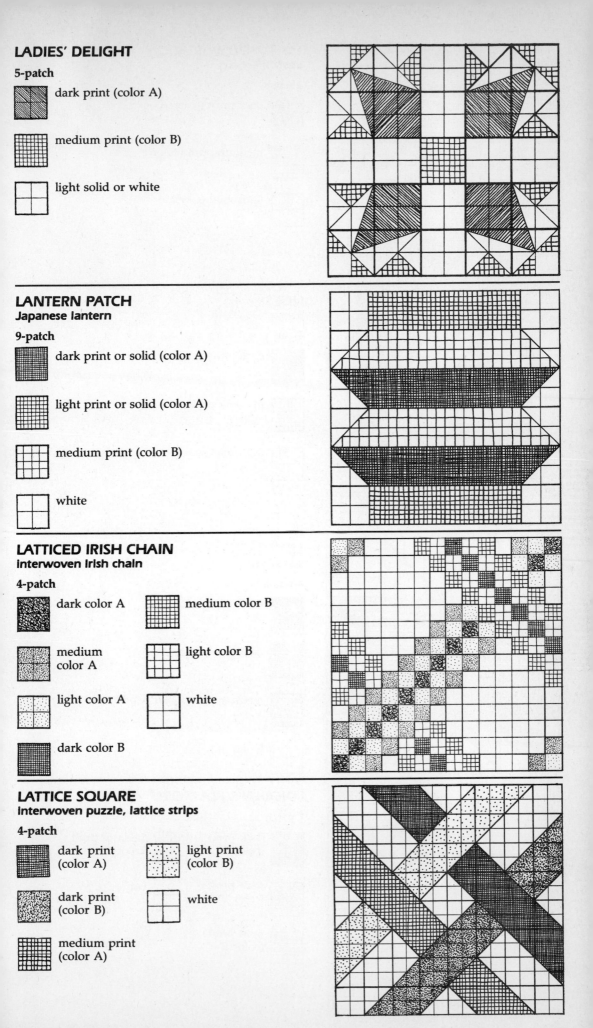

dark print (color A)

medium print (color B)

light solid or white

# LANTERN PATCH
**Japanese lantern**

9-patch

dark print or solid (color A)

light print or solid (color A)

medium print (color B)

white

# LATTICED IRISH CHAIN
**interwoven Irish chain**

4-patch

dark color A          medium color B

medium color A        light color B

light color A         white

dark color B

# LATTICE SQUARE
**Interwoven puzzle, lattice strips**

4-patch

dark print (color A)          light print (color B)

dark print (color B)          white

medium print (color A)

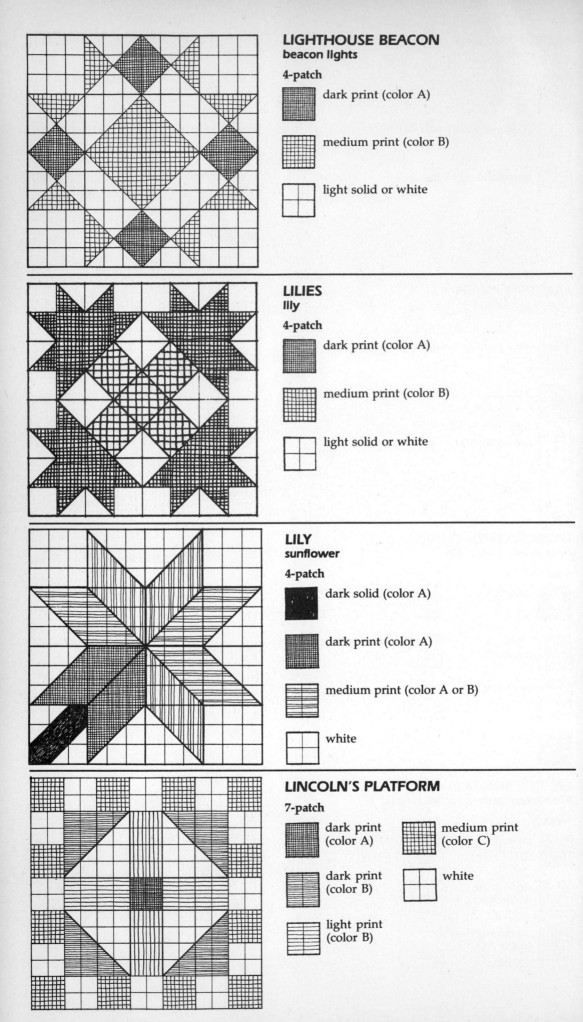

## LIGHTHOUSE BEACON
**beacon lights**

**4-patch**

dark print (color A)

medium print (color B)

light solid or white

## LILIES
**lily**

**4-patch**

dark print (color A)

medium print (color B)

light solid or white

## LILY
**sunflower**

**4-patch**

dark solid (color A)

dark print (color A)

medium print (color A or B)

white

## LINCOLN'S PLATFORM

**7-patch**

dark print (color A)

dark print (color B)

light print (color B)

medium print (color C)

white

## LINDY'S PLANE
**Lindy airplane**

**4-patch**

▨ dark print (color A)

☐ light solid or white

## LINTON

**5-patch**

▦ dark print (color A)

▦ medium print (color B)

▦ light print (color A)

## LITTLE GIANT BLOCK
**little giant, engine block**

**4-patch circle**

▦ dark print (color A)

▦ medium print (color B)

▦ medium print (color A)

☐ white

## LITTLE ROCK BLOCK
**Arkansas star, butterfly, Little Rock patch, star of the sea**

**9-patch**

▦ dark print (color A)

▦ medium print (color B)

☐ white

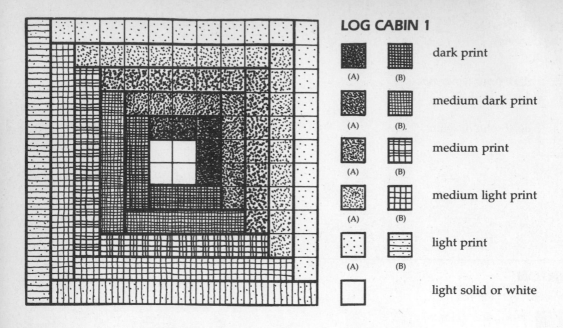

## LOG CABIN 1

| | | |
|---|---|---|
| (A) | (B) | dark print |
| (A) | (B) | medium dark print |
| (A) | (B) | medium print |
| (A) | (B) | medium light print |
| (A) | (B) | light print |
| | | light solid or white |

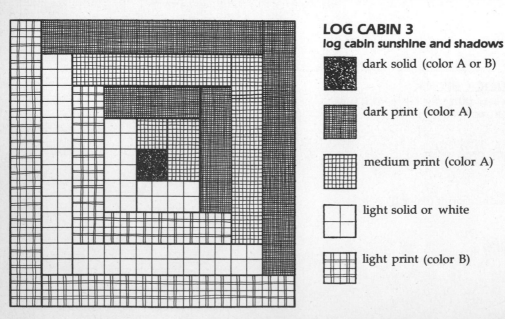

## LOG CABIN 2

| | | |
|---|---|---|
| (A) | (B) | dark print |
| (A) | (B) | medium dark print |
| (A) | (B) | medium print |
| (A) | (B) | medium light print |
| (A) | (B) | light print |
| | | light solid or white |

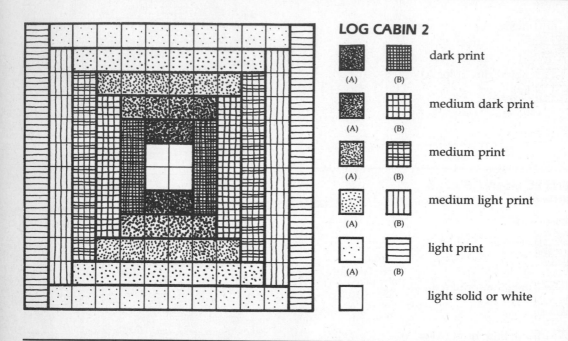

## LOG CABIN 3
**log cabin sunshine and shadows**

dark solid (color A or B)

dark print (color A)

medium print (color A)

light solid or white

light print (color B)

## LONDONTOWN ROADS
**London roads, London roads II**

**9-patch**

dark print (color A)

medium print (color B)

light solid or white

## LOUISIANA
**Louisiana block, Louisiana patch**

**4-patch**

dark print (color A)

medium print (color B)

light solid or white

## LOVE RING 1
**drunkard's path, love ring**

**9-patch circle**

dark print (color A)

light solid or white

## LOVE RING 2
**drunkard's path, love ring**

**9-patch circle**

dark print (color A)

white

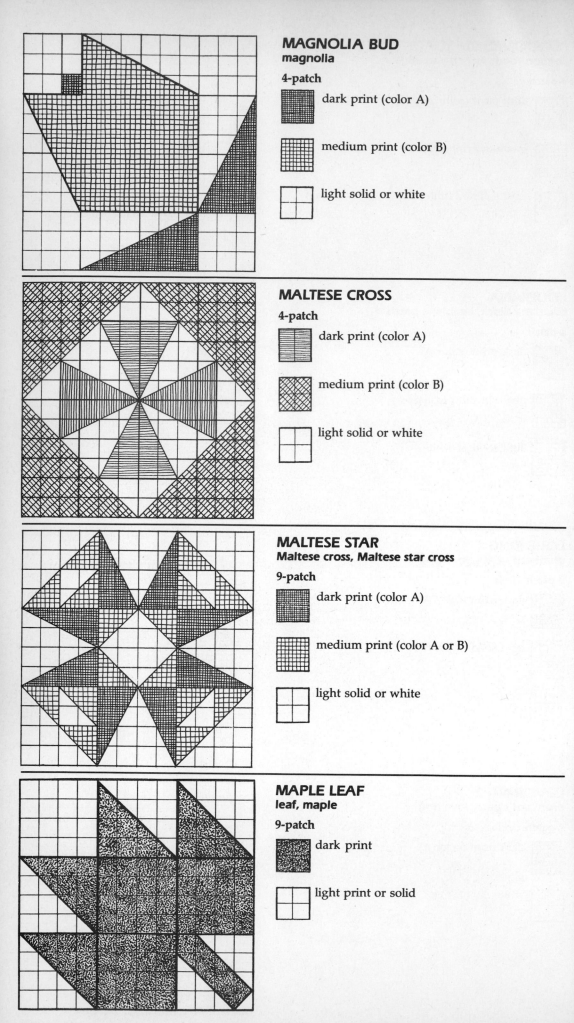

## MAGNOLIA BUD
**magnolia**

4-patch

- dark print (color A)
- medium print (color B)
- light solid or white

## MALTESE CROSS

4-patch

- dark print (color A)
- medium print (color B)
- light solid or white

## MALTESE STAR
**Maltese cross, Maltese star cross**

9-patch

- dark print (color A)
- medium print (color A or B)
- light solid or white

## MAPLE LEAF
**leaf, maple**

9-patch

- dark print
- light print or solid

## MARTHA WASHINGTON'S STAR
**Martha Washington, Washington star**

4-patch

dark print (color A)

medium print (color B)

light solid or white

## MARYLAND
**state of Maryland**

5-patch

dark print (color A)

medium print (color B)

light print (color A or C)

light solid or white

## MASSACHUSSETTS
**state of Massachusetts**

9-patch

dark print (color A)

light print (color A or B)

light solid or white

## MAY BASKET, THE
**May basket**

4-patch circle

dark print (color A)

medium print (color B)

light solid or white

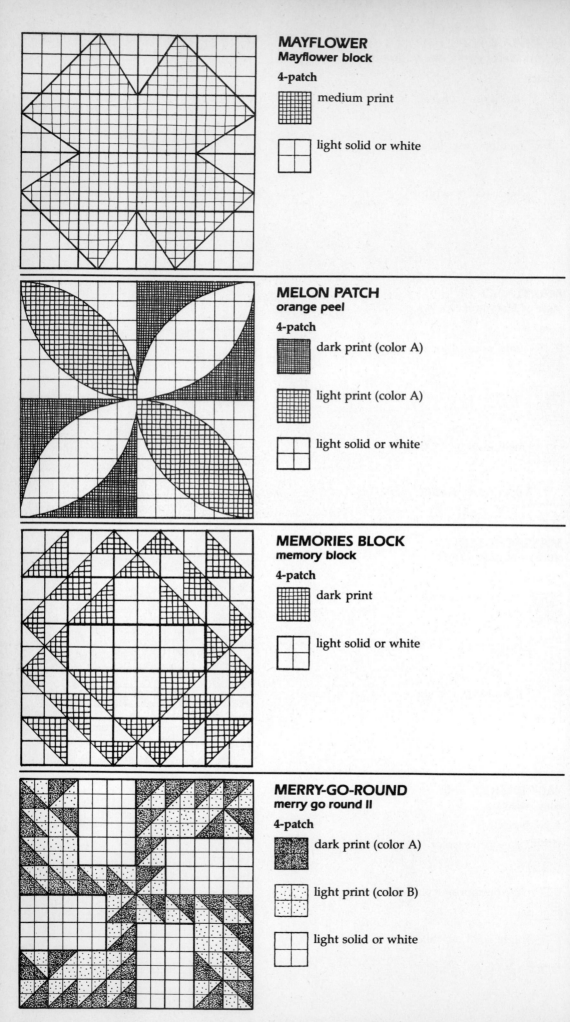

**MAYFLOWER**
**Mayflower block**
4-patch
medium print
light solid or white

**MELON PATCH**
**orange peel**
4-patch
dark print (color A)
light print (color A)
light solid or white

**MEMORIES BLOCK**
**memory block**
4-patch
dark print
light solid or white

**MERRY-GO-ROUND**
**merry go round II**
4-patch
dark print (color A)
light print (color B)
light solid or white

## MEXICAN CROSS 1
### Dallas star, Mexican rose, Mexican star

4-patch

dark print (color A)

medium print (color B)

light solid or white

## MEXICAN CROSS 2
### Mexican rose, Mexican star

4-patch

dark print or solid (color A)

dark print (color B)

medium print (color A)

white

## MILLWHEEL 1
### millwheel, mill wheel

4-patch

dark print or solid

light print or solid

## MILLWHEEL 2
### mill wheel

4-patch

dark print or solid

light solid or white

173

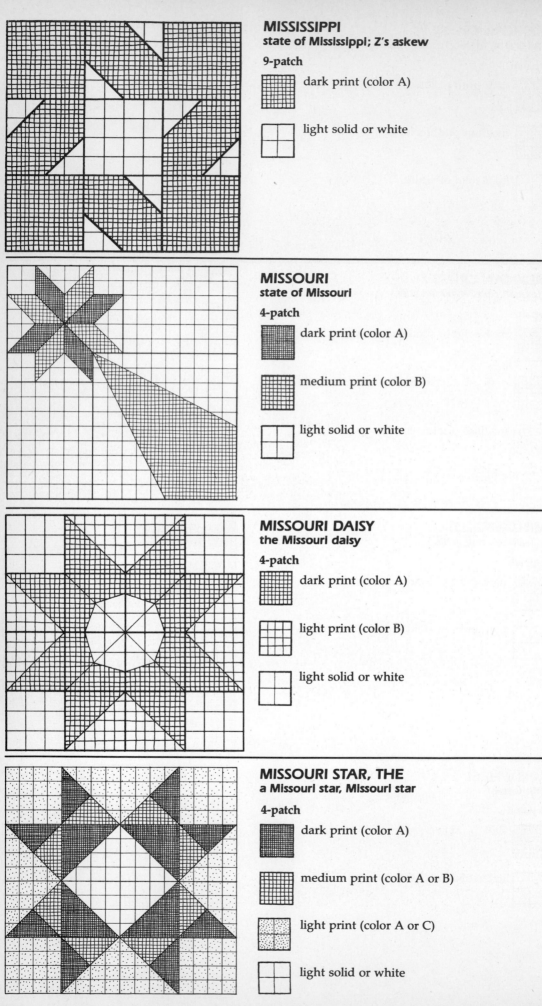

## MISSISSIPPI
**state of Mississippi; Z's askew**

**9-patch**

[dark print swatch] dark print (color A)

[light swatch] light solid or white

## MISSOURI
**state of Missouri**

**4-patch**

[dark print swatch] dark print (color A)

[medium print swatch] medium print (color B)

[light swatch] light solid or white

## MISSOURI DAISY
**the Missouri daisy**

**4-patch**

[dark print swatch] dark print (color A)

[light print swatch] light print (color B)

[light swatch] light solid or white

## MISSOURI STAR, THE
**a Missouri star, Missouri star**

**4-patch**

[dark print swatch] dark print (color A)

[medium print swatch] medium print (color A or B)

[light print swatch] light print (color A or C)

[light swatch] light solid or white

## MOHAWK TRAIL
### Mohawk trails

**4-patch**

▨ dark print (color A)

▨ medium print (color A)

▨ light print (color A)

☐ light solid or white

## MOLLIE'S CHOICE

**9-patch**

▥ dark print

☐ light solid or white

## MONKEY WRENCH

**4-patch**

▨ dark print or solid

☐ light solid or white

## MOON OVER THE MOUNTAIN
### moon over mountain

**4-patch circle**

▦ dark print (color A)

▤ medium print (color B)

☐ light solid

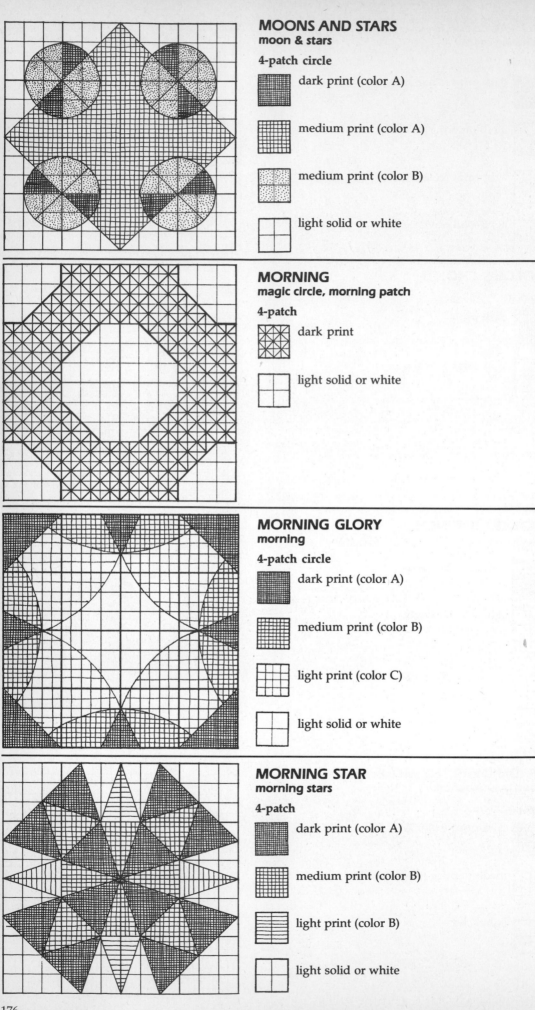

## MOONS AND STARS
moon & stars

4-patch circle

- dark print (color A)
- medium print (color A)
- medium print (color B)
- light solid or white

## MORNING
magic circle, morning patch

4-patch

- dark print
- light solid or white

## MORNING GLORY
morning

4-patch circle

- dark print (color A)
- medium print (color B)
- light print (color C)
- light solid or white

## MORNING STAR
morning stars

4-patch

- dark print (color A)
- medium print (color B)
- light print (color B)
- light solid or white

## MOSAIC STAR

**4-patch**

dark print (color A)

medium print (color A)

light print (color B)

light solid or white

## MOTHER'S CHOICE

**4-patch**

medium print

light solid or white

## MOTHER'S DREAM 1
**mother's dream**

**4-patch**

dark print (color A)

medium print (color B)

light solid or white

## MOTHER'S DREAM 2
**mother's dream I**

**9-patch**

dark print (color A)

medium print (color A or B)

light solid or white

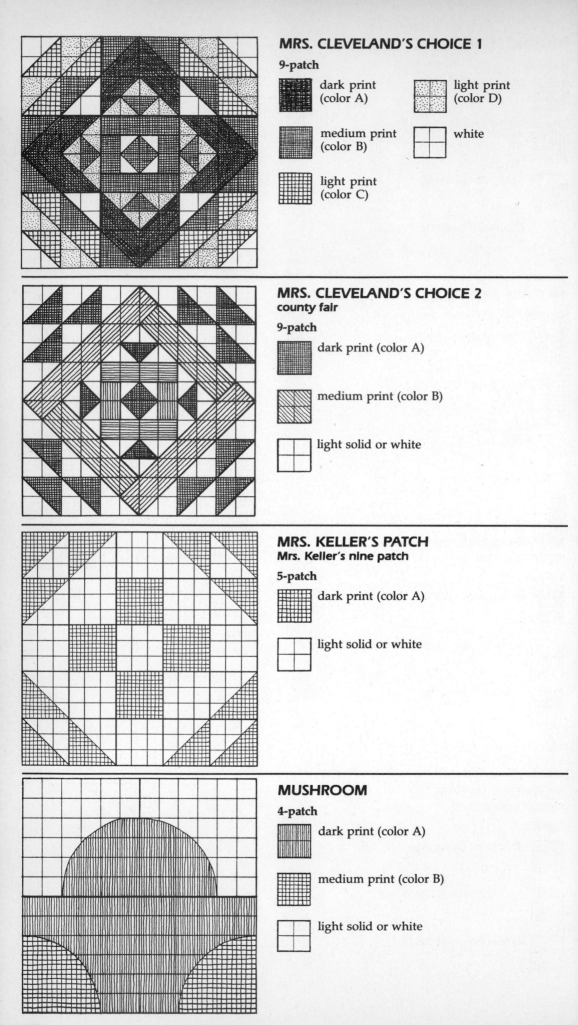

## MRS. CLEVELAND'S CHOICE 1

**9-patch**

▨ dark print (color A)

▦ medium print (color B)

▦ light print (color C)

░ light print (color D)

☐ white

## MRS. CLEVELAND'S CHOICE 2
**county fair**

**9-patch**

▦ dark print (color A)

▨ medium print (color B)

☐ light solid or white

## MRS. KELLER'S PATCH
**Mrs. Keller's nine patch**

**5-patch**

▦ dark print (color A)

☐ light solid or white

## MUSHROOM

**4-patch**

▥ dark print (color A)

▦ medium print (color B)

☐ light solid or white

# NAVAJO BLUES

- dark blue (darkest)
- dark blue (dark)
- dark blue (medium)
- medium blue
- medium light blue
- light blue

179

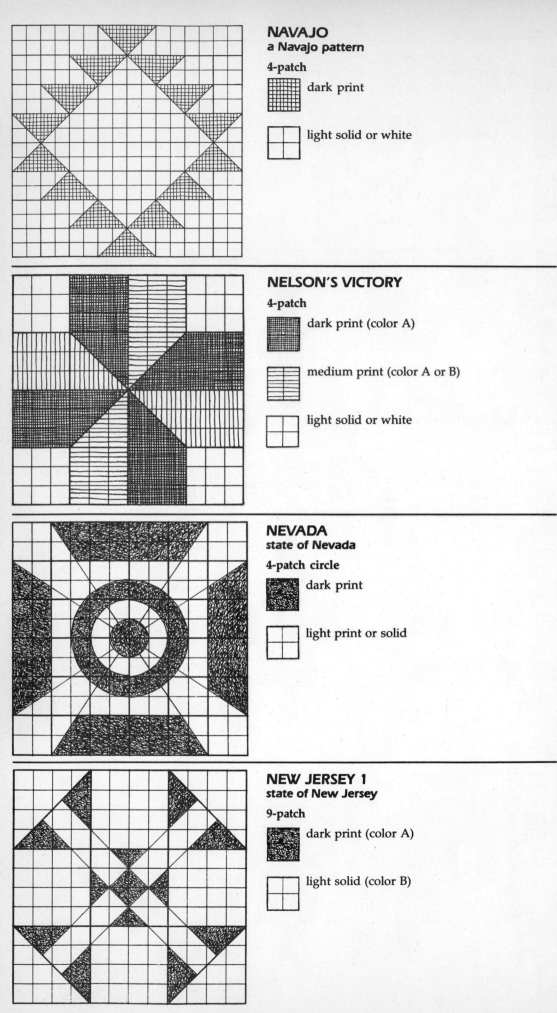

## NAVAJO
### a Navajo pattern

**4-patch**

dark print

light solid or white

## NELSON'S VICTORY

**4-patch**

dark print (color A)

medium print (color A or B)

light solid or white

## NEVADA
### state of Nevada

**4-patch circle**

dark print

light print or solid

## NEW JERSEY 1
### state of New Jersey

**9-patch**

dark print (color A)

light solid (color B)

## NEW JERSEY 2
### state of New Jersey
**9-patch**

dark print (color A)

medium print (color B)

light solid or white

## NEXT-DOOR NEIGHBOR 1
**4-patch**

dark print (color A)

medium print (color B)

light solid or white

## NEXT-DOOR NEIGHBOR 2
**4-patch**

dark print (color A)

medium print (color A or B)

light solid or white

## NEXT-DOOR NEIGHBOR 3
**4-patch**

dark print (color A)

medium print (color B)

light print (color C)

white

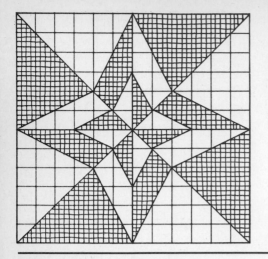

## NIGHT AND DAY
### night & day

**4-patch**

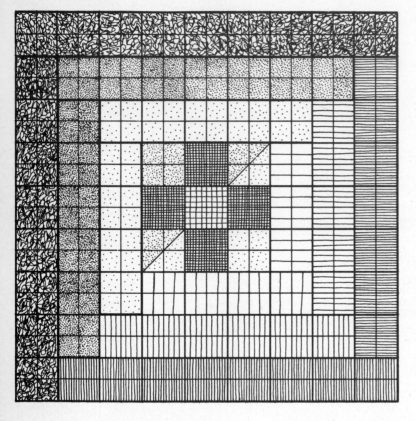 dark print (color A)

[ ] light print or solid (color A)

## NINE-PATCH LOG CABIN
### log cabin variation

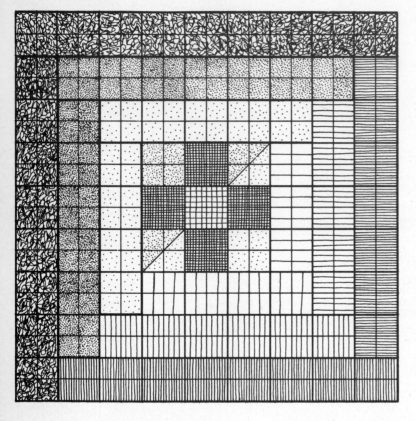

dark print
(color A)

medium print
(color A)

light print
(color A)

medium light
(color A)

dark print
(color B)

medium print
(color B)

light print
(color B)

very light print
(color B)

dark print
(color C)

medium print
(color C)

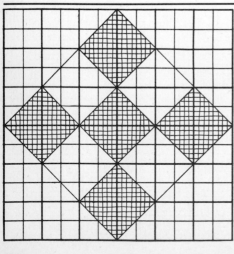

## NINE-PATCH VARIATION
### 9-patch variation

**9-patch**

dark print (color A)

light print or solid (color B)

## NINE-PATCH STAR 1
### 9-patch star, 9-patch star II

dark print (color A)

medium print (color D)

medium print (color A or B)

white

light print (color A or C)

## NINE-PATCH STAR 2
### 9-patch star

dark print (color A)

medium print (color B)

light solid or white

## NINE-PATCH STAR 3
### 9-patch star, nosegay

dark print (color A)

medium print (color B)

light solid or white

## NOCTURNE
### noctourne
### 5-patch

dark print (color A)

medium print (color A)

medium print (color B)

light solid or white

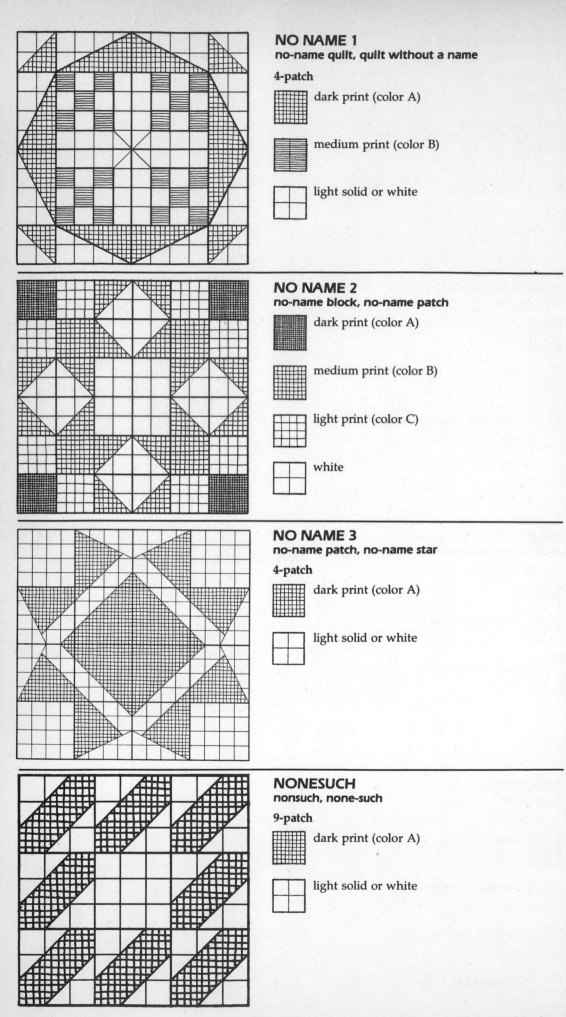

## NO NAME 1
**no-name quilt, quilt without a name**

4-patch

dark print (color A)

medium print (color B)

light solid or white

## NO NAME 2
**no-name block, no-name patch**

dark print (color A)

medium print (color B)

light print (color C)

white

## NO NAME 3
**no-name patch, no-name star**

4-patch

dark print (color A)

light solid or white

## NONESUCH
**nonsuch, none-such**

9-patch

dark print (color A)

light solid or white

## NONSUCH
**nonesuch**

9-patch

dark print (color A)

light print (color A)

medium print (color B)

white

## NOON LIGHT
**noon and light, noon & lights**

4-patch

dark print (color A)

medium print (color B)

light solid or white

## NORTH CAROLINA STAR 1
**North Carolina, state of North Carolina**

4-patch

dark print or solid (color A)

medium print (color B)

light solid or white

## NORTH CAROLINA STAR 2
**state of North Carolina**

4-patch

dark print (color A)

medium print (color A)

medium print (color B)

light solid (color B)

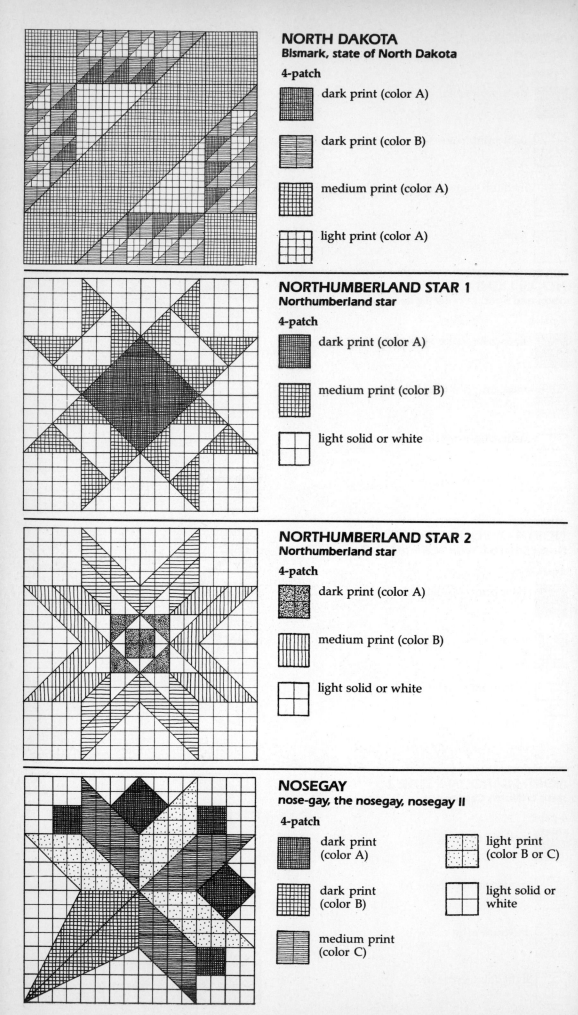

# NORTH DAKOTA
**Bismark, state of North Dakota**

4-patch

dark print (color A)

dark print (color B)

medium print (color A)

light print (color A)

# NORTHUMBERLAND STAR 1
**Northumberland star**

4-patch

dark print (color A)

medium print (color B)

light solid or white

# NORTHUMBERLAND STAR 2
**Northumberland star**

4-patch

dark print (color A)

medium print (color B)

light solid or white

# NOSEGAY
**nose-gay, the nosegay, nosegay II**

4-patch

dark print (color A)

dark print (color B)

medium print (color C)

light print (color B or C)

light solid or white

## OCEAN WAVE 1
**waves, whirlpool**

**4-patch**

dark print (color A)

light solid (color A or B)

## OCEAN WAVE 2
**whirlpool**

**4-patch**

dark print (color A)

light print (color A)

medium print (color B)

light solid or white

## OCTAGON 1
**Job's troubles, melon patch, snowball**

**9-patch**

dark print (color A)

medium print (color B)

light solid or white

## OCTAGON 2
**snowball variation**

**9-patch**

dark print (color A)

light print or solid (color B)

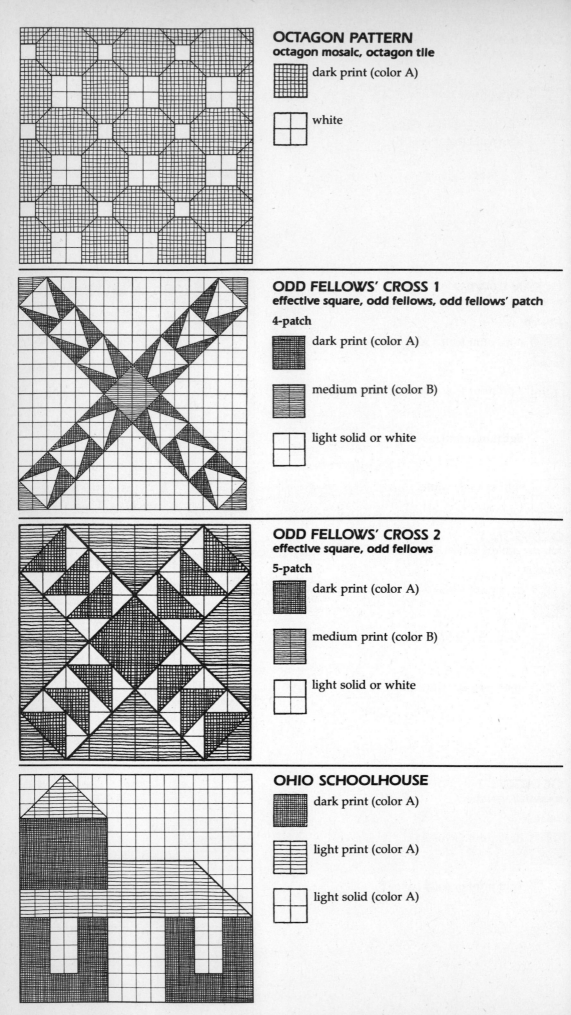

## OCTAGON PATTERN
**octagon mosaic, octagon tile**

dark print (color A)

white

## ODD FELLOWS' CROSS 1
**effective square, odd fellows, odd fellows' patch**

4-patch

dark print (color A)

medium print (color B)

light solid or white

## ODD FELLOWS' CROSS 2
**effective square, odd fellows**

5-patch

dark print (color A)

medium print (color B)

light solid or white

## OHIO SCHOOLHOUSE

dark print (color A)

light print (color A)

light solid (color A)

188

## OHIO STAR
**9-patch**

dark print (color A)

medium print (color A or B)

light solid or white

---

## OH SUSANNAH
**Susannah, Susannah III**

**4-patch**

dark print (color A)

medium light print (color A or B)

light solid or white

---

## OLD MAID'S PUZZLE 1
**old maid puzzle**

**4-patch**

dark print (color A)

light print (color A or B)

light solid

---

## OLD MAID'S PUZZLE 2
**old maid puzzle**

**4-patch**

dark print (color A)

medium print (color B)

light print (color C)

light solid or white

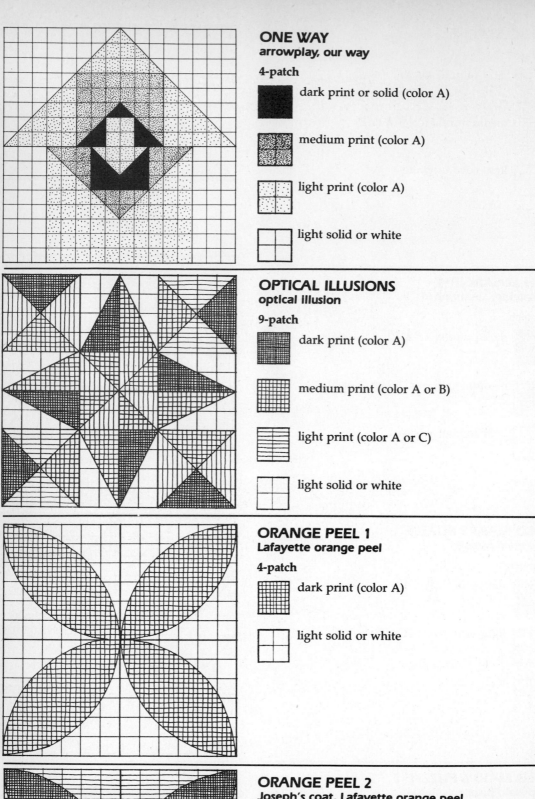

## ONE WAY
**arrowplay, our way**

4-patch

- dark print or solid (color A)
- medium print (color A)
- light print (color A)
- light solid or white

## OPTICAL ILLUSIONS
**optical illusion**

9-patch

- dark print (color A)
- medium print (color A or B)
- light print (color A or C)
- light solid or white

## ORANGE PEEL 1
**Lafayette orange peel**

4-patch

- dark print (color A)
- light solid or white

## ORANGE PEEL 2
**Joseph's coat, Lafayette orange peel**

4-patch

 dark print (color A)

 light print (color A)

190

## ORANGE PEEL 3
### Joseph's coat, Lafayette orange peel
4-patch

▦ dark print (color A)

▤ light print (color D)

▦ medium print (color B)

▦ white

▦ medium print (color C)

## ORANGE PEEL 4
### Joseph's coat, Lafayette orange peel
4-patch

■ dark print (color A)

□ white

## OREGON
### state of Oregon
5-patch

▦ dark print (color A)

□ light solid or white

## OZARK MAPLE
### leaves, Ozark maple leaf
4-patch

▦ dark print (color A)

□ light solid or white

191

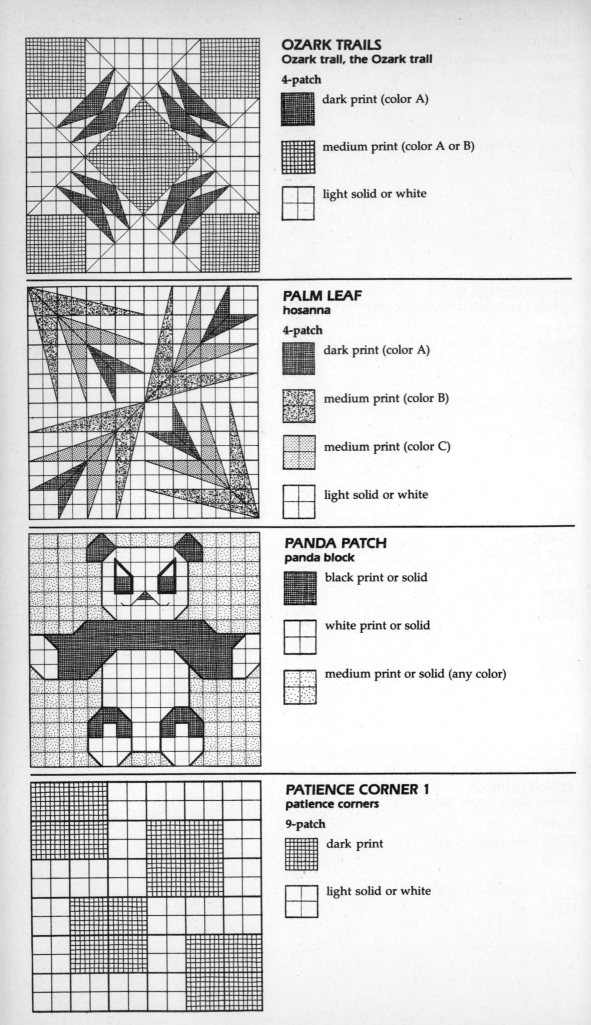

## OZARK TRAILS
**Ozark trail, the Ozark trail**

4-patch

dark print (color A)

medium print (color A or B)

light solid or white

## PALM LEAF
**hosanna**

4-patch

dark print (color A)

medium print (color B)

medium print (color C)

light solid or white

## PANDA PATCH
**panda block**

black print or solid

white print or solid

medium print or solid (any color)

## PATIENCE CORNER 1
**patience corners**

9-patch

dark print

light solid or white

## PATIENCE CORNER 2
**patience corners**

**9-patch**

dark print

light solid or white

## PATIENCE CORNER 3
**patience corners**

**9-patch**

dark print (color A)

light print (color A or B)

## PATIENCE CORNERS 1
**patience corner**

**4-patch**

dark print (color A)

light print (color A)

light solid or white

## PATIENCE CORNERS 2
**patience corner**

**4-patch**

dark print (color A)

light print (color B)

light solid or white

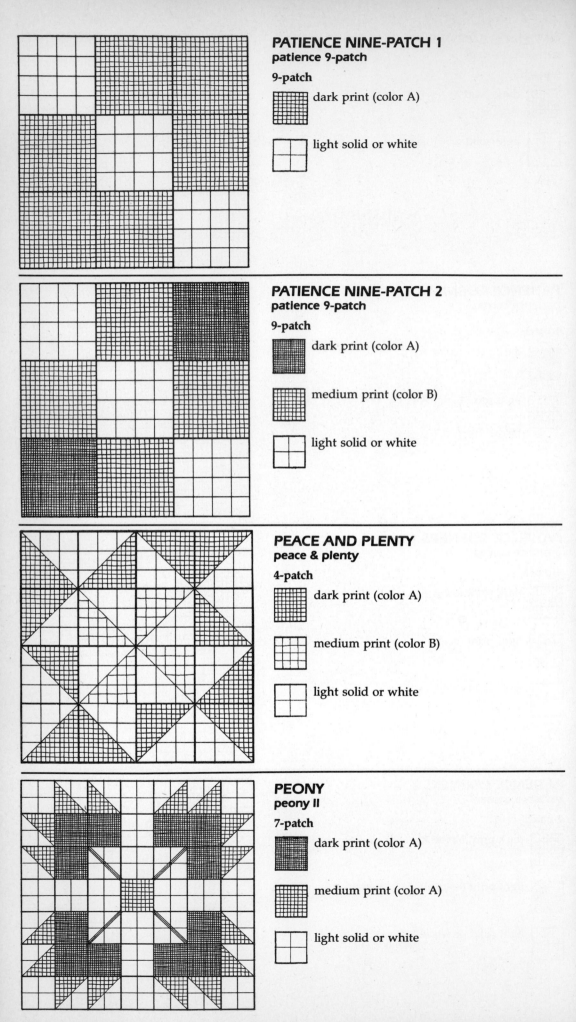

**PATIENCE NINE-PATCH 1**
patience 9-patch

9-patch

dark print (color A)

light solid or white

**PATIENCE NINE-PATCH 2**
patience 9-patch

9-patch

dark print (color A)

medium print (color B)

light solid or white

**PEACE AND PLENTY**
peace & plenty

4-patch

dark print (color A)

medium print (color B)

light solid or white

**PEONY**
peony II

7-patch

dark print (color A)

medium print (color A)

light solid or white

## PERIWINKLE
### Arkansas snowflake, four-point

**4-patch**

▨ dark print (color A)

☐ light solid or white

## PHILADELPHIA PAVEMENTS 1

**4-patch**

▨ dark print (color A)

▨ medium print (color B)

☐ light solid or white

## PHILADELPHIA PAVEMENTS 2

**5-patch**

▨ dark print (color A)

▨ medium print (color B)

☐ light solid or white

## PHILADELPHIA PAVEMENTS 3

**5-patch**

▨ dark print (color A)

▨ medium print (color B)

☐ light solid or white

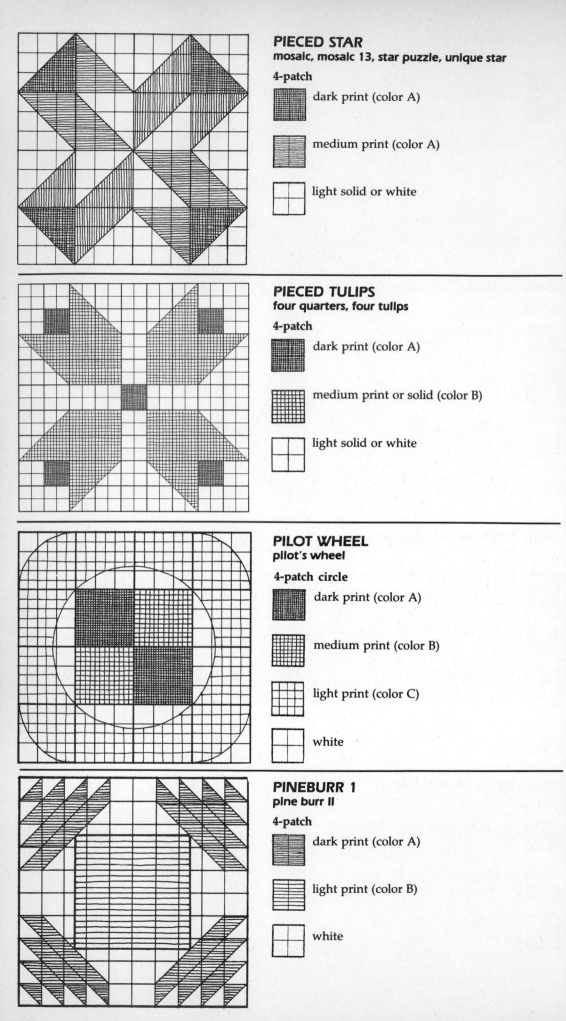

## PIECED STAR
### mosaic, mosaic 13, star puzzle, unique star

4-patch

■ dark print (color A)

▨ medium print (color A)

☐ light solid or white

## PIECED TULIPS
### four quarters, four tulips

4-patch

■ dark print (color A)

▦ medium print or solid (color B)

☐ light solid or white

## PILOT WHEEL
### pilot's wheel

4-patch circle

■ dark print (color A)

▦ medium print (color B)

▥ light print (color C)

☐ white

## PINEBURR 1
### pine burr II

4-patch

▥ dark print (color A)

▥ light print (color B)

☐ white

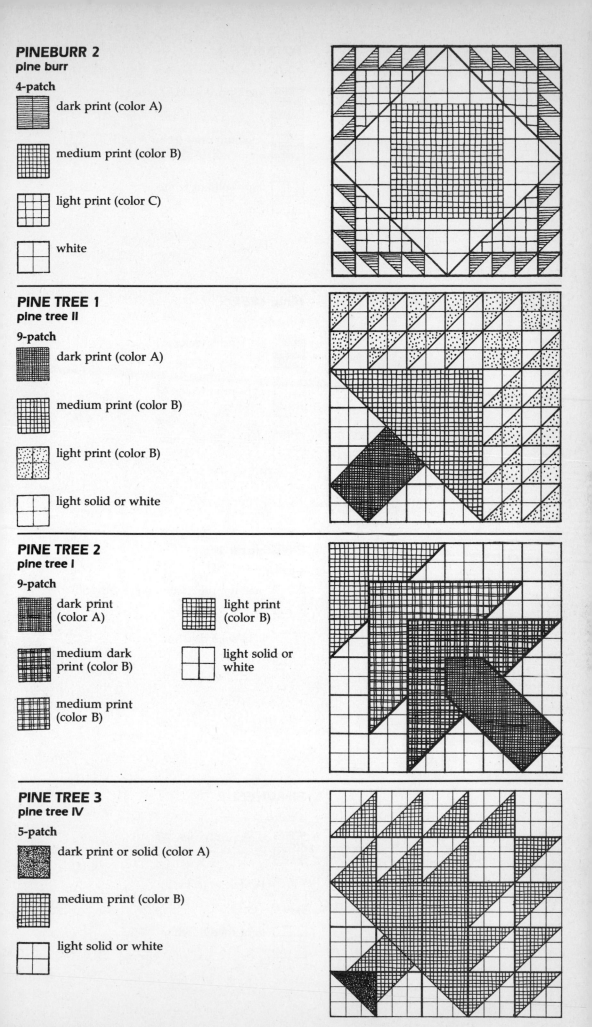

## PINEBURR 2
**pine burr**

**4-patch**

- dark print (color A)
- medium print (color B)
- light print (color C)
- white

## PINE TREE 1
**pine tree II**

**9-patch**

- dark print (color A)
- medium print (color B)
- light print (color B)
- light solid or white

## PINE TREE 2
**pine tree I**

**9-patch**

- dark print (color A)
- medium dark print (color B)
- medium print (color B)
- light print (color B)
- light solid or white

## PINE TREE 3
**pine tree IV**

**5-patch**

- dark print or solid (color A)
- medium print (color B)
- light solid or white

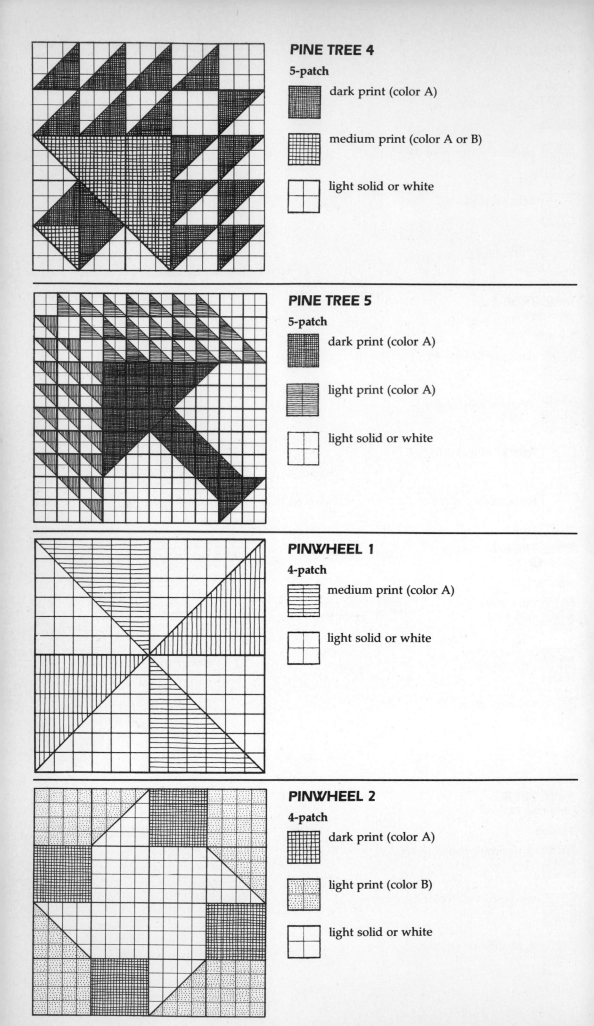

## PINE TREE 4

**5-patch**

dark print (color A)

medium print (color A or B)

light solid or white

## PINE TREE 5

**5-patch**

dark print (color A)

light print (color A)

light solid or white

## PINWHEEL 1

**4-patch**

medium print (color A)

light solid or white

## PINWHEEL 2

**4-patch**

dark print (color A)

light print (color B)

light solid or white

## PINWHEEL 3
### pinwheel variation 2

4-patch

dark print (color A)

light solid or white

## PINWHEEL 4
### broken pinwheel

4-patch

dark print (color A)

medium print (color B)

white

## PINWHEEL SQUARE 1
### follow-the-leader, pin wheel square

5-patch

dark print (color A)

medium print (color B)

light print or solid (color C)

white

## PINWHEEL SQUARE 2
### pin wheel square

5-patch

dark print (color A)

medium print (color B)

light print (color C)

light solid or white

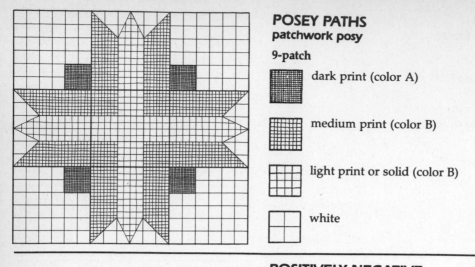

## POSEY PATHS
### patchwork posy

**9-patch**

dark print (color A)

medium print (color B)

light print or solid (color B)

white

## POSITIVELY NEGATIVE
### double pinwheels

**4-patch**

dark print or solid (color A)

light print or solid (color A)

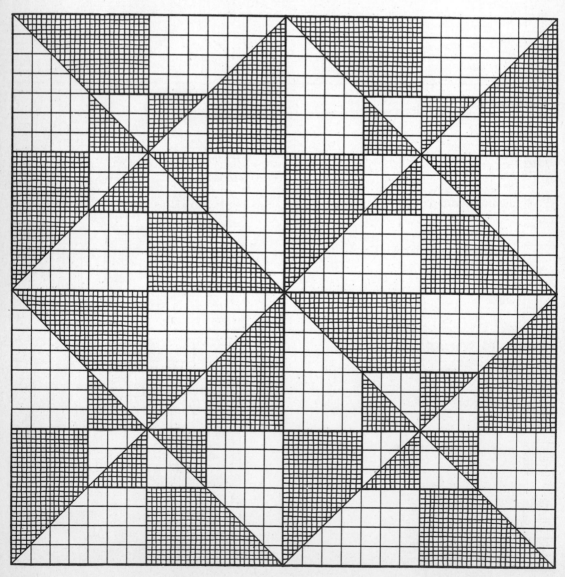

## POSTAGE STAMP BASKET
**postage stamp, stamp basket**

**4-patch**

medium print (color A)

medium print (color D)

medium print (color B)

light solid or white

medium print (color C)

## PRACTICAL ORCHARD
**a practical orchard, the practical orchard**

**9-patch**

dark print (color A)

light solid or white

## PRAIRIE QUEEN 1
**prairie queen**

**9-patch**

dark print (color A)

light print (color A)

light solid or white

## PRAIRIE QUEEN 2
**prairie queen**

**4-patch**

dark print (color A)

medium print (color B)

light print (color C)

white

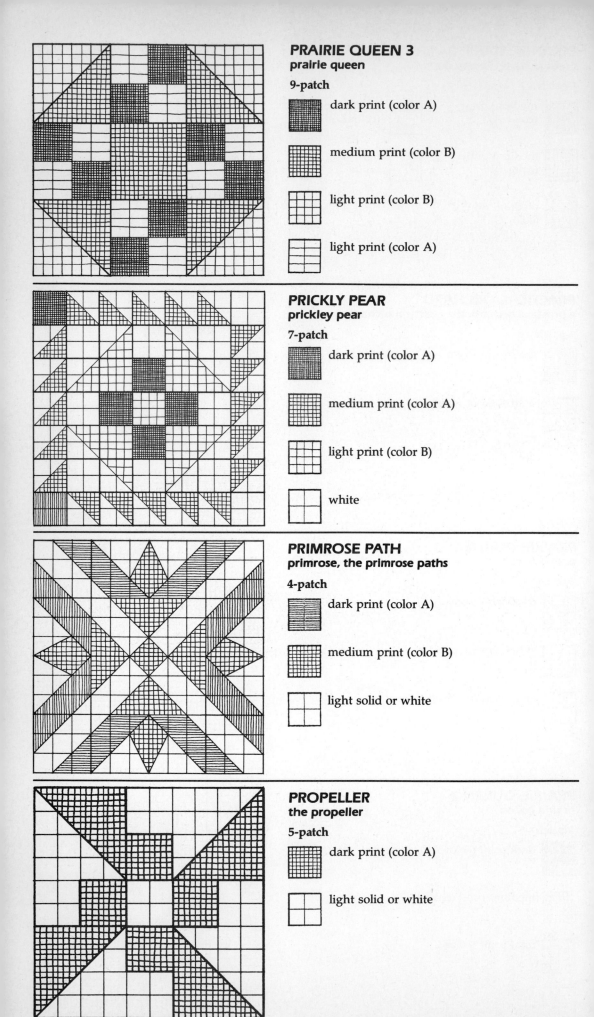

## PRAIRIE QUEEN 3
**prairie queen**

9-patch

dark print (color A)

medium print (color B)

light print (color B)

light print (color A)

## PRICKLY PEAR
**prickley pear**

7-patch

dark print (color A)

medium print (color A)

light print (color B)

white

## PRIMROSE PATH
**primrose, the primrose paths**

4-patch

dark print (color A)

medium print (color B)

light solid or white

## PROPELLER
**the propeller**

5-patch

dark print (color A)

light solid or white

## PROSPERITY
**empty spools, prosperity block**

**9-patch**

dark print (color A)

medium print (color A)

medium print (color B)

light solid or white

## PROVIDENCE BLOCK
**providence block II, providence quilt block**

**5-patch**

dark print (color A)

dark print (color B)

light print (color B)

light solid or white

## PULLMAN PUZZLE
**baseball**

**4-patch circle**

dark print (color A)

light solid or white

## PULLMAN PUZZLES

**4-patch circle**

dark print (color A)

light solid or white

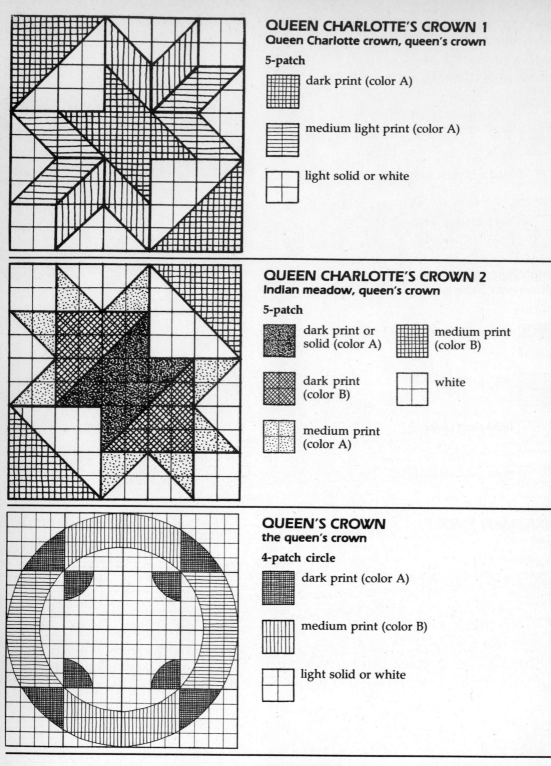

## QUEEN CHARLOTTE'S CROWN 1
**Queen Charlotte crown, queen's crown**

5-patch

dark print (color A)

medium light print (color A)

light solid or white

## QUEEN CHARLOTTE'S CROWN 2
**Indian meadow, queen's crown**

5-patch

dark print or
solid (color A)

medium print
(color B)

dark print
(color B)

white

medium print
(color A)

## QUEEN'S CROWN
**the queen's crown**

4-patch circle

dark print (color A)

medium print (color B)

light solid or white

## RAIL-FENCE 1
**lightning, rail fence II**

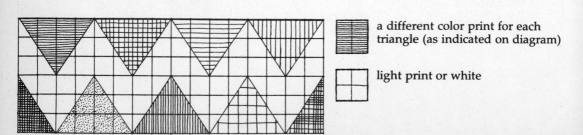

a different color print for each
triangle (as indicated on diagram)

light print or white

## RAIL-FENCE 2
### rail fence, fence rail

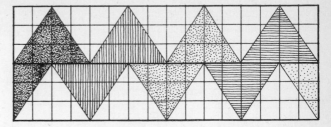

a different color print for each triangle (as indicated on diagram)

light solid or white

## RAILROAD CROSSING
### R.R. crossing I

**4-patch**

 dark print (color A)

 dark print (color B)

 light print (color C)

 light solid or white

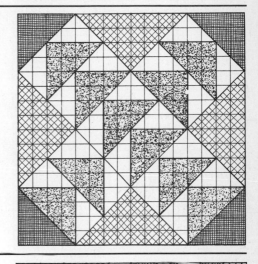

## RANDOM COUNTRY CALICO 1
### country calico, country charm

**1–2-patch**

 a different color print for each rectangle

## RANDOM COUNTRY CALICO 2
### country calico, woven country calico

**1–2-patch**

 a different print for each rectangle

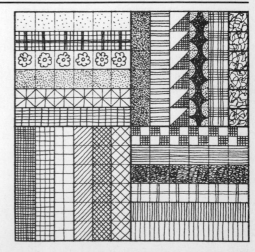

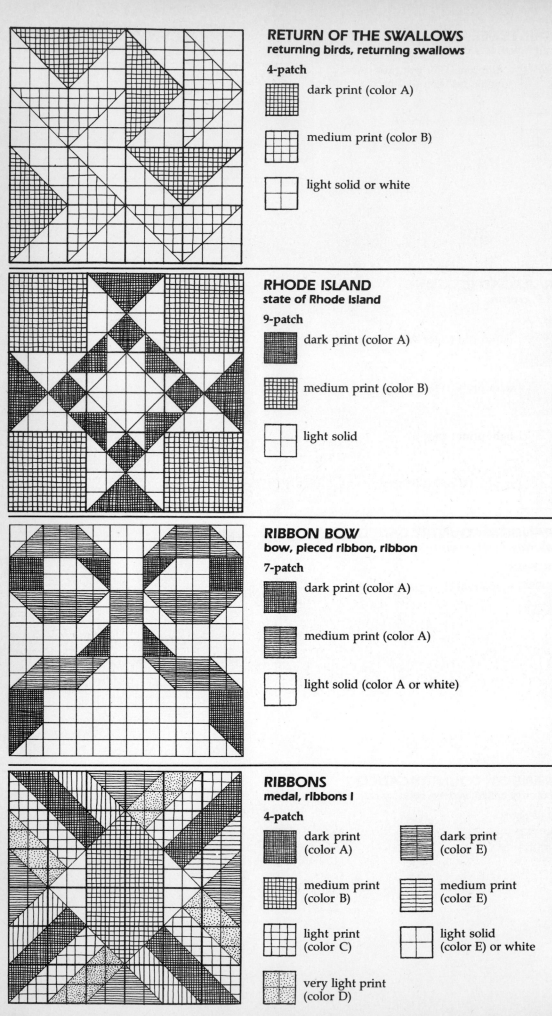

## RETURN OF THE SWALLOWS
### returning birds, returning swallows
4-patch

- dark print (color A)
- medium print (color B)
- light solid or white

## RHODE ISLAND
### state of Rhode Island
9-patch

- dark print (color A)
- medium print (color B)
- light solid

## RIBBON BOW
### bow, pieced ribbon, ribbon
7-patch

- dark print (color A)
- medium print (color A)
- light solid (color A or white)

## RIBBONS
### medal, ribbons I
4-patch

- dark print (color A)
- medium print (color B)
- light print (color C)
- very light print (color D)
- dark print (color E)
- medium print (color E)
- light solid (color E) or white

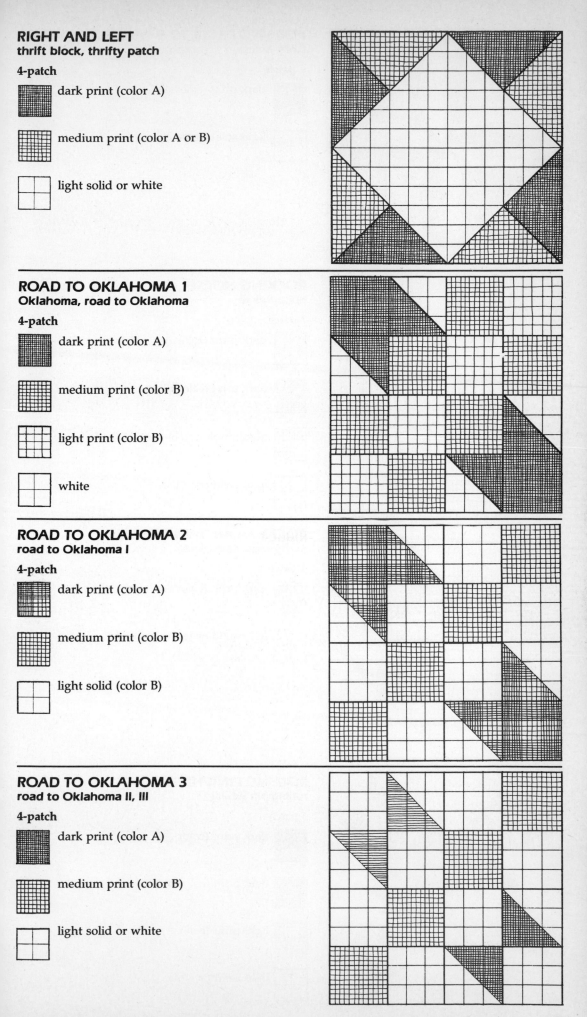

**RIGHT AND LEFT**
**thrift block, thrifty patch**

4-patch

- dark print (color A)
- medium print (color A or B)
- light solid or white

**ROAD TO OKLAHOMA 1**
**Oklahoma, road to Oklahoma**

4-patch

- dark print (color A)
- medium print (color B)
- light print (color B)
- white

**ROAD TO OKLAHOMA 2**
**road to Oklahoma I**

4-patch

- dark print (color A)
- medium print (color B)
- light solid (color B)

**ROAD TO OKLAHOMA 3**
**road to Oklahoma II, III**

4-patch

- dark print (color A)
- medium print (color B)
- light solid or white

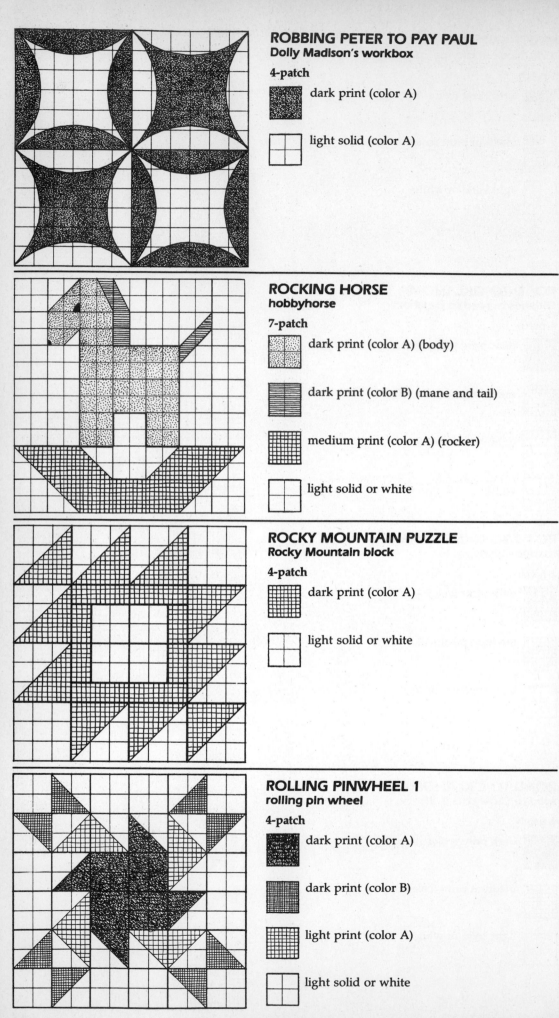

## ROBBING PETER TO PAY PAUL
**Dolly Madison's workbox**

4-patch

- dark print (color A)
- light solid (color A)

## ROCKING HORSE
**hobbyhorse**

7-patch

- dark print (color A) (body)
- dark print (color B) (mane and tail)
- medium print (color A) (rocker)
- light solid or white

## ROCKY MOUNTAIN PUZZLE
**Rocky Mountain block**

4-patch

- dark print (color A)
- light solid or white

## ROLLING PINWHEEL 1
**rolling pin wheel**

4-patch

- dark print (color A)
- dark print (color B)
- light print (color A)
- light solid or white

## ROLLING PINWHEEL 2
**rolling pin wheel**

**4-patch**

dark print (color A)

light solid or white

## ROLLING STONE 1
**rolling stone block**

**9-patch**

dark print (color A)

light solid or white

## ROLLING STONE 2
**rolling stone l**

**9-patch**

dark print (color A)

medium print (color A or B)

light solid or white

## ROSE BUDS
**rosebud**

**4-patch**

dark print (color A)

light solid or white

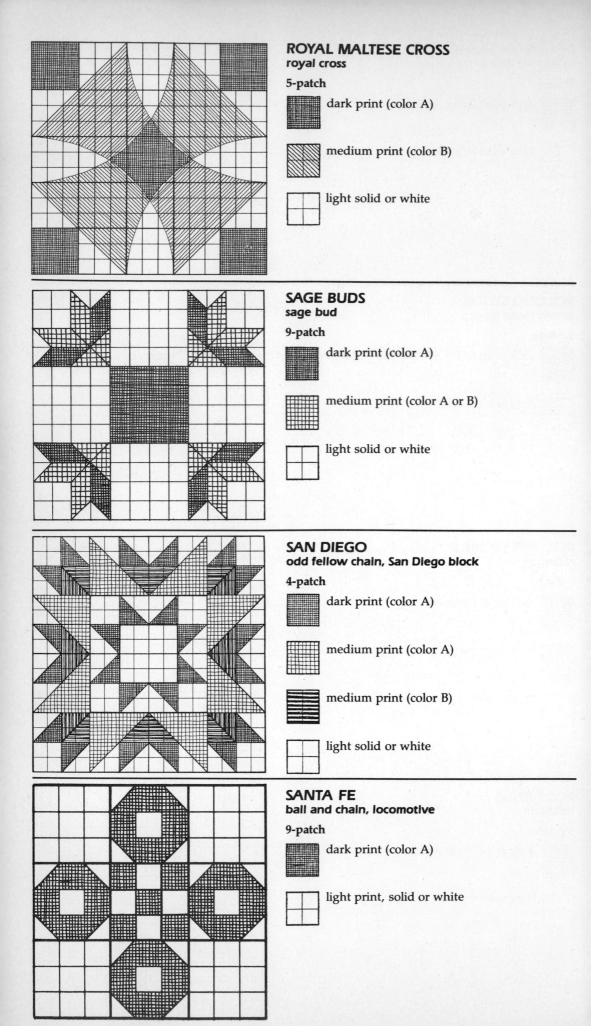

## ROYAL MALTESE CROSS
royal cross

5-patch

■ dark print (color A)

▨ medium print (color B)

□ light solid or white

## SAGE BUDS
sage bud

9-patch

■ dark print (color A)

▨ medium print (color A or B)

□ light solid or white

## SAN DIEGO
odd fellow chain, San Diego block

4-patch

▨ dark print (color A)

▨ medium print (color A)

▤ medium print (color B)

□ light solid or white

## SANTA FE
ball and chain, locomotive

9-patch

■ dark print (color A)

□ light print, solid or white

# SAVE ALL
**save-all chain**

**9-patch**

dark print
(color A)

light solid or white

medium print
(color B)

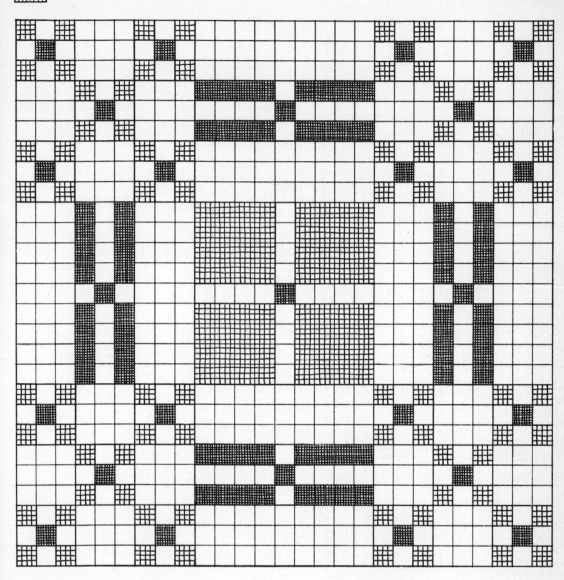

---

# SAWTOOTH 1
**saw-tooth**

**9-patch**

dark print (color A)

light solid or white

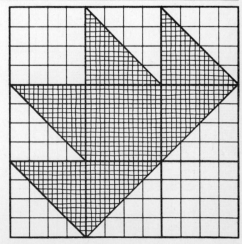

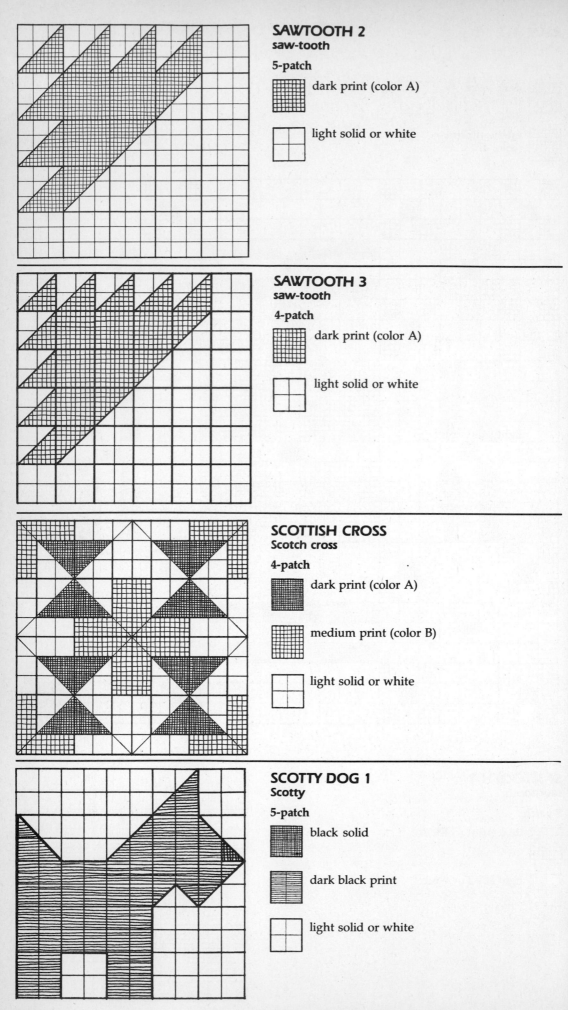

## SAWTOOTH 2
**saw-tooth**

**5-patch**

dark print (color A)

light solid or white

## SAWTOOTH 3
**saw-tooth**

**4-patch**

dark print (color A)

light solid or white

## SCOTTISH CROSS
**Scotch cross**

**4-patch**

dark print (color A)

medium print (color B)

light solid or white

## SCOTTY DOG 1
**Scotty**

**5-patch**

black solid

dark black print

light solid or white

## SCOTTY DOG 2
**Scotty**

**9-patch**

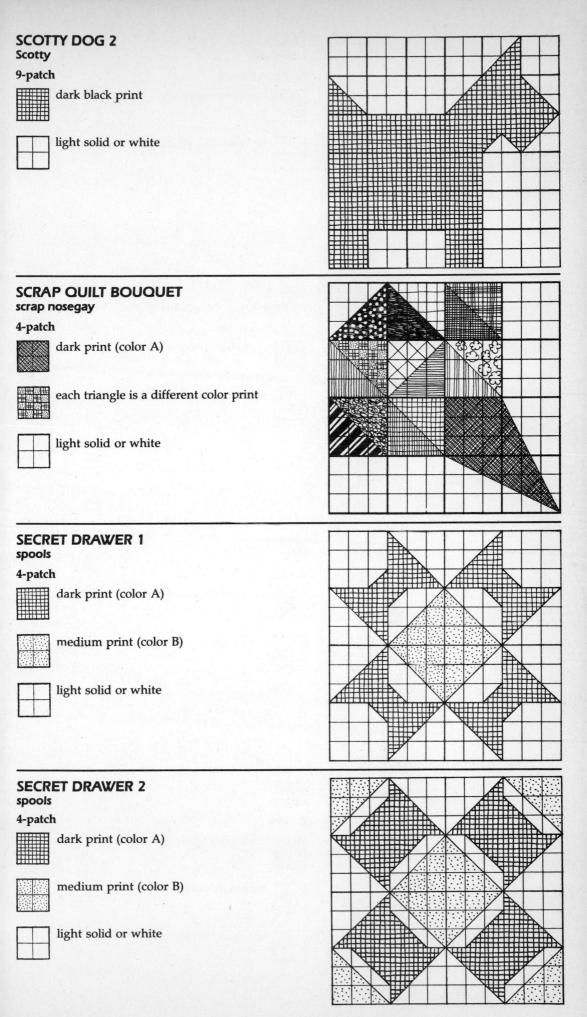

⊞ dark black print

☐ light solid or white

## SCRAP QUILT BOUQUET
**scrap nosegay**

**4-patch**

▧ dark print (color A)

▨ each triangle is a different color print

☐ light solid or white

## SECRET DRAWER 1
**spools**

**4-patch**

⊞ dark print (color A)

⊡ medium print (color B)

☐ light solid or white

## SECRET DRAWER 2
**spools**

**4-patch**

⊞ dark print (color A)

⊡ medium print (color B)

☐ light solid or white

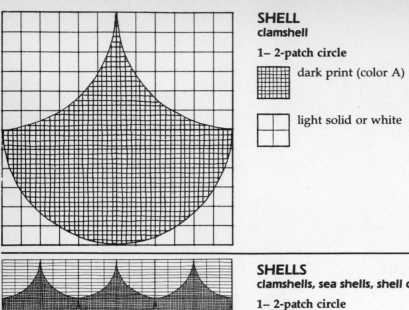

## SHELL
**clamshell**

### 1– 2-patch circle

 dark print (color A)

light solid or white

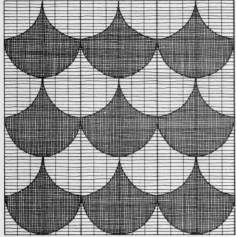

## SHELLS
**clamshells, sea shells, shell chain**

### 1– 2-patch circle

 dark print (color A)

light print or solid (color B)

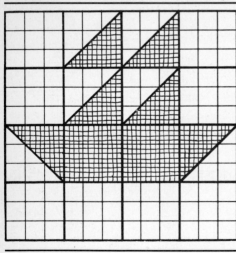

## SHIP 1
**boat**

### 4-patch

 dark print (color A)

light solid or white

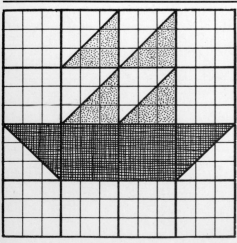

## SHIP 2
**boat**

### 4-patch

 dark print (color A)

 light print (color B)

 light solid or white

# SHIP 3
**boat, ship-on-seas**

**4-patch**

- dark print (color A)
- light print (color B)
- dark print (color C)
- medium print (color C)
- light print (color C)
- light solid or white

# SHIP 4
**boat, tall ships**

**4-patch**

- dark print (color A)
- light print (color B)
- light solid or white

# SHOO FLY
**shoo-fly**

**9-patch**

- dark print (color A)
- light solid or white

# SINGLE STAR
**easy star, simple star**

**4-patch**

- dark print (color A)
- light solid or white

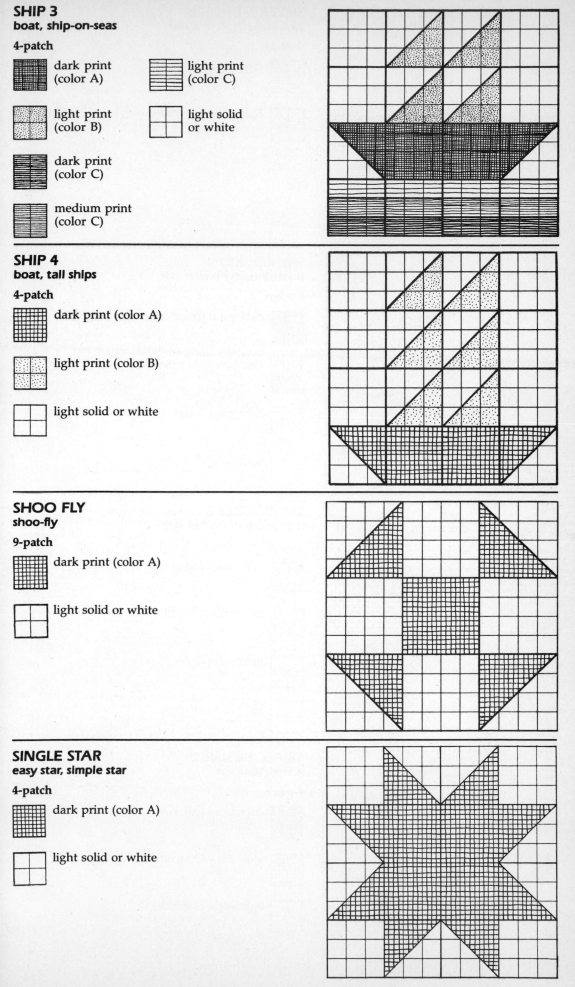

215

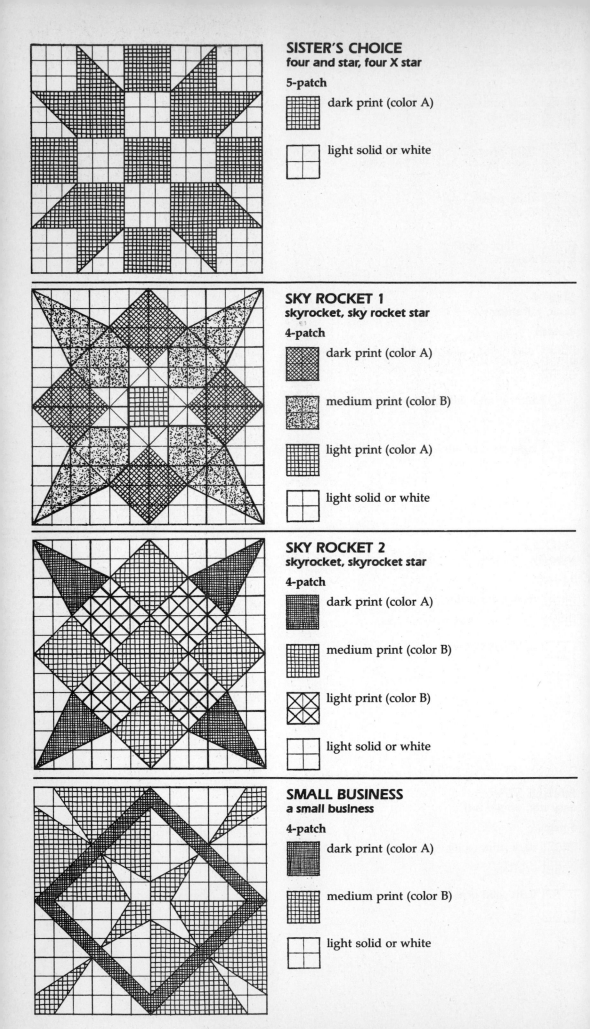

### SISTER'S CHOICE
**four and star, four X star**

**5-patch**

- dark print (color A)
- light solid or white

### SKY ROCKET 1
**skyrocket, sky rocket star**

**4-patch**

- dark print (color A)
- medium print (color B)
- light print (color A)
- light solid or white

### SKY ROCKET 2
**skyrocket, skyrocket star**

**4-patch**

- dark print (color A)
- medium print (color B)
- light print (color B)
- light solid or white

### SMALL BUSINESS
**a small business**

**4-patch**

- dark print (color A)
- medium print (color B)
- light solid or white

## SOUTH DAKOTA
### state of South Dakota

**9-patch**

dark print (color A)

medium print (color A)

light print (color B)

light solid or white

## SPIDER WEB 1
### a spider's web

**4-patch**

dark print (color A)

medium print (color A)

light print (color A)

light solid or white

## SPIDER WEB 2
### crazy quilt spider web

each patch made in a different scrap color

light solid or white

## SPOOL 1
### spools II, wood spools

**1–2-patch**

dark print (color A)

light print (color B)

light solid or white

217

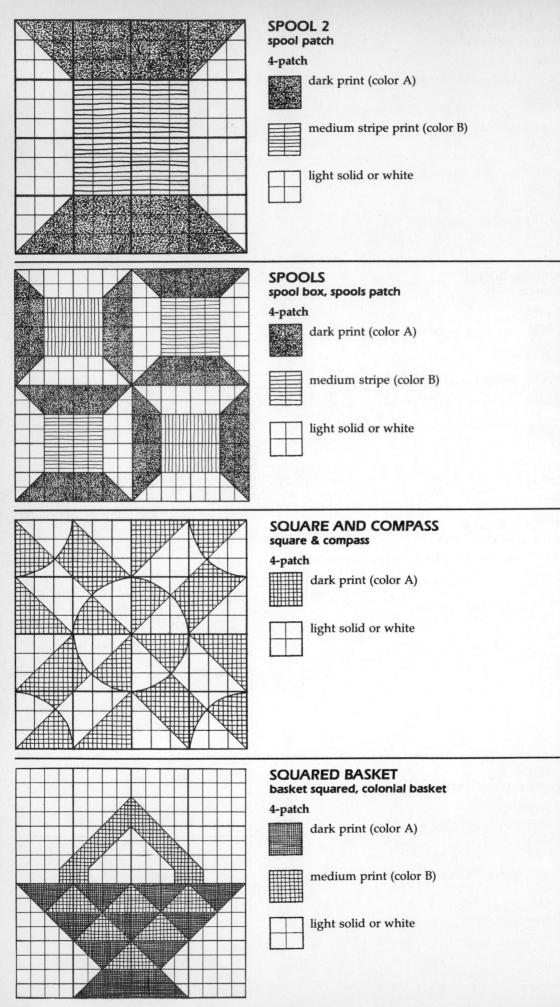

## SPOOL 2
### spool patch
**4-patch**

dark print (color A)

medium stripe print (color B)

light solid or white

## SPOOLS
### spool box, spools patch
**4-patch**

dark print (color A)

medium stripe (color B)

light solid or white

## SQUARE AND COMPASS
### square & compass
**4-patch**

dark print (color A)

light solid or white

## SQUARED BASKET
### basket squared, colonial basket
**4-patch**

dark print (color A)

medium print (color B)

light solid or white

## SQUARE WITHIN A SQUARE
**Amish square**

**4-patch**

 dark solid (color A)

 medium solid (color B)

 light solid (color C)

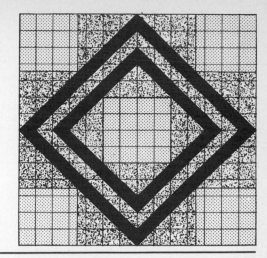

## STAR AND CRESCENTS 1
**star & crescent**

**4-patch**

 dark print (color A)

light solid or white

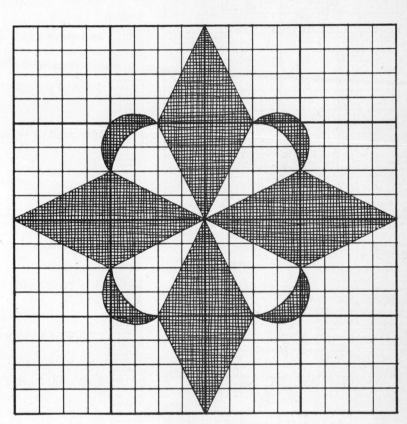

## STAR AND CRESCENTS 2
**star & crescent**

**9-patch**

 dark print (color A)

 medium print (color B)

 light solid or white

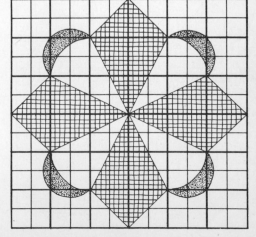

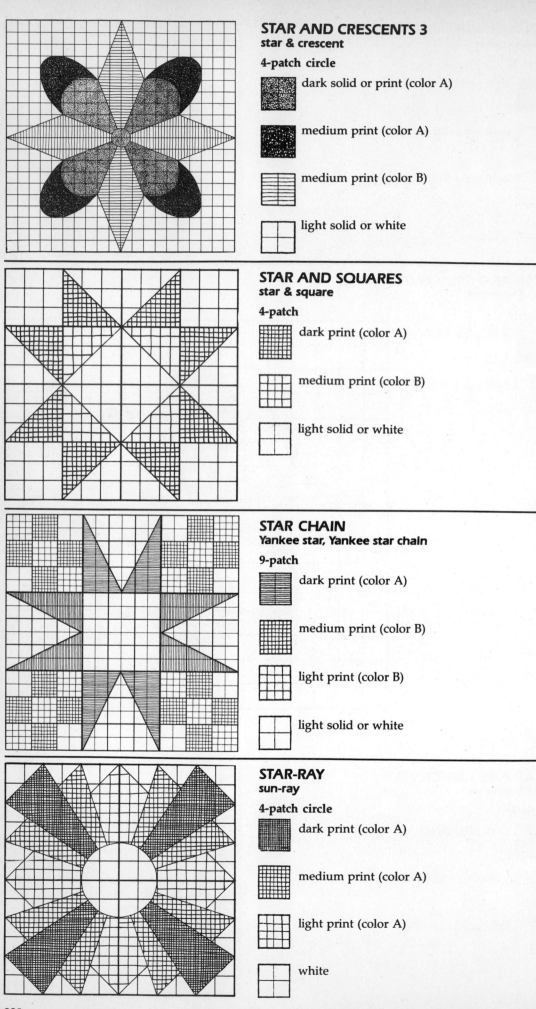

## STAR AND CRESCENTS 3
**star & crescent**

4-patch circle

dark solid or print (color A)

medium print (color A)

medium print (color B)

light solid or white

## STAR AND SQUARES
**star & square**

4-patch

dark print (color A)

medium print (color B)

light solid or white

## STAR CHAIN
**Yankee star, Yankee star chain**

9-patch

dark print (color A)

medium print (color B)

light print (color B)

light solid or white

## STAR-RAY
**sun-ray**

4-patch circle

dark print (color A)

medium print (color A)

light print (color A)

white

## STARRY PATH
### galaxy, star path

**4-patch**

dark print (color A)

medium print (color B)

light solid or white

## STARSHIP
### star ship, Trenton quilt block

**4-patch circle**

dark print (color A)

light solid or white

## STATE FAIR 1
### state fair

**4-patch circle**

dark print (color A)

medium print (color B)

light solid or white

## STATE FAIR 2
### moons and stars, state fair block

**4-patch circle**

dark print (color A)

medium print (color B)

light solid or white

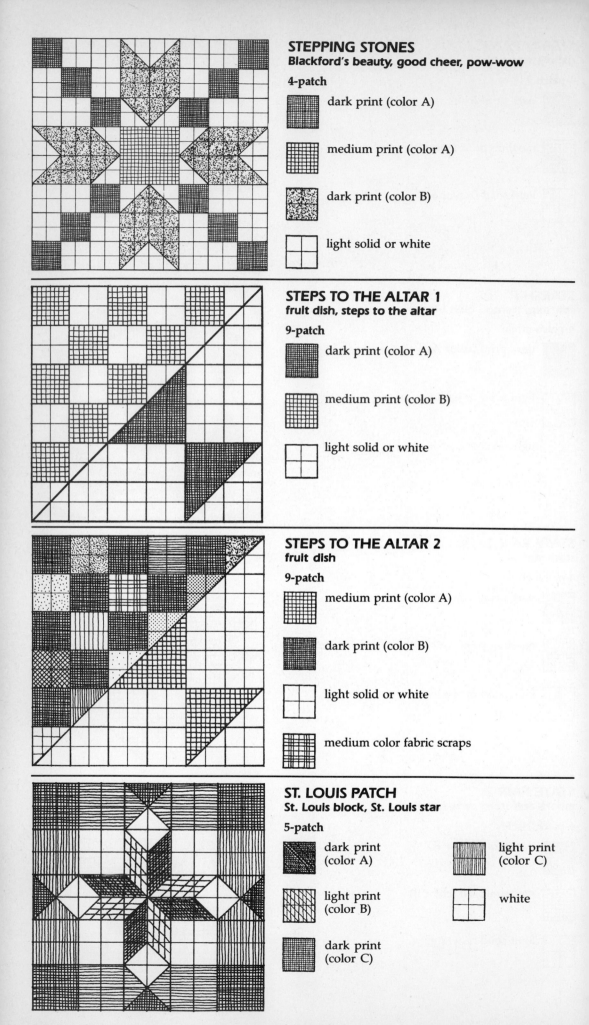

## STEPPING STONES
**Blackford's beauty, good cheer, pow-wow**

4-patch

- dark print (color A)
- medium print (color A)
- dark print (color B)
- light solid or white

## STEPS TO THE ALTAR 1
**fruit dish, steps to the altar**

9-patch

- dark print (color A)
- medium print (color B)
- light solid or white

## STEPS TO THE ALTAR 2
**fruit dish**

9-patch

- medium print (color A)
- dark print (color B)
- light solid or white
- medium color fabric scraps

## ST. LOUIS PATCH
**St. Louis block, St. Louis star**

5-patch

- dark print (color A)
- light print (color B)
- dark print (color C)
- light print (color C)
- white

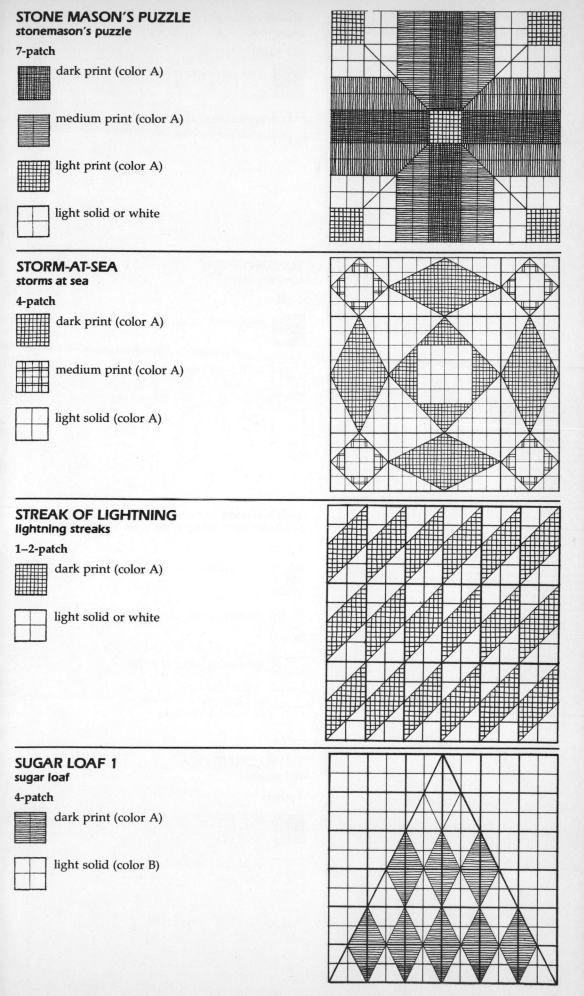

## STONE MASON'S PUZZLE
**stonemason's puzzle**

**7-patch**

dark print (color A)

medium print (color A)

light print (color A)

light solid or white

## STORM-AT-SEA
**storms at sea**

**4-patch**

dark print (color A)

medium print (color A)

light solid (color A)

## STREAK OF LIGHTNING
**lightning streaks**

**1–2-patch**

dark print (color A)

light solid or white

## SUGAR LOAF 1
**sugar loaf**

**4-patch**

dark print (color A)

light solid (color B)

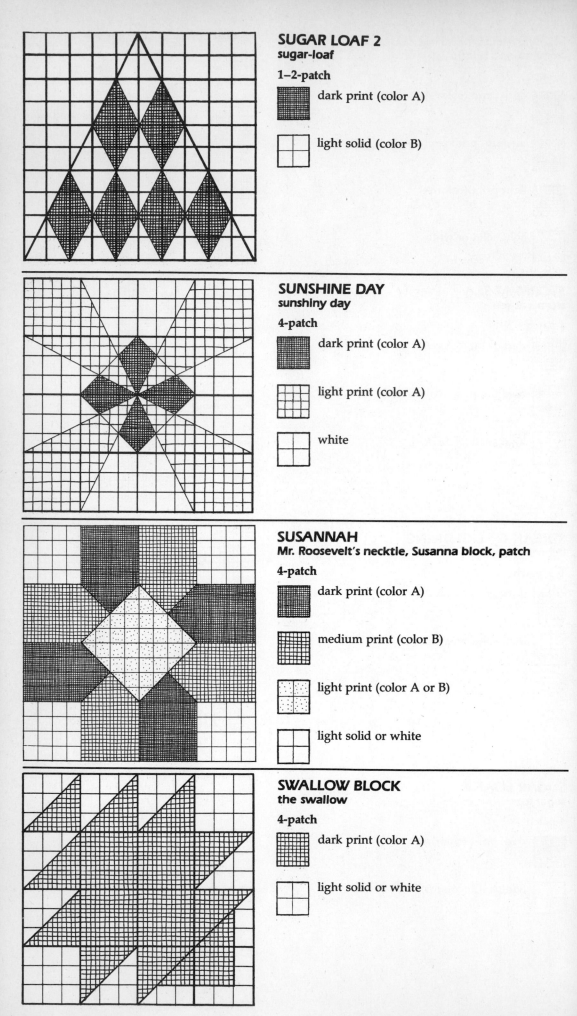

**SUGAR LOAF 2**
sugar-loaf

1–2-patch

dark print (color A)

light solid (color B)

**SUNSHINE DAY**
sunshiny day

4-patch

dark print (color A)

light print (color A)

white

**SUSANNAH**
Mr. Roosevelt's necktie, Susanna block, patch

4-patch

dark print (color A)

medium print (color B)

light print (color A or B)

light solid or white

**SWALLOW BLOCK**
the swallow

4-patch

dark print (color A)

light solid or white

## SWALLOWS
### the swallows

**5-patch**

dark print (color A)

medium print (color A)

dark print (color B)

light solid or white

## SWALLOWS ON A STAR
### flying swallows

**4-patch**

dark print (color A)

light print (color B)

white

## SWAN BLOCK
### duck adaptation

**5-patch**

dark print (color A)

light print (color A)

light print (color B)

bright solid (bill)

light solid or white

## SWASTIKA 1
### swastika I, swastika II

**4-patch**

dark print (color A)

light solid or white

225

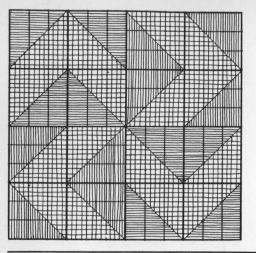

## SWASTIKA 2

**4-patch**

 dark print (color A)

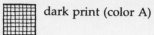 light print (color A or B)

## SWASTIKA 3
**swastika patch, wind power of Osages**

**7-patch**

 dark print (color A)

 light solid or white

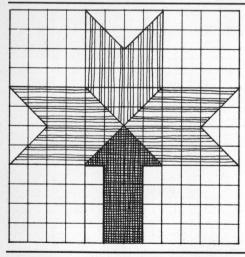

## SWEET GUM LEAF
**sweet gum**

**9-patch**

 dark print (color A)

 medium print (color B)

 light solid or white

## SWING-IN-THE-CENTER
**swing in the center block**

**9-patch**

 dark print (color A)

 medium print (color B)

 light solid or white

226

## TALLAHASSEE
**Tallahassee block, quilt block**

**4-patch**

dark print (color A)

light print (color A)

## TALL PINE TREE
**tall pine**

**4-patch**

dark print (color A)

medium print (color B)

light print (color B)

light solid or white

## TANGLED GARTER
**garter**

**9-patch**

dark print or solid

light solid or white

## TANGLED PINWHEELS
**tangled lines**

**4-patch**

dark print (color A)

medium print (color B)

light solid or white

227

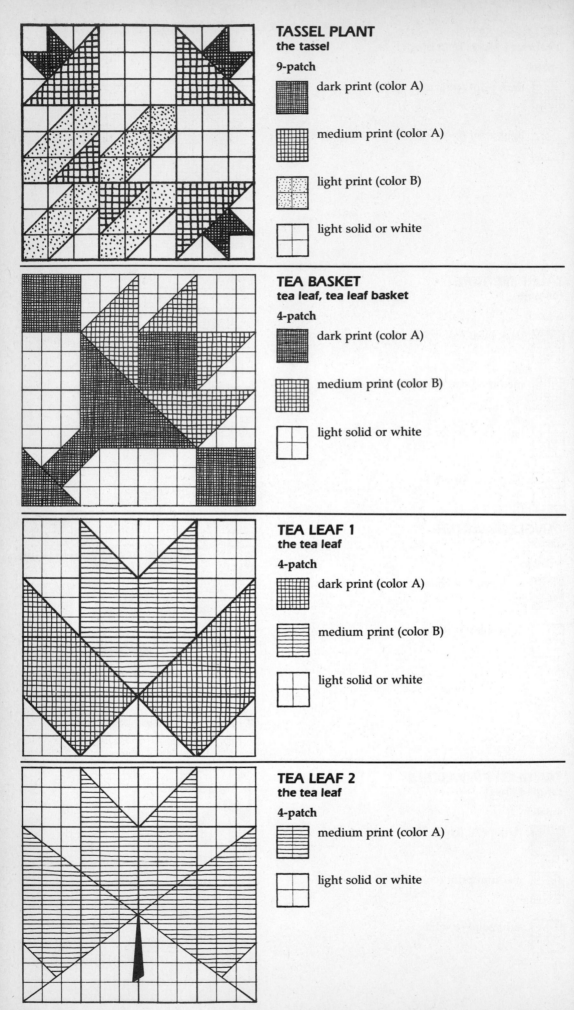

**TASSEL PLANT**
the tassel

9-patch

dark print (color A)

medium print (color A)

light print (color B)

light solid or white

**TEA BASKET**
tea leaf, tea leaf basket

4-patch

dark print (color A)

medium print (color B)

light solid or white

**TEA LEAF 1**
the tea leaf

4-patch

dark print (color A)

medium print (color B)

light solid or white

**TEA LEAF 2**
the tea leaf

4-patch

medium print (color A)

light solid or white

## TEA LEAF 3
**the tea leaf, tea leaves**

**4-patch**

dark print (color A)

light solid or white

## TEMPLE COURT

**4-patch**

dark print (color A)

light solid or white

## TILE PUZZLE
**tile**

**9-patch**

dark print (color A)

light solid or white

## TIPPE-CANOE AND TYLER TOO 1
**Tippecanoe & Tyler too**

**9-patch**

dark print or solid (color A)

light print (color B)

dark print (color B)

light solid or white

medium print (color B)

medium light print (color B)

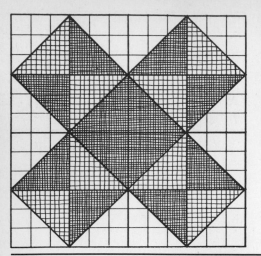

## TIPPE-CANOE AND TYLER TOO 2
**Tippecanoe & Tyler too**

**9-patch**

 dark print (color A)

 medium print (color A or B)

light solid or white

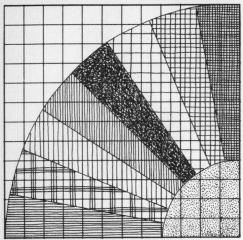

## TRADITIONAL FAN
**grandmother's fan**

**circle-patch**

 each fan blade patch made in a different color and print

 medium print or solid

light solid or white

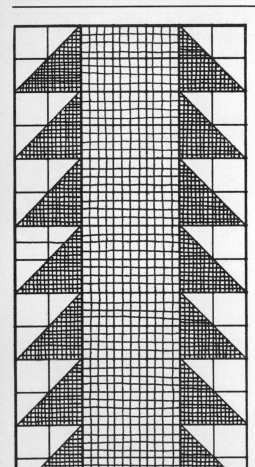

## TREE EVERLASTING
**everlasting tree**

**1–2-patch**

 dark print (color A)

 medium print or solid (color B)

light solid or white

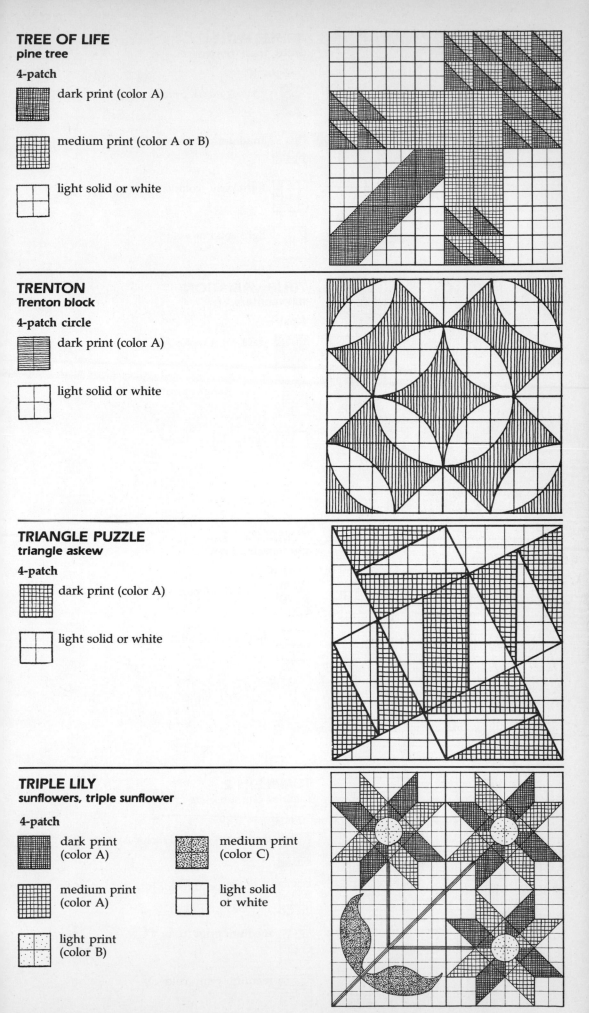

# TREE OF LIFE
## pine tree

**4-patch**

    dark print (color A)

    medium print (color A or B)

    light solid or white

# TRENTON
## Trenton block

**4-patch circle**

    dark print (color A)

    light solid or white

# TRIANGLE PUZZLE
## triangle askew

**4-patch**

    dark print (color A)

    light solid or white

# TRIPLE LILY
## sunflowers, triple sunflower

**4-patch**

    dark print (color A)

    medium print (color C)

    medium print (color A)

    light solid or white

    light print (color B)

231

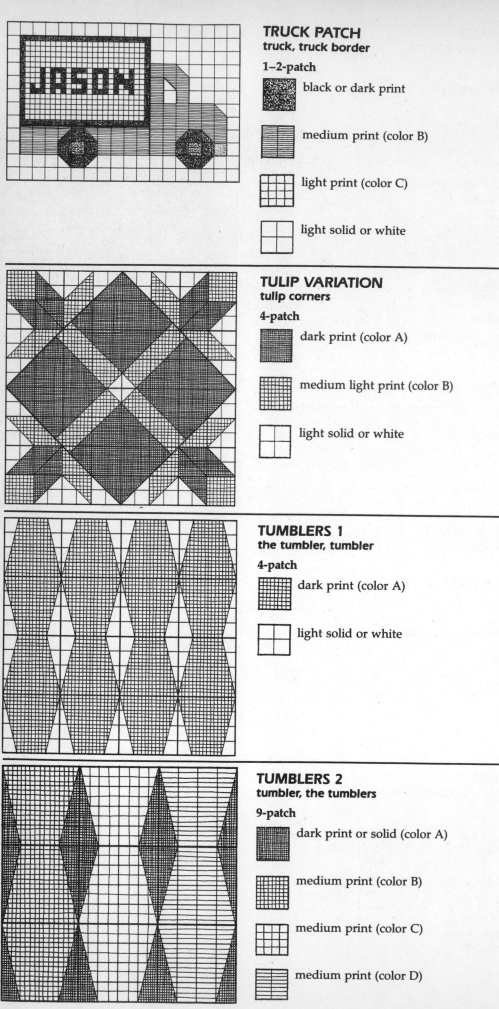

## TRUCK PATCH
**truck, truck border**

1–2-patch

- black or dark print
- medium print (color B)
- light print (color C)
- light solid or white

## TULIP VARIATION
**tulip corners**

4-patch

- dark print (color A)
- medium light print (color B)
- light solid or white

## TUMBLERS 1
**the tumbler, tumbler**

4-patch

- dark print (color A)
- light solid or white

## TUMBLERS 2
**tumbler, the tumblers**

9-patch

- dark print or solid (color A)
- medium print (color B)
- medium print (color C)
- medium print (color D)

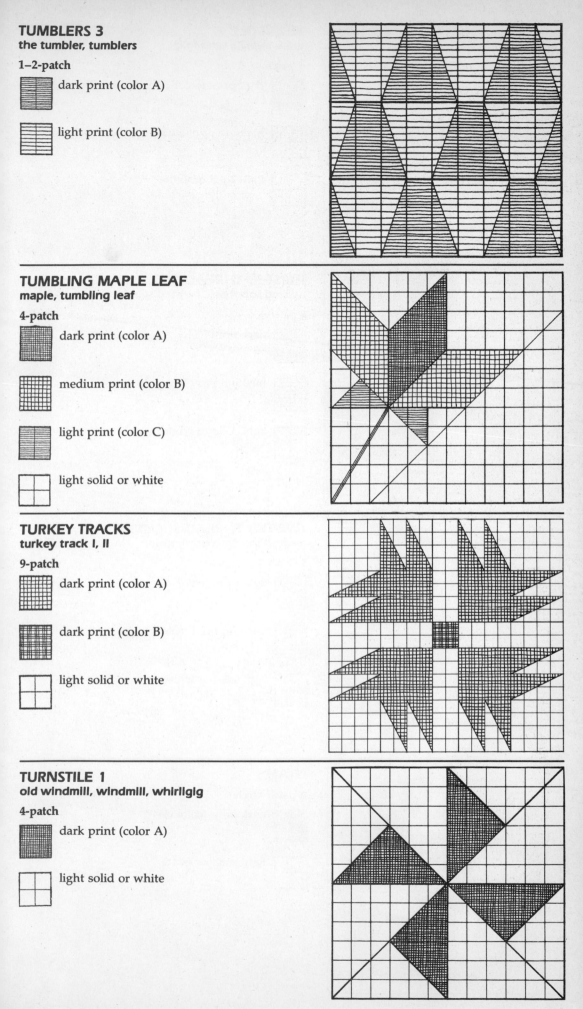

## TUMBLERS 3
**the tumbler, tumblers**

**1–2-patch**

dark print (color A)

light print (color B)

## TUMBLING MAPLE LEAF
**maple, tumbling leaf**

**4-patch**

dark print (color A)

medium print (color B)

light print (color C)

light solid or white

## TURKEY TRACKS
**turkey track I, II**

**9-patch**

dark print (color A)

dark print (color B)

light solid or white

## TURNSTILE 1
**old windmill, windmill, whirligig**

**4-patch**

dark print (color A)

light solid or white

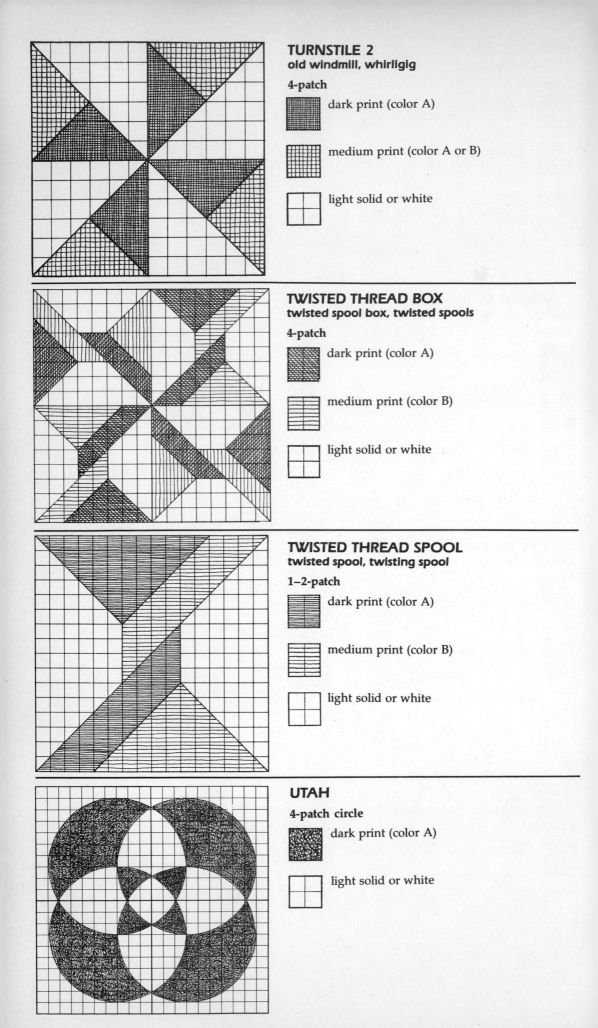

## TURNSTILE 2
### old windmill, whirligig
**4-patch**

dark print (color A)

medium print (color A or B)

light solid or white

## TWISTED THREAD BOX
### twisted spool box, twisted spools
**4-patch**

dark print (color A)

medium print (color B)

light solid or white

## TWISTED THREAD SPOOL
### twisted spool, twisting spool
**1–2-patch**

dark print (color A)

medium print (color B)

light solid or white

## UTAH
**4-patch circle**

dark print (color A)

light solid or white

## VERMONT BLOCK
**state of Vermont**

**4-patch**

dark print (color A)

medium print (color B)

light solid or white

## VIRGINIA
**Virginia star, state of Virginia**

**9-patch**

dark print (color A)

medium print (color B)

light solid or white

## WASHINGTON
**state of Washington**

**4-patch**

dark print (color A)

medium print (color A or B)

light solid or white

## WASHINGTON SIDEWALKS
**sidewalks**

**4-patch**

dark print (color A)

medium print (color B)

light solid or white

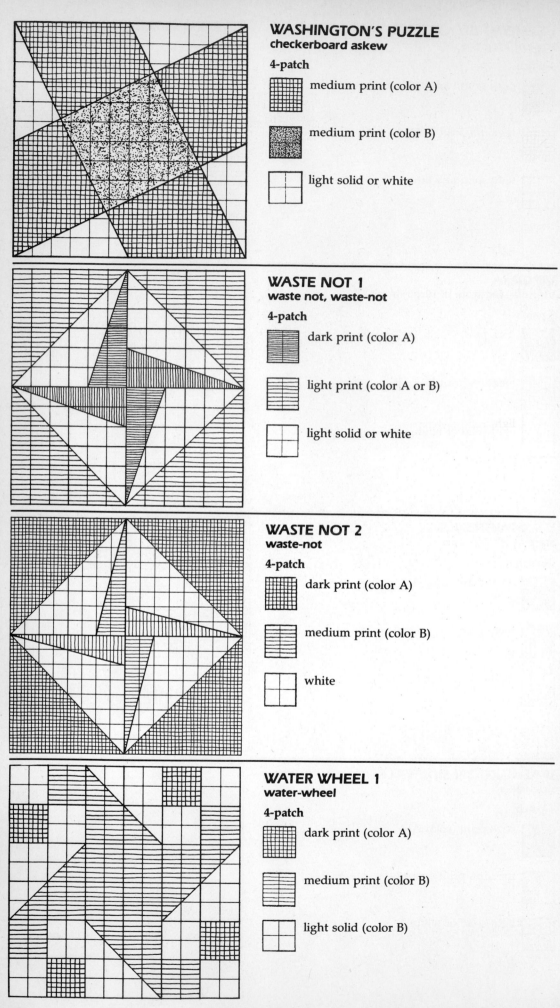

**WASHINGTON'S PUZZLE**
checkerboard askew

4-patch

medium print (color A)

medium print (color B)

light solid or white

**WASTE NOT 1**
waste not, waste-not

4-patch

dark print (color A)

light print (color A or B)

light solid or white

**WASTE NOT 2**
waste-not

4-patch

dark print (color A)

medium print (color B)

white

**WATER WHEEL 1**
water-wheel

4-patch

dark print (color A)

medium print (color B)

light solid (color B)

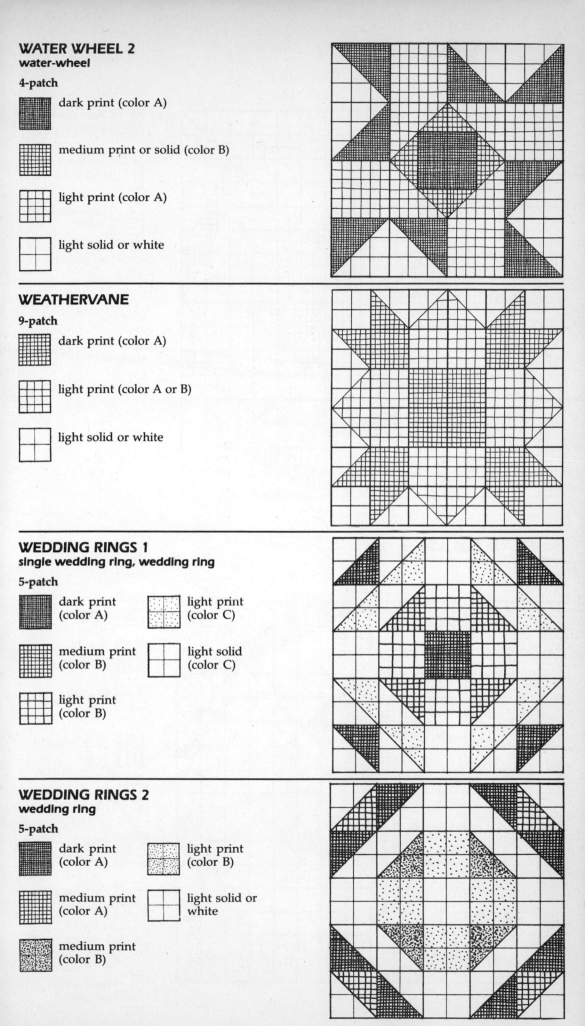

## WATER WHEEL 2
water-wheel

**4-patch**

dark print (color A)

medium print or solid (color B)

light print (color A)

light solid or white

## WEATHERVANE

**9-patch**

dark print (color A)

light print (color A or B)

light solid or white

## WEDDING RINGS 1
single wedding ring, wedding ring

**5-patch**

dark print
(color A)

light print
(color C)

medium print
(color B)

light solid
(color C)

light print
(color B)

## WEDDING RINGS 2
wedding ring

**5-patch**

dark print
(color A)

light print
(color B)

medium print
(color A)

light solid or
white

medium print
(color B)

# WHEEL OF FORTUNE 1
**wheel-of-fortune**

**4-patch**

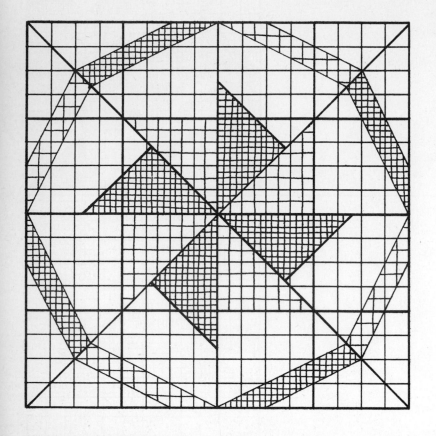

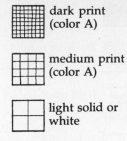

dark print
(color A)

medium print
(color A)

light solid or
white

# WHEEL OF FORTUNE 2
**wheel-of-fortune**

**4-patch**

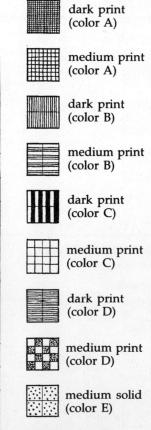

dark print
(color A)

medium print
(color A)

dark print
(color B)

medium print
(color B)

dark print
(color C)

medium print
(color C)

dark print
(color D)

medium print
(color D)

medium solid
(color E)

light solid
or white

## WHIRLWIND
### lone star, twin sister, windmill

**4-patch**

dark print (color A)

light solid or white

## WHIRLWIND REVERSE
### whirlwind

**4-patch**

dark print (color A)

light solid or white

## WHITE ROSE
### rose circle

**4-patch circle**

dark print (color A)

medium print (color A)

white

## WIDOWER CHOICE
### widower's choice, widow choice

**5-patch**

dark print (color A)

light solid or white

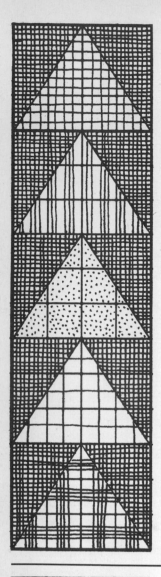

 dark print or solid (color A)

 each triangle a different color print

## WILD GOOSE 2
**wild goose chase**

**1–2-patch**

 dark print or solid (color A)

 each triangle a different color print

240

## WILD GOOSE 3
### wild goose chase

**5-patch**

dark print or solid (color A)

light print or solid (color B)

## WILLOW
### weeping willow, willow tree

**4-patch**

dark print or solid (color A)

light print (color B)

dark print (color B)

light solid or white

medium dark print (color B)

medium print (color B)

## WINDBLOWN SQUARE 1
### Balkan puzzle, whirlwind square, whirlwind, windblown star

**4-patch**

dark print (color A)

light solid or white

medium print (color B)

medium print (color C)

## WINDBLOWN SQUARE 2
### whirlwind, whirlwind square, windblown star

**4-patch**

dark print (color A)

light solid or white

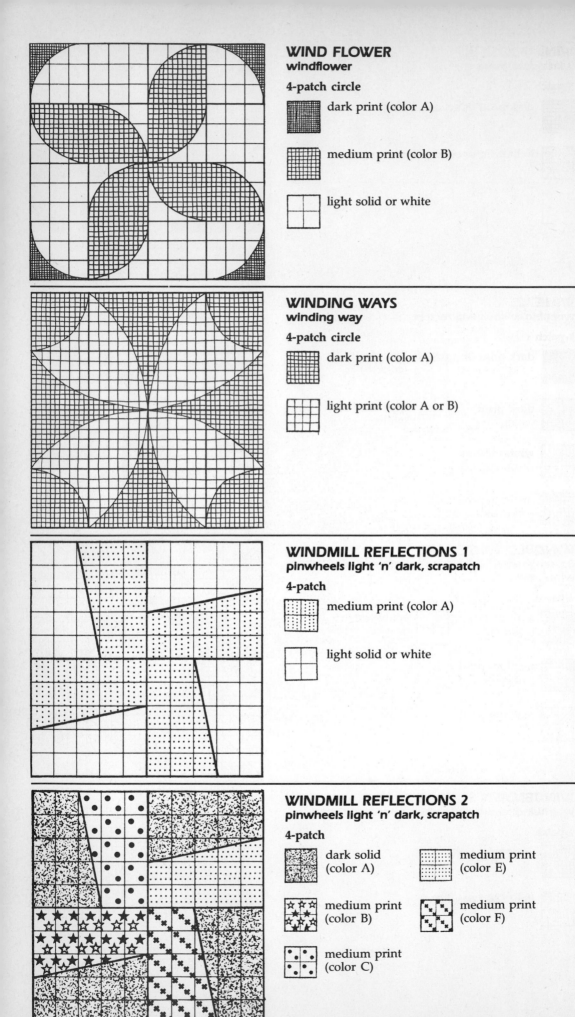

**WIND FLOWER**
windflower

4-patch circle

dark print (color A)

medium print (color B)

light solid or white

**WINDING WAYS**
winding way

4-patch circle

dark print (color A)

light print (color A or B)

**WINDMILL REFLECTIONS 1**
pinwheels light 'n' dark, scrapatch

4-patch

medium print (color A)

light solid or white

**WINDMILL REFLECTIONS 2**
pinwheels light 'n' dark, scrapatch

4-patch

dark solid
(color A)

medium print
(color B)

medium print
(color C)

medium print
(color E)

medium print
(color F)

## WINDMILL STARS
**windmill star**

**4-patch**

dark print (color A)

medium print (color B)

light solid or white

## WING
**wing block, wings**

**9-patch circle**

dark print (color A)

medium print (color A or B)

white

## WING SQUARE
**winged square, winged square II**

**9-patch**

dark print (color A)

medium print (color A)

medium print (color B)

medium light print (color B)

light solid or white

## WOMEN'S CHRISTIAN TEMPERANCE UNION
**W.C.T.U., women's C.T.U.**

**9-patch**

dark print (color A)

medium print (color B)

light solid or white

243

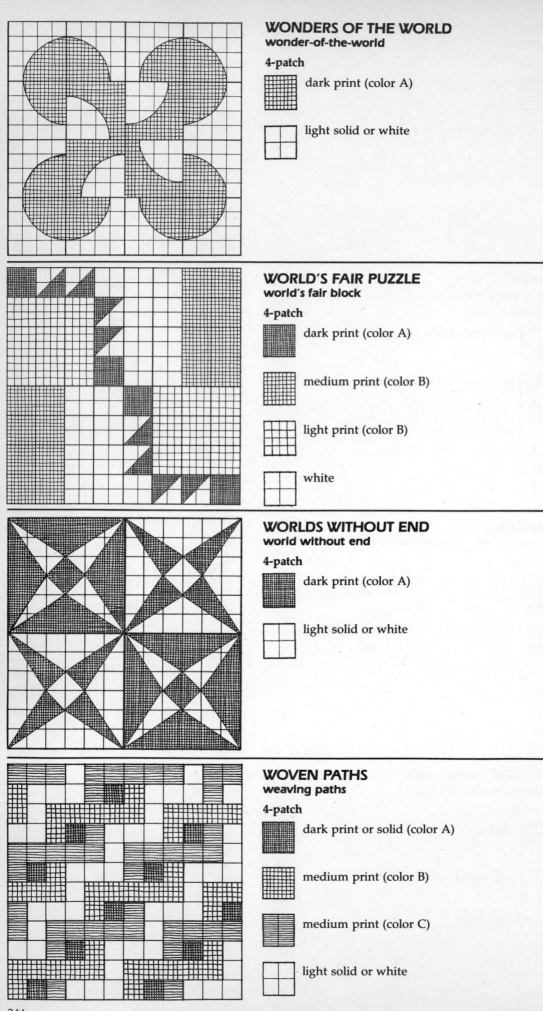

## WONDERS OF THE WORLD
**wonder-of-the-world**

4-patch

dark print (color A)

light solid or white

## WORLD'S FAIR PUZZLE
**world's fair block**

4-patch

dark print (color A)

medium print (color B)

light print (color B)

white

## WORLDS WITHOUT END
**world without end**

4-patch

dark print (color A)

light solid or white

## WOVEN PATHS
**weaving paths**

4-patch

dark print or solid (color A)

medium print (color B)

medium print (color C)

light solid or white

# WOVEN X
**basketweave X, flying cloud**

4-patch

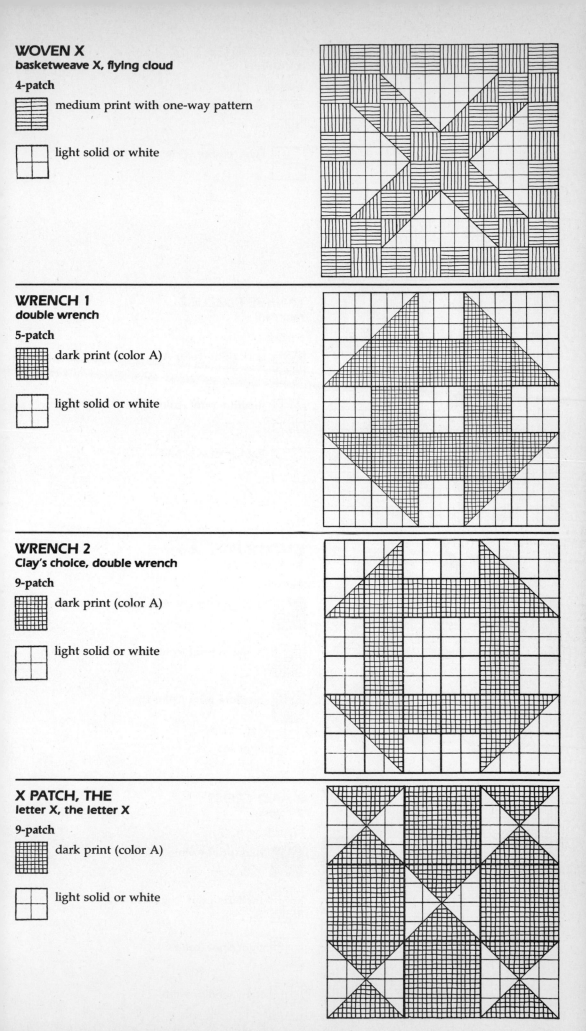

medium print with one-way pattern

light solid or white

# WRENCH 1
**double wrench**

5-patch

dark print (color A)

light solid or white

# WRENCH 2
**Clay's choice, double wrench**

9-patch

dark print (color A)

light solid or white

# X PATCH, THE
**letter X, the letter X**

9-patch

dark print (color A)

light solid or white

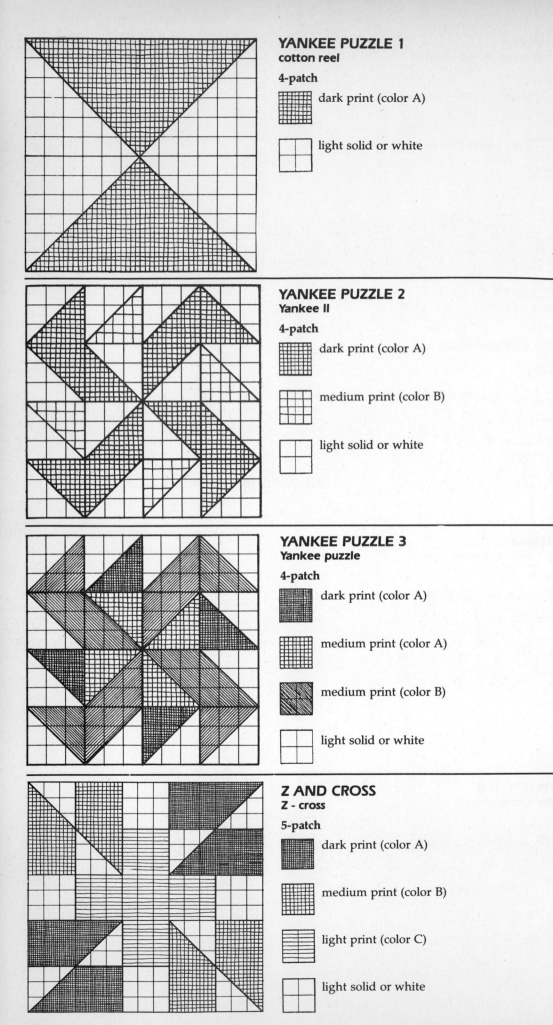

## YANKEE PUZZLE 1
**cotton reel**

**4-patch**

- dark print (color A)
- light solid or white

## YANKEE PUZZLE 2
**Yankee II**

**4-patch**

- dark print (color A)
- medium print (color B)
- light solid or white

## YANKEE PUZZLE 3
**Yankee puzzle**

**4-patch**

- dark print (color A)
- medium print (color A)
- medium print (color B)
- light solid or white

## Z AND CROSS
**Z - cross**

**5-patch**

- dark print (color A)
- medium print (color B)
- light print (color C)
- light solid or white

246

# PATCHWORK BLOCK ALPHABET

This alphabet can be used as a border on a crib or youth quilt or as individual blocks in a memory or album quilt.

A wonderful set of soft blocks can be made for your favorite baby, using six letters for each block.

## PATTERNS: A TO Z

**5-patch**

This legend is used for all letters.

 **medium print or solid**

 **light solid**

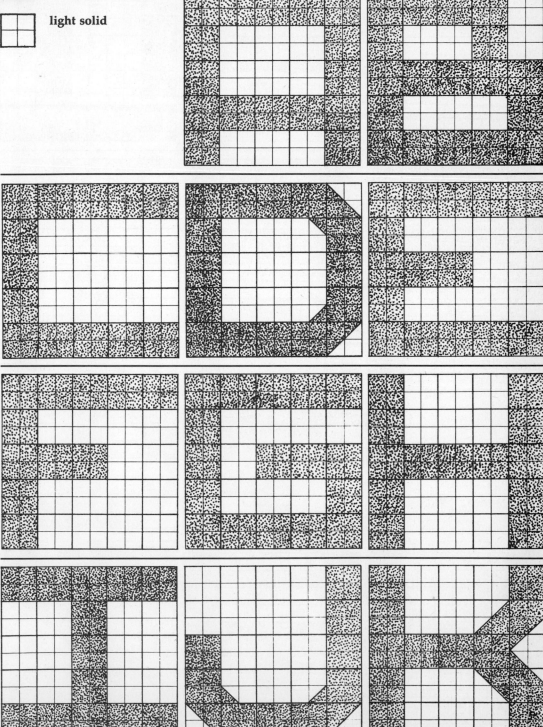

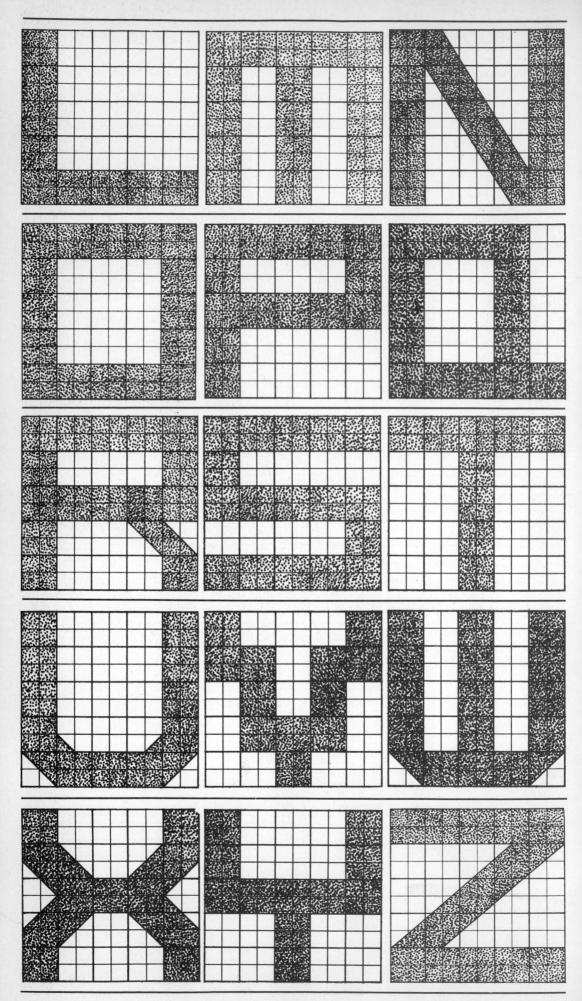

248

# PHOTOGRAPHS OF PATTERNS

Airplane 3

Attic Windows

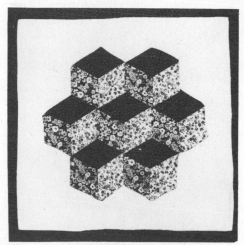

Baby blocks

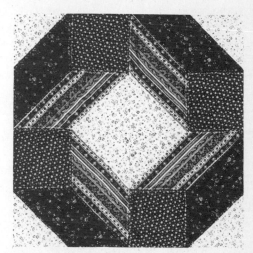

Bachelor's Puzzle

Basic Nine-Patch

Bear's Paw

249

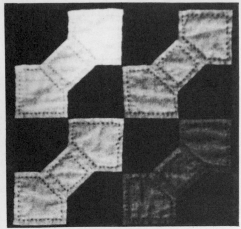

Bow Ties

Bow Ties Quilt

Box Kite

Card Tricks

Christmas Fruit Basket

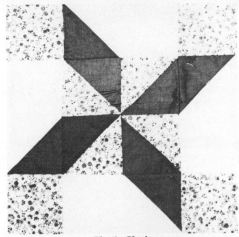

Clay's Choice

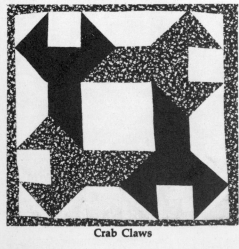

Crab Claws

Doe and Darts

Double Pinwheel

Dresden Plate

Drunkard's Path 6

Dutchman Puzzle

Eight-Pointed Star

Evening Star—Morning Star

Feather Star and Square

Flower Basket 2

251

**Flying Squares Block**

**Four-Patch**

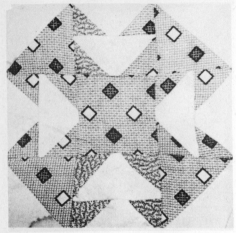

**Four T Square (antique)**

**Grandmother's Flower Garden**

**Grape Basket**

**Guiding Star**

**Honey Bee**

**House 7 (miniature quilt)**

**House 7 (in heart)**

**Interlaced Star**

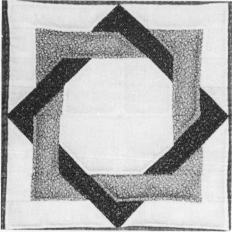

**Interlocked Squares**

**Interlocked Squares with Star**

**Jack in the Box**

**Jacob's Ladder 1**

**Jacob's Ladder (four-block)**

**Log Cabin 1**

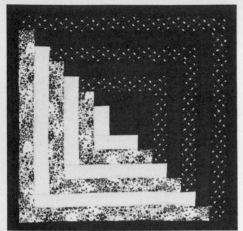

**Log Cabin 3**

**Louisiana**

**Love Ring 2**

**Maple Leaf**

**Mexican Cross 2**

**Monkey Wrench**

**Moon Over the Mountain (with geese)**

**Mosaic Star**

254

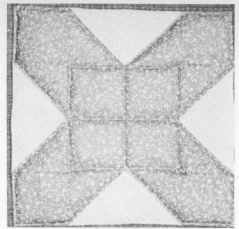

Mother's Choice

Mrs. Cleveland's Choice

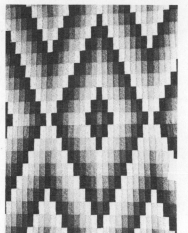

Navajo Blues

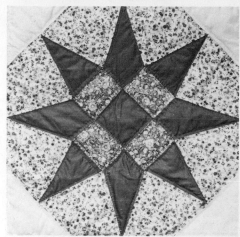

North Carolina Star

Nosegay

Ohio Schoolhouse

Ohio Star

Oh Susannah

One Way

Philadelphia Pavements 2

Pine Tree 1

Pinwheel 1

Positively Negative

Postage Stamp Basket

Random Country Calico

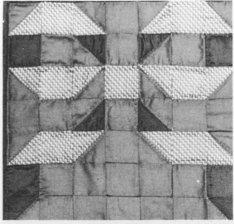

Ribbon Bow

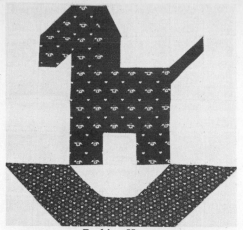

Rocking Horse

Ship 3

Spider Web

Star and Crescents 3

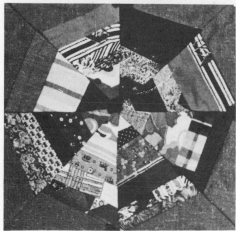

Star and Squares

Storm-at-Sea

Swallows on a Star

Traditional Fan

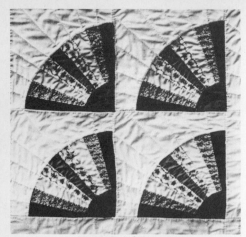

**Traditional Fans**

**Triple Lily**

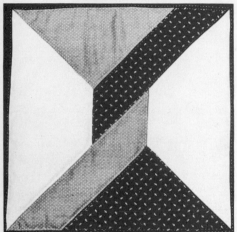

**Twisted Thread Spool**

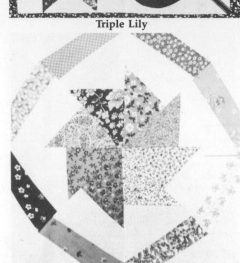

**Wheel of Fortune 2**

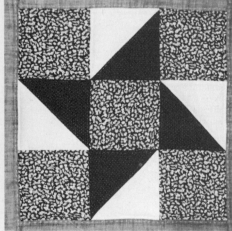

**Windmill**

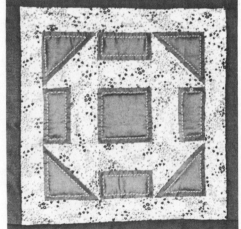

**Wrench 2**

# Templates

A template is a full-size pattern shape or quilting outline, made of cardboard, plastic, or lightweight sheet metal. It is used to trace the pattern outline on the fabric, and can be used many times.

This book is designed to generate the working templates. The patterns are all drafted on graph paper. These can be enlarged to full-scale working drawings. (See "Enlarging and Reducing Patterns," page 18.)

A template is now made of each pattern shape by tracing. This will ensure a perfect fit to the pattern and enable the quilter to custom-size every pattern by changing the grid size of the graph paper used to prepare the full-scale working drawing.

On the following pages I have included some basic full-scale template shapes that can be traced and used for working some of the patterns. However, due to space limitations and, more important, the desire to provide pattern draftings that could adjusted in size to suit quilters' individual needs, I have not provided a complete set of working templates. The templates provided are for visual recognition of the standard shapes and the ability to alter the size of these shapes in direct proportion.

**Note:** Never use a photocopy machine to reproduce any template pattern for use as a template. In most cases, the copy will shrink the size of the original and therefore become inaccurate for this purpose.

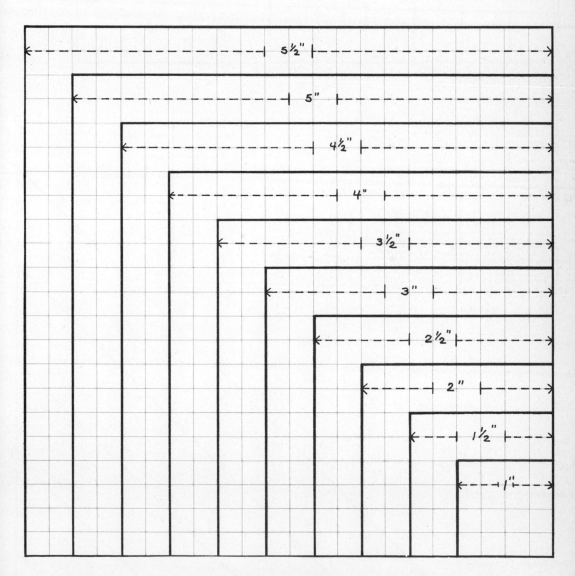

**Square Templates**

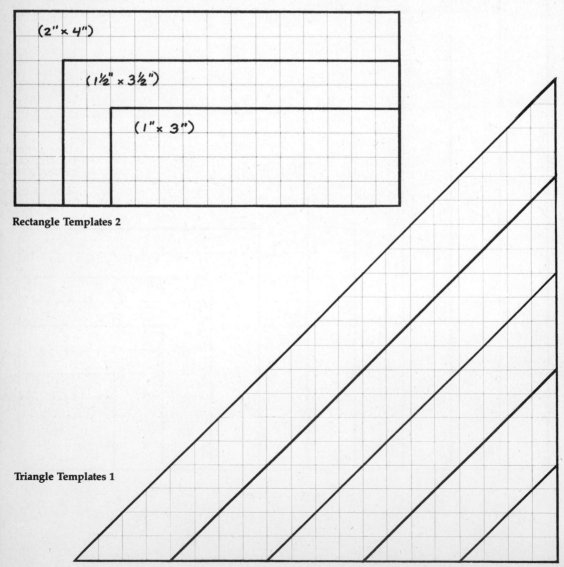

(4" x 5")

(3½" x 4½")

(3" x 4")

(2½" x 3½")

(2" x 3")

(1½" x 2½")

(1" x 2")

**Rectangle Templates 1**

(2" x 4")

(1½" x 3½")

(1" x 3")

**Rectangle Templates 2**

**Triangle Templates 1**

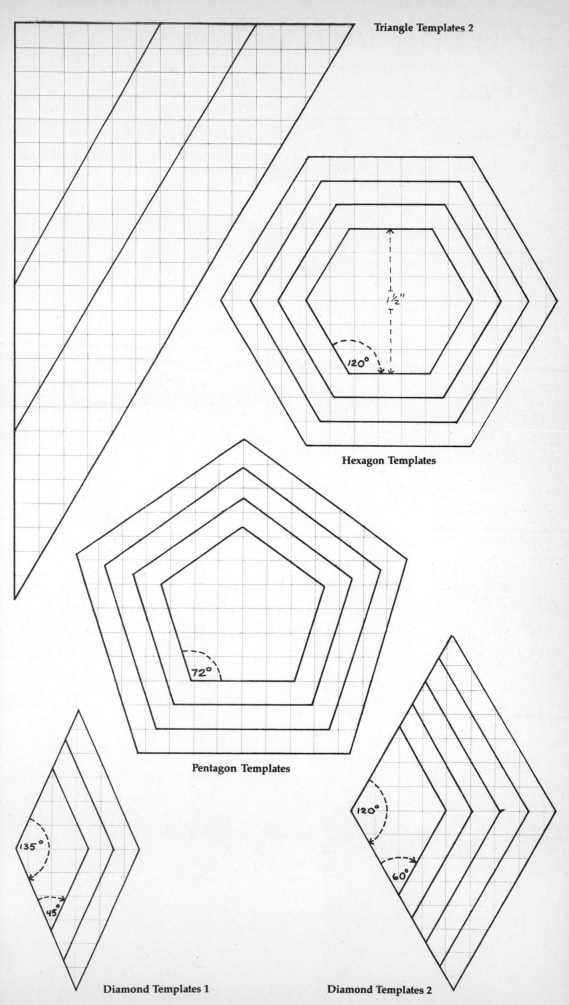

Triangle Templates 2

1½"

120°

Hexagon Templates

72°

Pentagon Templates

135°

45°

Diamond Templates 1

120°

60°

Diamond Templates 2

261

# Finishing Techniques

## BINDINGS

### BIAS BINDING

Bias binding is used to finish the edges of a quilt or quilted fabric. The following method will enable the quilter to create a bias binding from any fabric used for quilting.

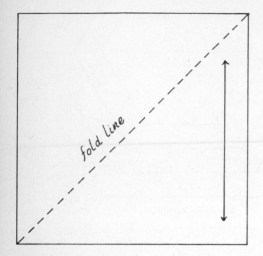

**Step 1**  Cut the fabric into a square (36" fabric = 1 square yard, 45" fabric = 1¼ square yards, etc.). Fold on the diagonal.

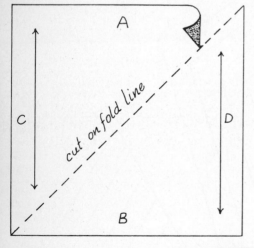

**Step 2**  Cut on fold.

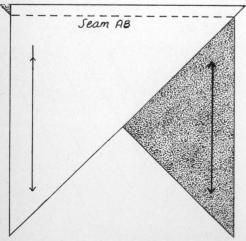

**Step 3**  Put A and B *right sides* together. Sew with a ½" seam allowance.

**Step 4** Place the fabric wrong side up on a flat surface. Using a yardstick, mark the desired finished *cut* width of bias binding. (For example, ¾" to 4"). Move the yardstick and mark again. Connect these marks with a straight line.

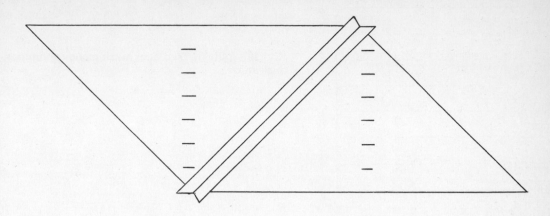

**Step 5** Place C and D together, dropping down one bias width at the top and bottom.

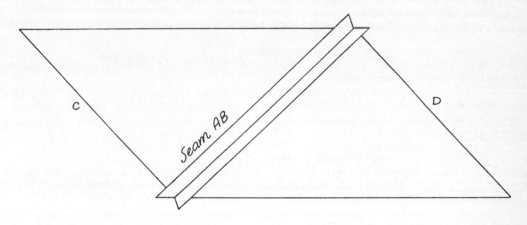

**Step 6** Carefully matching the marked lines, pin and stitch along the seam line C–D.

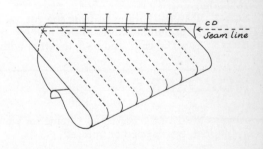

**Step 7** You have now formed a tube.

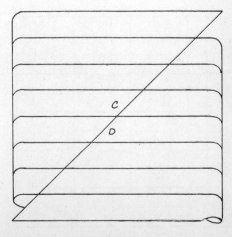

263

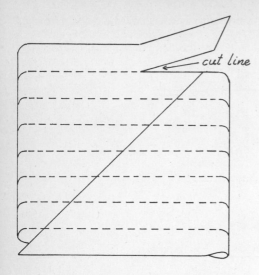

Cut along the marked line, making one continuous bias strip.

## To Attach a Double Bias Binding

**Step 1**  Baste together the outside raw edges of the quilt sandwich to even the edges and avoid pulling the fabric.

**Step 2**  Take the bias binding strip (purchased or handmade) and fold it in half lengthwise (raw edges together) and press.

**Step 3**  Place the binding strip on the basted edge, with the raw edges aligned to the raw edge of the quilt and the folded edge toward the center of the quilt. Stitch to the quilt top by hand or machine, leaving a ¼" to ½" seam allowance.

**Step 4**  Clip the corners of the quilt sandwich about ½". Curve the bias binding gently around the curve as you reach each corner.

**Step 5**  When the binding is firmly attached to the quilt top on four sides, carefully roll the folded edge over the raw edges to the back. Slip-stitch to the backing just over the stitching line.

## ROLLED HEM

**Step 1**  Cut the backing 1" larger than the quilt top.

**Step 2**  Turn the edge ¼" to the inside, roll it over the raw edges to the front, and slip-stitch in place.

**Note:** This can be reversed (to have the slip stitch on the backing) by making the border on the quilt top 1" larger than the backing.

## SELF-EDGE

You can work a self-finished edge on a quilt if there are no quilting stitches within an inch of the raw edges.

**Step 1**  Trim the batting ¼" from the edge of the quilt.

**Step 2**  Turn the raw edges of the quilt top *and* backing ¼" in toward the batting. Pin in place.

**Step 3**  Sew the front and back together with a fine running stitch.

# BORDERS

Always think of the border as a frame for your quilting work. It can be thin or wide, pieced, plain, or appliquéd, overlapped or mitered.

## PIECED BORDER

The pieced border is constructed in the same way as a pieced block. The design is often a duplication of a segment of the central pattern (repeat of one or more of the geometric shapes).

## APPLIQUÉ BORDER

The appliqué border is usually an adaptation of the appliqué design on the body of the quilt or a winding stemlike floral repeating some element of the pattern. Leaves are a very popular addition to the winding stem.

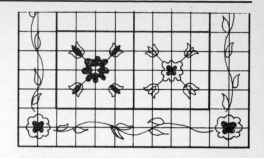

## PLAIN BORDER

Plain borders are usually quilted with complicated or ornate patterns. (See "Border Quilting Patterns," page 76.)

## PATCHWORK BORDER PATTERNS

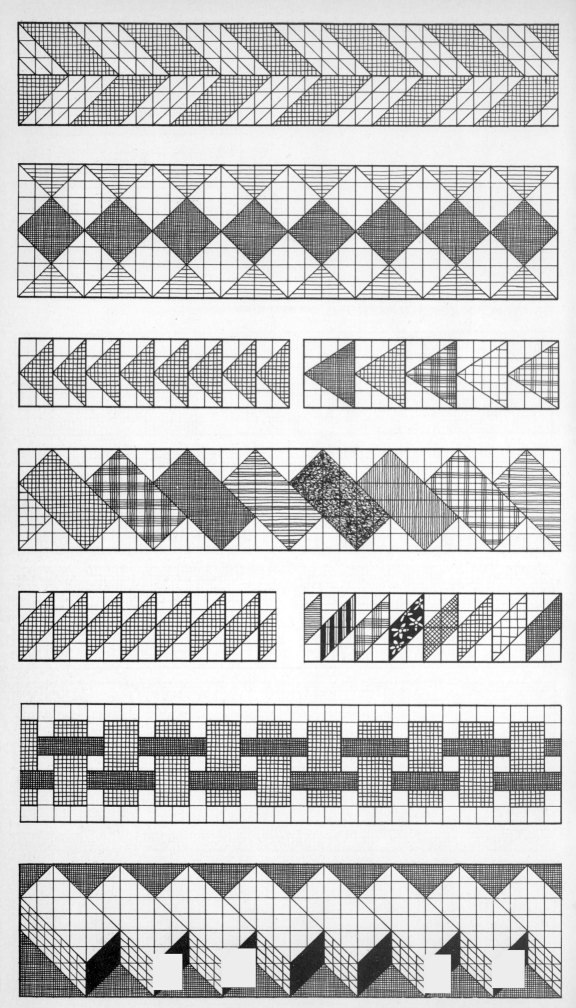

266

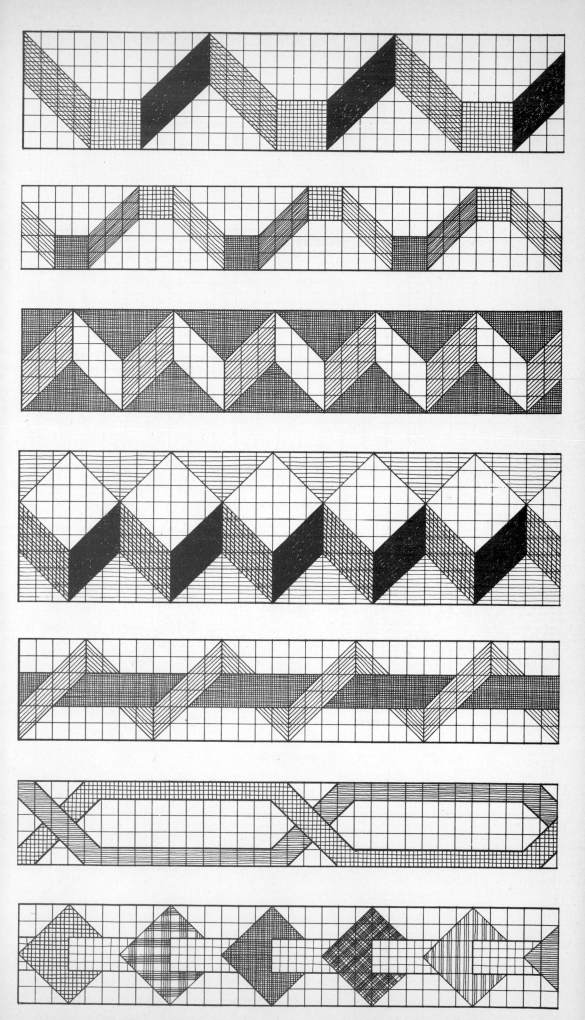

Juvenile and baby quilts are very popular with quilters of all ages. The following border patterns were especially designed for the little ones.

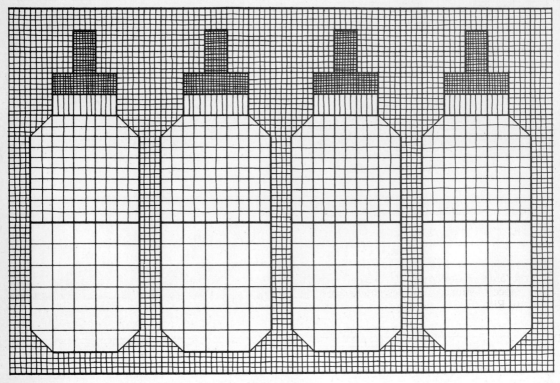

**Baby Bottles**

**Small World**

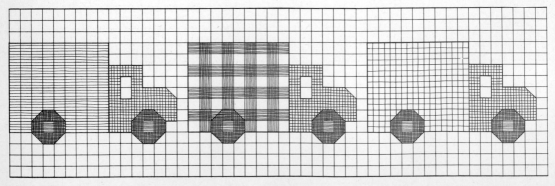

**Trucks**

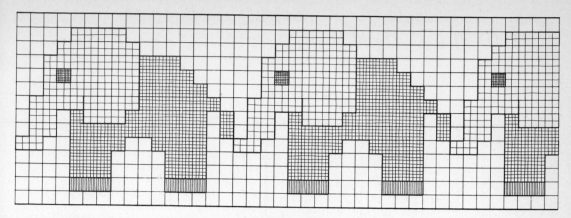

**Elephants**

# THE FINAL TOUCH

Always sign and date your work. The signature can
be embroidered directly on the fabric, or embroidered
on a piece of muslin or cross-stitched on hardanger
cloth or Ribband™ and appliquéd to a corner of the
work.

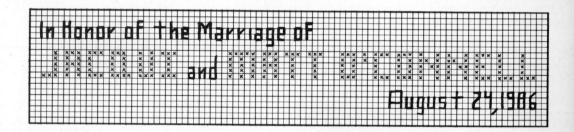

# Graph Paper

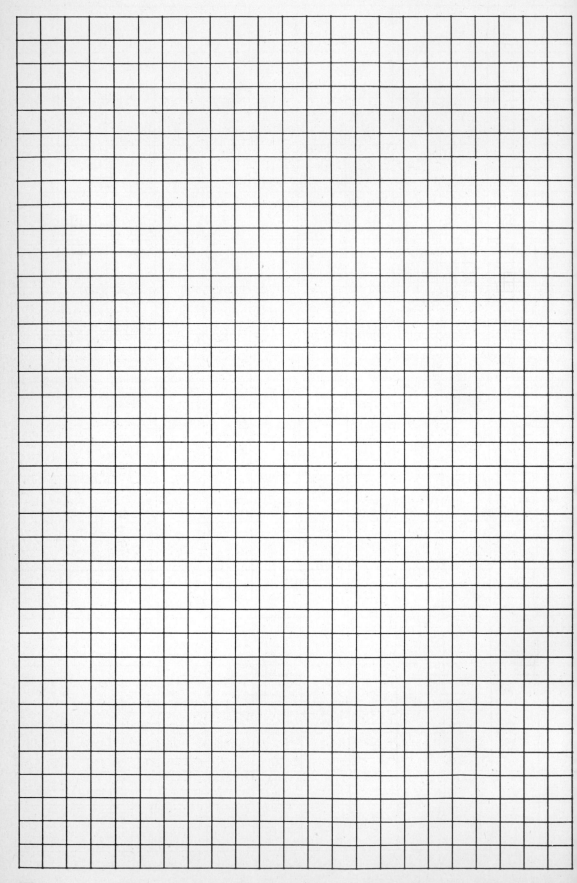

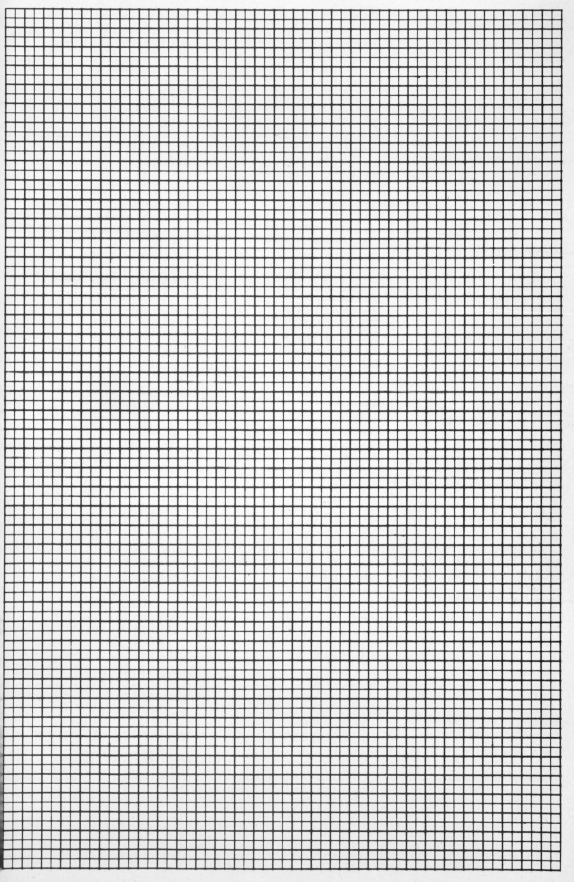

# INDEX OF PATCHWORK PATTERNS